Philosophical Tales

Martin Cohen is a teacher and writer specializing in philosophy, ethics, and education, with a special interest in computing. His books include *101 Philosophy Problems* (3rd ed., 2007) and *101 Ethical Dilemmas* (2nd ed., 2007), *Political Philosophy* (2001), *No Holiday* (2006), and *Wittgenstein's Beetle* (2005). He has been editor of *The Philosopher* since 1995.

Philosophical Tales

Being an alternative history revealing the
characters, the plots, and the hidden scenes that
make up the True Story of Philosophy

Martin Cohen

Illustrations by
Raúl Gonzáles III

Blackwell
Publishing

BLACKWELL PUBLISHING
350 Main Street, Malden, MA 02148-5020, USA
9600 Garsington Road, Oxford OX4 2DQ, UK
550 Swanston Street, Carlton, Victoria 3053, Australia

First published 2008 by Blackwell Publishing Ltd

2   2008

Library of Congress Cataloging-in-Publication Data

Cohen, Martin, 1964–
Philosophical tales / Martin Cohen.
      p.   cm.
Includes bibliographical references and index.
ISBN 978-1-4051-4036-2 (hardcover : alk. paper) – ISBN 978-1-4051-4037-9
(pbk. : alk. paper)   1. Philosophy–History.   I. Title.
B72.C58 2008
190–dc22
2007038433

A catalogue record for this title is available from the British Library.

Set in 11 on 13 pt Dante
by SNP Best-set Typesetter Ltd., Hong Kong
Printed and bound in the United Kingdom
by TJ International Ltd, Padstow, Cornwall

For further information on
Blackwell Publishing, visit our website at
www.blackwellpublishing.com

CONTENTS

CONTENTS

Philosophers are kind-hearted sorts of chaps, willing to help others into "the paragraphs," but there is still something mad about them, with their "ludicrous stiff solemnity and air of paragraph-importance." They pity past generations, who lived when the System was presumably not finished, and when therefore unbiased objectivity was not yet possible. But when you ask them about the new System they always put you off with the same excuse: "No, it is not yet quite ready. The System is almost finished, or at least under construction, and will be finished by next Sunday."

(Søren Kierkegaard, *Postscript*)

FORWARD!

Why does anyone start to read philosophy? Yet I myself was introduced to philosophy by three books. The first was André Malraux's *Man's Estate* (*La Condition Humaine*) in translation. The second was Bertrand Russell's *History of Western Philosophy*, and the third was Plato's *Republic*.

Naturally one did not read these books. *Man's Estate* is a typically French ornate work of little purpose. Wordy, complex, and dull. Russell is far, far too long, like a lecture that should have ended an hour ago. And Plato's *Republic*, although full of ideas, seems to be written in a kind of code. Nonetheless, each book served a useful purpose. The first, although unreadable, was small and imposing enough to carry around. The second was informative, if rather soporific, and the third was somehow fascinating if rather strange and resolutely obscure.

But here we have *Philosophical Tales*, which I hope can combine all three functions. The three positive ones, that is. It is small enough to carry around (and impress people). It is quite informative, and lastly (most importantly), it is full of strange and obscure philosophical titbits.

Now some people will say that they are too advanced to need titbits, they want full-blown lengthy treatises. Why should someone who wants to read Kant's *Critique of Pure Reason* in the original gobbledegook need to know that he considered coffee to be poisonous and rolled himself three times in his sheets every night before sleeping? Why would someone who could understand Hegel's *Die Phänomenologie des Geistes* (*Phenomenology of Spirit*) want to know that he came up with his theory that society is rooted in conflict while working as a schoolteacher? Or why even that that quintessential British rationalist, John Stuart Mill, exponent of the dry theory known as 'utilitarianism', actually considered poetry to be the "most philosophic of all writing"? So what, if Mill wrote to his friend, Wordsworth, author of the "daffodils" poem, to say that he had shown him that poetry "is truth," not individual and local, but general; not "standing upon external testimony, but carried alive into the heart by passion." For this, the conventional histories tell us, was an aberration, a momentary weakness.

So here is an alternative account of philosophers with human frailties, a portrait that may sometimes undermine their status as moral arbiters, sometimes as path-breaking theorists. But then, for all people tell us, philosophers are not a separate race. They are creatures like the rest of us, created on this planet (even if they often claim authority over it), children growing into men and women with experiences, influences, and most evidently, prejudices. Aristotle did not reflect Greek views of racial superiority – he invented them. (John Locke and Bishop Berkeley were also aware of the dubious nature of their profits from the slave trade.) Marx did not spend his time solely in the British Library, but liked his cigars, his beer, and his women too, more so in fact than providing for his children (several of whom died of malnutrition).

These personal details do not speak only of unimportant trivialities, but give insights into the 'big picture'. For as Sherlock Holmes remarked, in the *Case of Identity*, "It has long been an axiom of mine that the little things are infinitely the most important."

At the same time, the 'true story' of philosophy is less the story of individuals than of ideas, and more particularly, ideas being stolen, borrowed, and twisted. It is interesting to see that Descartes's great *cogito* really came from Augustine, whose interests were not the foundations of knowledge at all. (Augustine was content to think his thoughts were divinely inspired.) Or more recently that Wittgenstein borrowed his mysterious category of 'things that must remain silent' from another Austrian fantasist called Otto Weininger.

And it is the story of ideas lost too, so that although Plato had raised the possibility that women might have the 'same souls' as men, Aristotle successfully came up with good philosophical reasons as to why only men's ideas should hold court (explaining that women have fewer teeth, no souls, and their hearts do not beat), and it is his assumptions that have shaped philosophy ever since. So here women will play only a bit part. Hypatia, Harriet Taylor Mill, Mrs. Marx, and Sartre's companion appear, but only fleetingly, only in the background. Would that it were not so! But men wrote the history of philosophy, and history is where our tales come from.

HOW TO USE THIS BOOK

Did Plato really write those Socratic Dialogues – or was it Socrates?
Why is it a bit doubtful that Descartes ever really said "I think therefore I am"?
– and what has Sartre got against waiters anyway?

Philosophical tales: stories, fictions, falsehoods. Untruths, misrepresentations, canards, lies, fibs, whoppers. Or merely mis-statements, prevarications, narratives not entirely based on fact. This is a book that collects, deconstructs, and relates the great philosophical tale. And although I have tried to be 'scrupulously accurate', there is far less agreed upon about philosophers, let alone philosophy, than its professors and luminaries would have us believe, and so nothing in this book can be taken uncritically, as the end of the matter. It is, instead, an attempt to open up the debates, to open up the decisions that the 'powers-that-be' like to impose. In other words, it is a kind of 'alternative' history of philosophy – the philosophical approach applied to philosophy itself. Do not look here for the generally accepted view, the 'everyone agrees' version – that is for the other ten thousand books, the ten thousand experts to repeat. Here we want something interesting precisely because it is different. After all, philosophy is a lot more interesting than many of its dull exponents would have us believe.

Where do great philosophers come from? And where do they get their ideas? Who decides what is important, and what is not? Is it just happenstance that there are almost no women, just lots of wealthy, aristocratic men? Did the Chinese and Indian philosophers really have so little influence on Europe? Why is Descartes's 'modern' philosophy full of backwards-looking references to God? Is Hegel (as Schopenhauer alleged) a fool who could not write, or simply too difficult for most of us? Or is there a need for some Marxist-style deconstruction of the whole edifice of knowledge to be undertaken?

Philosophy is supposed to be about asking difficult questions, taking 'nothing for granted'. Yet this is not, it turns out, the approach that philosophy wants applied to itself. Instead, the 'debates' of the subject are handed down from on high, carved in stone, as are the great philosophers.

We follow a tidy and predictable course with the landmarks being Plato and Aristotle, followed along the way by Descartes and Kant. No women, not many non-Europeans. Left on the sidelines are Confucius, Lao Tzu, Mencius, Buddha . . . And the 'questions' of philosophy likewise have long ago settled into a comfortable pattern, the parameters set, the range of acceptable responses proscribed . . .

It seems that, with the institutionalization of the subject, philosophers increasingly debate the exact interpretations of so-and-so, or such-and-such, while all around, to borrow a famous sentiment, the great sea of philosophy lies unexplored.

So this book is an attempt to dip a toe into that great sea, or perhaps even to 'jostle' the philosophical pantheon somewhat in order to allow a few new faces in. The aim, naturally, is the reinvigoration of philosophy, not its 'destruction'. But if one must precede the other, and many of the tales offered here create doubts where before all was splendid consensus, then so be it. For that is still, and always has been, the true spirit of philosophy.

The book consists of summaries of the most celebrated and the most philosophically interesting tales (categories which are not necessarily describing the same things), the backgrounds to their telling, and assessments of the leading players. The entries consider both individual philosophers and schools of thought; each offers one key philosophical text which (as a rule) is also quoted briefly. In this way, the book provides a solid grounding in philosophical ideas and individuals.

Yet, in this procession of philosophers, it is perhaps unfortunate that so many fall by the wayside. It turns out that philosophy is not so much a series of footnotes to Plato as Plato himself follows Pythagoras (who in turn borrowed his ideas from the East). Here is the great Aristotle, insisting that women do not have minds and that all non-Greek humans should be treated as domestic cattle. And over there, in the shallow end, are Wittgenstein and Sartre copying out other people's theories and hoping that they are now their own. But building on ideas is, after all, what philosophy should be all about. Plato is straightforwardly presenting the ideas and arguments of his time, rarely making claims to originality for himself. If Descartes himself turns out to be less 'modern' than he is 'medieval', with his most famous discovery turning out to be only a slight restatement of a religious dictum, he was 'modern' in his enthusiasm for science. (The *Meditations* starts with an account of his dissection of a monkey . . .) Yet one difference between 'modern' and 'ancient' philosophy is that the early philosophers wanted to acknowledge their sources and influences, whereas the later philosophers seem to feel the need to claim originality pressing heavily upon them.

And if to be a philosopher does not rule out learning from previous ones, under the microscope, as it were, it still seems as if the Great Philosophers turn out not to be so great, indeed, to be rather ordinary. We can't avoid their vanities, and their prejudices, their foolishness and their dishonesty. Seeing this, some will think to dismiss them (or philosophy itself), but that would be to exhibit a profoundly unreflective turn of mind. The point is not that 'philosophers' need to be different from the rest of us, or either they are not true philosophers, or philosophy itself is all applesauce, blather, bunkum, claptrap, and piffle. The point is that philosophy is a much more communal process, and a much more subtle one than those who like to construct hierarchies of knowledge (with themselves invariably somewhere near the top) want people to know. The point is that philosophers may be great, in their way, and yet also very ordinary. The point is that philosophers are people like you and me.

PHILOSOPHICAL ILLUSTRATIONS

Raúl Gonzáles is co-founder of the world famous art collective, the Miracle Fire, and teaches at the Museum of Fire Art, Boston. His work has been displayed both nationally and internationally and he can be found today creating art with Princess Die and their cat Mao Mao at the Miracle Fortress in Somerville, Massachussets.

I
THE ANCIENTS

CHAPTER 1
SOCRATES THE SORCERER
(469–399 BCE)

There is a curious drawing, made in the thirteenth century, of Socrates with a funny hat on, seated at a lectern, with a feather quill in one hand. Behind him is a short, bossy Plato, prodding his master impatiently. We know it is them as there are little labels pointing to each saying "Socrates" and "Plato." Otherwise . . . the picture is a mystery.

When the twentieth-century philosopher Jacques Derrida came across it during a visit to the Bodleian Library in Oxford, England, in 1978, he was shocked. Derrida wrote in one of his long, pompous books (of which more later) that after he "stumbled across it" he "stopped dead, with a feeling of hallucination . . . and of revelation at the same time, an apocalyptic revelation."

It seems as if Plato is dictating to his teacher, Socrates, who is reduced to child-like obedience (hence the funny hat). Derrida says the picture symbolizes a kind of Freudian patricide, and makes several rather vulgar references to the picture (and Plato's finger) to prove his point. Yet there is nothing in the image to prove that Socrates is being humiliated rather than helped. It is rather the staid hierarchy of Western Philosophy that may have been being pushed and prodded. Perhaps that is why Derrida, a distinguished French philosopher, was so shocked!

For certainly, if you read conventional histories of philosophy, you would think Socrates rather a dull fellow. Little is known about him, it seems, apart from the fact that he was born in Athens in the year 469 BCE, and that his father was a sculptor and his mother a midwife. There remain only a few other fragments of writing to throw a little more light on the man himself. Let one such historian, Professor Hugh Tredennick, take up the story:

> Portraits and descriptions make it clear that he had a heavy, rather ugly, face, with a snub nose, prominent eyes beneath shaggy eyebrows, and a large full mouth. He was bearded and (in his later years at any rate) bald. His thickset body had great powers of endurance. He strutted as he walked, always went barefoot, and would often stand in a trance for hours. . . . On the other hand his mind, though not creative, was exceptionally clear,

3

critical and eager. It tolerated no pretence; and since his will was as strong as his convictions, his conduct was as logical as his thinking. In a sceptical age he believed firmly in moral goodness as the one thing that matters; and he identified it with knowledge, because to his straightforward nature it seemed inconceivable that anyone would see what is right without doing it.

This is reassuring stuff. Yet none of this fits that funny, thirteenth-century picture . . .

The Philosophical Tale

Yet, if there is little enough that is agreed about Socrates, there is perhaps one thing. And that is that he is the most influential philosopher of them all. This despite the fact that no one is quite sure what he said – let alone thought. There are scraps enough to be sure, but the real Socrates remains an elusive figure. His footprints are everywhere, yet the man himself, like Macavity the mystery cat,* is nowhere to be found.

There are stories: of the dogmatic Socrates instructing a young and naive Plato to destroy his youthful attempts at poetry; of the fanatical Socrates standing for a day and a night rooted to the spot (wrestling with

FIGURE 1 He stood till dawn came and the Sun rose, then walked away, after offering a prayer to the Sun.

*In T. S. Eliot's poem of the same name.

a thought), while others brought up mattresses to watch and take bets on how long he'd stay there, and of course there is that "famous-last-words" scene (described so eloquently in the *Phaedo*) shortly before he sips his last drink of hemlock.

> For let me tell you, Gentlemen, that to be afraid of death is only another form of thinking that one is wise when one is not. It is to think that one knows what one does not know.

Historians consider Diogenes Laertius to be the most, indeed the only, reliable source about the 'historical Socrates'. Otherwise, all the accounts of this miasmic figure say more about their author's preferences than they do about Socrates. Xenophon, the devious soldier-of-fortune, draws a picture of a dull, practical Socrates, holding forth in a harmless but insignificant way. Hegel, the philosopher of 'historical determinism' and of the dialectic, sees Socrates as a pivotal figure in the tide of world history, a Janus God with two faces, one surveying the past and the other facing the future.[1] And Nietzsche, writing in the *Gay Science*, describes Socrates as a "mocking and enamoured monster," a kind of philosophical "pied piper of Athens."

Yet overshadowing them all, it is the Platonic picture that has created the Socrates we know. Plato, the idealist, offers an idol, a master-figure for philosophy. A saint, a prophet of "the Sun-God," a teacher condemned for his teachings as a heretic. It is he who tells the most eloquent Socratic story. In the dialogue the *Symposium*, for instance, Plato writes:

> Immersed in some problem at dawn, he stood in the same spot considering it, and when he found it a tough problem, he would not give it up but stood there trying to understand it. Time drew on until midday, and the men began to notice him, saying to one another in wonder: "Socrates has been standing there in contemplation, since dawn!" The result was that in the evening, after they had eaten their suppers, this being summer, some of the Ionians brought out their rugs and mattresses and took their sleep in the cool: thus they waited to see if Socrates would go on standing all night too. He stood till dawn came and the sun rose, then walked away, after offering a prayer to the Sun.

Elsewhere in the same dialogue, the good and bad twins, Aristodemus and Alcibiades, offer two more, opposing, views, which Plato uses to paint a picture of Socrates as 'Eros', the God of sexuality, and a figure beyond everyday categories. Socrates here is neither ignorant nor wise, neither tragic nor comic, male nor female – but outside all such distinctions. He can walk barefoot on ice during winter, drink wine without becoming drunk. Even his supposed ugliness now becomes an advantage, for having eyes set towards the sides of his head enables him to perceive a wider field of vision, just as having a flat distorted nose allows him to receive scents from all directions. And those disproportionately thick lips, can of course, now be seen as able to receive all the more kisses.

But is any of this the 'real Socrates' – or just the one we want to believe in?

In Plato's dialogues, Socrates appears, as one contemporary writer, Sarah Kofman, has put it very nicely, as something of a "seductive sorcerer," party to some mystical insight that he never is to reveal.

> Like an uncanny double, he seems to appear and disappear at will, immobilising himself, mesmerising himself and others through some magic trick, like a sorcerer with more power to charm than the finest flute player or the most eloquent narrator. He is more powerful than Gorgias, and his rhetoric more powerful than Agathon's, who hurls his Gorgon-like speeches at listeners to frighten them and to hide the vacuity of his own thought.

Socrates is a good philosopher to launch the project of deconstructing philosophy with: is he the "sculptor's son" who frittered away his inheritance, or the midwife's boy who brought philosophy as critical dialogue screaming into the world? Socrates' ugliness, his demonic voice, his ability to stay immobile for several days on end all contribute to the myth. Or is it a legend? Out of them all, Socrates is the hardest to deconstruct . . . Indeed, he may just be indeconstructible.

Pompous Footnote

1   The same concept lives on in the name of the month of January, the month that faces both the old year and the new one.

CHAPTER 2
THE DIFFERENT FORMS OF PLATO
(ca. 427–347 BCE)

If Socrates is really a bit of a mystery, Plato seems to be plain as a pikestaff. Or so, at least, it is for Richard Robinson writing in *The Concise Encyclopaedia of Western Philosophy and Philosophers*. As he tidily puts it:

> Plato's publications are all preserved, and make five large modern volumes. They constitute not merely the greatest philosophical work there is, but also one of the greatest pieces of literature in the world.

Indeed, he continues confidently, if anyone asks what philosophy is, "the best answer is: 'read Plato'. For it was Plato who brought the word 'philosophy' into use; and it was he who mainly invented and first practiced the sort of study for which 'philosophy' is the name."[1]

The Philosophical Tale

Amongst all of the philosophical constructions, those of Plato seem to stand a little bit taller, a little bit undeniably grander, than all the rest. And amongst these, it is perhaps the *Republic* that stands tallest and grandest of all: the blueprint of the philosophical State, the original utopia, to be built on a clear understanding of the nature of justice, and a glimpse of the world of the Platonic Forms.

But first, here is a bit more on the man himself.

Plato was born, studied, taught, and eventually died in Athens. His real name was Aristocles, but in his school days he received the nickname 'Platon' (meaning "broad") because of his broad shoulders, and that is how history has remembered him. He came of aristocratic lineage (perhaps even seeing himself as of 'kingly' stock) and, as was normal at the time, trained both in poetry and in warfare. He was interested in politics, but considered democracy to be the rule of the unwise, which limited his options in Athens, then a democracy.

Instead, he toured the Greek colonies in Africa and Italy, absorbing Pythagorean notions, and traveled several times to Syracuse, the capital

FIGURE 2 Justice will be found, said Plato, when everyone does their own job and minds their own business.

of Greek Sicily, to advise the new king, Dionysius II, hoping there to put his political ideas into practice. He fell out with the king, however, and only just managed to return to Athens in 387 where he settled down to establishing the famous 'Academy' for the study of philosophy, what some like to consider the first 'university'. He is said to have died in his sleep at the age of 80 after enjoying the wedding feast of one of his students.

Anyway, the *Republic* contains within it the well-known allegory of the Cave, a kind of thought experiment in which chained prisoners face a wall on which they can see only shadows passing before them, but which they take to be reality. Some of the prisoners eventually escape to see the real world, but on their return to the Cave, fail to convince their shackled companions that the things they think they can see in the Cave are in fact only misleading and distorted shadows. It is a paean to 'reason' over convention and mere belief. In the same spirit, the *Republic* opens with Socrates confidently declaring that Justice is to be understood as the correct ordering of things, as a kind of harmony, and one most easily seen by considering the planning of that largest of all human artifacts – the State. Here justice will be found, says Plato, when everyone does their own job and minds their own business. And if the blueprint for his State seems rather impractical, that is of no significance, for:

. . . perhaps in the other world, it is laid up as a pattern, one which those who desire to may behold, and in so doing, be able to put their own city in order. Whether such a city exists – or ever in fact will exist – is of no matter, for such a person will live after the manner of the ideal city, having nothing to do with any other.

Yet amongst all the mysteries and uncertainties of the dialogue, one aspect seems much neglected. For the *Republic is not ideal at all.* It is stated quite plainly early on: in fact, it is the *Luxurious State.* It is a response to Glaucon's demand for a few of the "ordinary conveniences" of life, or as he apologetically puts it to Socrates, "a relish to the meal."

Here is how Plato introduces his State. It starts off well enough . . .

SOCRATES: Let us then consider, first of all, what will be the citizens' way of life, now that we have thus established them. Will they not produce corn, and wine, and clothes, and shoes, and build houses for themselves? And when they are housed, they will work, in summer, commonly, stripped and barefoot, but in winter substantially clothed and shod. They will feed on barley-meal and flour of wheat, baking and kneading them, making noble cakes and loaves; these they will serve up on a mat of reeds or on clean leaves, themselves reclining the while upon beds strewn with yew or myrtle. And they and their children will feast, drinking of the wine which they have made, wearing garlands on their heads, and hymning the praises of the gods, in happy conversation with one another. And they will take care that their families do not exceed their means; having an eye to poverty or war.

GLAUCON: But, you have not given them a relish to their meal.

SOCRATES: True, I had forgotten; of course they must have a relish – salt, and olives, and cheese, and they will boil roots and herbs such as country people prepare; for a dessert we shall give them figs, and peas, and beans; and they will roast myrtle-berries and acorns at the fire, drinking in moderation. And with such a diet they may be expected to live in peace and health to a good old age, and bequeath a similar life to their children after them.

But Socrates has missed the point entirely. Figs and peas indeed! Glaucon's objection runs much deeper. "Yes, Socrates," he now says with sarcasm, "and if you were providing for a city of pigs, how else would you feed the beasts?"

SOCRATES: But what would you have, Glaucon?

GLAUCON: Why, you should give them the ordinary conveniences of life. People who are to be comfortable are accustomed to lie on sofas, and dine off tables, and they should have sauces and sweets in the modern style.

SOCRATES: Yes, now I understand. The question which you would have me consider is, not only how a State, but how a luxurious State is created; and possibly there is no harm in this, for in such a State we shall be more likely to see how justice and injustice originate. In my opinion the true and healthy constitution of the State is the one which I have described. But if you wish also to see a State affected by fever heat, I have no objection. For I suspect that many will not be satisfied with the simpler way of life. They will be for adding sofas, and tables, and other furniture; also dainties, and perfumes, and incense, and courtesans, and cakes, all these not of one sort only, but in every variety.

Shame! But Socrates is up to the unwholesome task set him.

SOCRATES: So, we must go beyond the necessaries of which I was at first speaking, such as houses, and clothes, and shoes: the arts of the painter and the embroiderer will have to be set in motion, and gold and ivory and all sorts of materials must be procured.

GLAUCON: True.

SOCRATES: Then we must enlarge our borders; for the original healthy State is no longer sufficient. Now will the city have to fill and swell with a multitude of callings which are not required by any natural want; such as the whole tribe of hunters and actors, of whom one large class have to do with forms and colours; another will be the votaries of music – poets and their attendant train of rhapsodists, players, dancers, contractors; also makers of divers kinds of articles, including women's dresses. And we shall want more servants. Will not tutors be also in request, and nurses wet and dry, and barbers, as well as confectioners and cooks; and swineherds, too, who were not needed and therefore had no place in the former edition of our State, but are needed now? They must not be forgotten: and there will be animals of many other kinds, if people eat them.

GLAUCON: Certainly.

SOCRATES: And living in this way we shall have much greater need of physicians than before?

GLAUCON: Much greater.

SOCRATES: And the country which was enough to support the original inhabitants will be too small now, and not enough?

GLAUCON: Quite true.

SOCRATES: Then a slice of our neighbours' land will be wanted by us for pasture and tillage, and they will want a slice of ours, if, like ourselves, they exceed the limit of necessity, and give themselves up to the unlimited accumulation of wealth?

GLAUCON: That, Socrates, will be inevitable.

SOCRATES: And so we shall go to war, Glaucon. Shall we not?

GLAUCON: Most certainly.

SOCRATES: Then without determining as yet whether war does good or harm, thus much we may affirm, that now we have discovered war to be derived from causes which are also the causes of almost all the evils in States, private as well as public.

GLAUCON: Indubitably.

It is only greed and materialism that require not only the division of labor generally, but class distinctions, an army, and the creation of a ruling elite – the famous Platonic guardians.

But is the most important question whether only vegetarians can do philosophy – or whether, in fact, philosophy is only necessary for non-vegetarians?

Critics of Plato who complain that his "ideal" society is apparently also a militaristic, indeed, a fascist State, with censorship and a rigidly controlled economy – not ideal at all – might be surprised to see in this alternative reading of the *Republic* a Plato quite happy to agree with them. What they may have failed to take into account is that the republic he describes is *not* his ideal one – it is merely the result that follows on from Glaucon's (in the name of the citizens) demand for meat, a constitutional error (so to speak) which Socrates himself avoids.

And indeed the ancient Greeks numbered amongst them many vegetarians. As well as Plutarch, one of the Greek priests at Delphi (whose essay "On Eating Flesh" is considered a literary, if not a philosophical, classic), there is Pythagoras, whose words seem to eerily pre-herald Plato's. "Oh, my fellow men!" exclaimed Pythagoras:

Do not defile your bodies with sinful foods. We have corn. We have apples bending down the branches with their weight, and grapes swelling on the vines. There are sweet flavored herbs and vegetables which can be cooked and softened over the fire. Nor are you denied milk or thyme-scented honey. The earth affords you a lavish supply of riches, of innocent foods, and offers you banquets that involve no blood-shed or slaughter.

So was the *Republic* not so much about Plato's own conception of the State – or more about Pythagoras'? An attempt by Plato to join in a long lost debate amongst the Greek vegetarians, rather than the piece of political planning it is now taken to be? The answer is lost in the mists of Mount Olympus. What seems certain, however, is that Plato's *Republic*, although magnificent, does not have to be treated as a consistent philosophical thesis. Perhaps it, like the other dialogues, could be read instead just as a collection of amusing bits and pieces and anecdotes put together by someone who would actually rather have been doing poetry.

And (stranger and stranger), although we mostly think of Plato as the stern puppet-master of Socrates, who is found in the *Republic* busy banning music and poetry, discouraging love and confining sex only to producing children, in another slightly later dialogue called the *Symposium* or 'drinking party', Plato paints a very different picture. Here, a merry Socrates recalls the words of the wise woman, Diotima, correcting his youthful views on philosophy and teaching him instead that love, and poetry about it, was a step on the way to the understanding and appreciation of beauty and goodness. Indeed, not only that, but the only way to perceiving the *ideal forms of* beauty and goodness. Here, the Theory of Forms itself, forever after to be attributed to Plato, is straight-forwardly credited to Diotima. And not content with that piece of self-demolition, Plato has this out-of-character-Socrates (for historians think that Socrates at this time never left Athens, and the drinking party is set in the countryside) praise personal love in a way that makes a shocking contrast to his usual stern advocacy of 'Platonic' relationships. After describing the psychological fevers that the physical presence of a lover can create, the fevers condemned in the *Republic* as a 'tyrant', he says here that it is only this that prevents the 'wings of the soul' from becoming parched and dry!

Or again, maybe it is something to do with a letter, sometimes attributed to Plato, in which he declares that the texts everyone assumes to be by him were in fact written by Socrates. Here, in the controversial so-called 'Second Epistle', Plato reveals himself as the true philosopher, and Socrates becomes the (if rather elderly) apprentice. Here it is Plato, and not (as conventionally noted in the Philosophical Histories) Socrates at all, that wisely eschews the inferior written form.

Pompous Footnote

1 Uniquely for the ancient Greeks, all Plato's writings seem to have survived. This is lucky as if he had a coherent philosophical system, it is not presented as such. Instead every bit of his writings needs to be considered, and a picture created from various pieces. And many pictures can be made.

CHAPTER 3
ARISTOTLE THE ARISTOCRAT
(384–ca. 322 BCE)

There is a suitably grand oil painting depicting the 'two great' Greek philosophers in the Academy surrounded by the other Greek alumni. *The
School of Athens*, painted by the Renaissance artist Raphael in the sixteenth
century, when such things were back in vogue, shows Plato, remembered
for teaching the virtues of the mysterious world of the Forms, gesticulating
with his hand directed upwards as if saying, "Look to the perfection of the
heavens for truth." Aristotle, by contrast, whose philosophy is supposed
to start with observation of earthly phenomena, is pointing downwards,
as if to say, "look around you at what is if you would know the truth."

That's an idealized picture of Aristotle, of course. Diogenes Laertius,
in his *Lives and Opinions of Eminent Philosophers*, offers a rather more down-
to-earth one. Aristotle, he says, had a lisping voice, very thin legs, and
small eyes, and used to indulge in very conspicuous dress, wearing lots
of rings and arranging his hair elaborately. Diogenes reminds us that
Lycon had revealed that the philosopher used to bathe in a bath of warm
olive oil, and, what's worse, to sell the oil afterwards. In fact, Aristotle's
reputation during his lifetime, and for a long period afterwards, was
nowhere near as elevated as that of Plato's. Writers such as the renowned
'sceptic' Timon of Philus sneered at "the sad chattering of the empty
Aristotle" while Theocritus of Chios wrote a rather unkind epigram on
him which runs:

> *The empty-headed Aristotle rais'd*
> *This empty tomb to Hermias the Eunuch,*
> *The ancient slave of the ill-us'd Eubulus.*
> *(Who for his monstrous appetite, preferred*
> *The Bosphorus to Academia's groves.)*

The Philosophical Tale

As a small boy, Aristotle was introduced to the mysteries of the natural
world by his father, who was the official doctor and herbalist for the

Macedonian king. Surely these would have been happy days, for Aristotle's parents were well-to-do and Aristotle was always eager to learn. Alas, this time was cut short by the early deaths of both his parents, and instead Aristotle found himself the ward of one Proxenus, the husband of his sister, Arimneste.

Proxenus, it seems, was a friend of Plato and so it was that in 367, at the age of 17, Aristotle left home, to become a student of Plato at the renowned Academy at Athens. If he arrived there intending to learn simply how to practice medicine, he soon became caught up instead with all the other debates there at the time, concerning mathematics, astronomy, laws, and politics.

His sharp and well-observed contributions made him a figure of note, and Plato called him, perhaps acerbically, the "intellect" of the school, yet, nonetheless, after Plato's death in 347 BCE, it was Speusippus, Plato's nephew, who was named head of the Academy and not Aristotle the Macedonian. Shortly afterwards Aristotle left mainland Greece, with his friend, Xenocrates, to set up a mini-academy of his own in the city of Assos in what is today northwestern Turkey and was then a mini-statelet ruled by Hermias.

Comfortably ensconced there, Aristotle and Xenocrates concentrated on the 'sciences', particularly biology. Fascinated by the huge variety of animal life, Aristotle worked energetically on arranging them into hierarchies and in fact, about a quarter of all his writing is concerned with categorizing nature, including the different forms the soul takes in different creatures. Over time he identified over five hundred animal species, carefully dissecting nearly fifty of them. He was best at classifying sea life and, on moving to Mytilene in the island of Lesvos, just off the Turkish coast, even observed that since the dolphin gave birth in the manner of certain land animals, it belonged with the mammals, not with the other fish. He also studied sharks, noting that some of these give birth to live young and puzzled over the ability of the torpedo fish to stun its prey without, understandably, realizing that this was by means of an electric shock. However, away from the sea, as often as not, his observations led him astray. He declared wrongly that plants reproduced only asexually, and that for humans the heart was the center of consciousness, and that it beat only in men's breasts. He asserted that the left side of the body was colder than the right, and that the brain was there merely to cool the blood, although there was an 'empty space' in the back of every man's head, for the soul.

He denied the power of thought to animals, maintaining that they were capable only of sensation and appetite, and that they needed the rule of humankind in order to survive. Unlike Pythagoras, who had seen the immortal soul in everything, in Aristotle's view plants and animals existed solely for the use of humans.

Although Aristotle is sometimes credited with anticipating Darwin in his theory that the design of everything in nature can be understood by considering its final 'purpose' or 'end', Plato too had explained the world by talking of the inclination of objects to regain their proper place – stones to fall, fire to rise, and so on. Indeed, in one of his dialogues, the *Timaeus*, Plato offers a theory of backwards evolution, in which Man, created directly by the Gods, rapidly degenerates: first into woman, and then into all the various strata of the animal world.

At least Aristotle does not follow Plato in this. But when he describes the nature of space and time, his cosmology is always conservative. He thought that the 'heavenly spheres' of Ptolemy were not just metaphorical but literal crystal ones, and then went on to calculate that for the heavens to function properly, there must be a few more of them, arriving eventually at the inelegant total of fifty-four spheres. The motion of heavenly objects was steady, even, and circular, as the spheres rotated smoothly in what he called the 'aether'. A 'vacuum', he asserted, was nonsensical, and even if somehow there were to be such a thing, certainly motion in it would be impossible.

As the Earth was the center of the universe, everything was arranged around it in layers. On Earth all things are changeable and corrupt, while in the heavens all is permanent and unchanging, Water was above earth, air above water, and fire highest of all. That this was so was borne out by observation: an object composed largely of earth, such as a rock, would, if suspended in air, fall downward; droplets of water fall as rain; bubbles of air trapped under water rise upwards, as do flames in a fire.

It also seemed obvious to Aristotle that the heavier an object was, the faster it would fall. Simple practical experiment can prove this is false, but instead this error blocked progress in physics until Galileo and Newton managed to demonstrate it as a logical and not just an empirical impossibility.

Likewise, Aristotle considered but rejected Democritus' theory that things were made up of atoms, holding up chemistry for two thousand years. By a queer symmetry, as the scientist John Tyndall noted in the nineteenth century, it almost seemed as though his statements were most accepted when they were most incorrect.

He put words in the place of things, subject in the place of object. He preached Induction without practicing it, inverting the true order of inquiry by passing from the general to the particular, instead of from the particular to the general. He made of the universe a closed sphere, in the centre of which he fixed the earth, proving from general principles, to his own satisfaction and to that of the world for near 2,000 years, that no other universe was possible. His notions of motion were entirely unphysical. It was natural or unnatural, better or worse, calm or violent, with no real mechanical conception regarding it lying at the bottom of his mind. He affirmed that a vacuum could not exist, and proved that if it did exist motion in it would be impossible. He determined *a priori* how many species of animals must exist, and shows on general principles why animals must have such and such parts.

Or, as Karl Popper would later put it: "The development of thought since Aristotle could, I think, be summed up by saying that every discipline, as long as it used the Aristotelian method of definition, has remained arrested in a state of empty verbiage and barren scholasticism, and that the degree to which the various sciences have been able to make any progress depended on the degree to which they have been able to get rid of this essentialist method." Popper adds that Aristotle's emphasis on definitions leads first to empty 'scholastic' hair-splitting, but then – worse – to disillusionment with reason itself. This, says Popper, is Aristotle's great crime.

Perhaps it was fortunate, then, for progress that Aristotle's studies were interrupted by a royal injunction to return to Macedonia to help educate Alexander the Great, the heir to the Macedonian throne. His main activity seems to have been preparing and copying out a special version of the *Iliad* for the young warrior. But Alexander seems not to have shared any of Aristotle's other interests.

Returning at last to Athens, Aristotle set up the new college which became known as the 'peripatetic school', after the Greek for 'walk about', because Aristotle, it was said, used to walk about whilst giving his lectures in the open air. Whether he did or not, he seems to have made sure that all his thoughts were committed to paper. Over time the 'walkabout' school built up a considerable library of manuscripts, which, it is said, eventually served as the kernel for the great Library at Alexandria. That Library was destroyed in 391, however, on the orders of Bishop Theophilus of Alexandria who said it was a "pagan temple," but fortunately for Aristotle, a separate collection of his manuscripts was found in a pit in Asia Minor about 80 BCE by soldiers of the Roman army. Being well

FIGURE 3 Fortunately, perhaps, for progress, Aristotle's studies were interrupted by a royal injunction to return to Macedonia.

organized, the Romans had them taken back to Italy where they were carefully recopied.

When, in the early fifth century, Rome itself fell to the 'barbarians', the manuscripts found their way to Persia, where they were preserved by the Arabs through the 'Dark Ages' in Europe. Thus it was that a reformed Christianity was later able to regain them from the 'infidel', translating the books into Latin in the twelfth and thirteenth centuries. And it is now that Aristotle begins to supplant Plato as 'the Philosopher'. Indeed, his views came to be regarded as possessing an almost divine authority, so that if Aristotle said it was so, it was so. In his heyday, according to Brother Giles of Rome, there were even churches in which Aristotle's *Ethics* was read every Sunday morning to the people instead of the Gospel.

So what was in the Aristotelian advice, that the Persians had guarded so carefully for centuries and had now become the foundation text for European culture? For if Aristotle had little influence on Alexander the Great, he certainly had a thousand years later.

Aristotle's secret

As we have seen, Aristotle's excellently simple method was to observe the world around him and explain what he saw from how it seemed to be. Women, he saw, were treated much worse than men. This, he explained, was because "Women are defective by nature" and this, he decided, is in turn best explained by the fact that they cannot produce the male fluid (semen). The Greeks thought this fluid contained little seeds which, when planted in the woman, in time grew into full human beings. During sex, the man supplies the substance of a human being, the soul, which is to say, 'the form', while the woman can only provide later the nourishment, that is to say, 'the matter'.

This all made sense to Aristotle as the world of 'matter', as Plato had taught, is generally inferior to the world of Forms. (Aristotle frequently attempts to differentiate himself from Plato, usually by unkind criticism, but in reality, Aristotle is Plato revisited.)

> . . . if we were discussing a couch or the like, we should try to determine its form rather than its matter (e.g. bronze or wood) . . . for the formal nature is of greater importance than the material nature.

Aristotle realized that the gods had wisely split humanity into two halves, in order to leave the man untainted.

Greek society followed the same principle. Women were confined within the parental home until a husband was chosen for them – at which time they would be in their mid-teens. The wife would then be trans-ferred to the home of her husband where she was expected to fulfill her principal function, of bearing and rearing children, or to be more precise, boys.

Usually, only one daughter, at most, would be wanted. Surplus girl children might even be left on the hillside to die. Athenian men had plenty of other ways to satisfy their sexual drive apart from with wives. There were courtesans or *hetairai*, prostitutes or their own slave women, not to mention of course plenty of boys and other men. The wife's function was primarily that of bringing up a son.

Naturally, the wife could not socialize with her husband and his friends. Social gatherings, even if held in her own home, were strictly off-limits. Well-off women were not permitted to leave the house to go to the mar-ketplace or communal well: these were activities reserved for men or for women slaves. Actually, women slaves had in some ways more rights than their mistresses, as slaves were considered as being so low in any case that the distinction between men and women ceased to matter.

But not everyone thought like this. In the *Republic*, Plato controversially foresees an upper class of 'guardians' among whom the chattel status of women is abolished (i.e., she is no longer owned by her husband) and in which women were to receive equal education to men. On the other hand, in the *Timaeus*, he notes:

> It is only males who are created directly by the gods and are given souls. Those who live rightly return to the stars but those who are cowards or lead unrighteous lives may with reason be supposed to have changed into the nature of women in the second generation.

Aristotle adopts the latter approach, adding that a man needs to take charge over woman, because he has superior intelligence. Mind you, this arrangement will, he thinks, of course also profit women. He compares the relationship between men and women to that between human beings and domesticated animals.

> It is the best for all tame animals to be ruled by human beings. For this is how they are kept alive. In the same way, the relationship between the male and the female is by nature such that the male is higher, the female lower, that the male rules and the female is ruled.

Slavery is a similar case, benefiting both slaves and masters. It is best and natural because some people are 'by nature' intended to be slaves. Most foreigners are like this, although like wild animals, they will need to be conquered first. Among barbarians, remarks Aristotle, showing his cosmopolitanism, no distinction is made between women and slaves, because there is no natural ruler among them: they are a community of slaves, male and female. "That is why the poets say: 'It is correct that Greeks rule Barbarians'," he adds, for "'by nature what is barbarian and what is slave are the same.'"

Then, in one of his occasional contrary thrusts, Aristotle asks, "But is there any one thus intended by nature to be a slave?" For whom "such a condition is expedient and right," or rather is not "all slavery a violation of nature?" Fortunately, he finds there is "no difficulty in answering this question, on grounds both of reason and of fact. For that some should rule and others be ruled is a thing not only necessary, but expedient; from the hour of their birth, some are marked out for subjection, others for rule." And he goes on:

That person is by nature a slave who can belong to another person and who only takes part in thinking by recognizing it, but not by possessing it. Other living beings (animals) cannot recognize thinking; they just obey feelings. However, there is little difference between using slaves and using tame animals: both provide bodily help to do necessary things.

Slaves should be looked after properly – for economic reasons. But like women, they have no right to leisure, no free time. They can own nothing and should not be allowed to take decisions. They are not members of the community.

Indeed the use made of slaves and of tame animals is not very different; for both with their bodies minister to the needs of life. Nature would like to distinguish between the bodies of freemen and slaves, making the one strong for servile labour, the other upright, and although useless for such services, useful for political life in the arts both of war and peace. But the opposite often happens – that some have the souls and others have the bodies of freemen. And doubtless if men differed from one another in the mere forms of their bodies as much as the statues of the Gods do from men, all would acknowledge that the inferior class should be slaves of the superior. And if this is true of the body, how much more just that a similar distinction should exist in the soul? But the beauty of the body is seen, whereas the beauty of the soul is not seen. It is clear, then, that some men are by nature free, and others slaves, and that for these latter slavery is both expedient and right.

A possible weakness with this theory, Aristotle soon realized, is that the right kind of souls and bodies do not necessarily go together. So, potentially one could have the soul of a slave and the body of a freeman, or vice versa. Only centuries later did Saint Augustine come up with a solution to the problem. Augustine explains that, since God decides who will win battles, capture in battle followed by enslavement is the way God punishes people for their sins. The failure to realize this is one of Aristotle's lesser faults.

The broad outlines of Aristotle's political theory, then, are that society should be constructed around higher and lower forms of human being.

- Women are inferior to men.
- Barbarians ('foreigners') are inferior to the civilized races.
- Slaves are inferior to everyone.

Certainly that is how most of his fellow aristocrats in Greece at the time thought, if not perhaps the slaves too. But Aristotle's contribution has been to ensure that the same basic approach dominated the Western world during the Middle Ages and leaves its echoes today, especially in conservative Islam.

So much for Aristotle's science and his politics – what though (following his own systematic approach) of Aristotle's logic and ethics, considered by many to be his most important contributions to philosophy? The first of these rests on the secure-sounding foundation of the 'laws of thought':

- The law of identity: whatever is, is.
- The law of non-contradiction: nothing can both be and not be.

And

- The law of the excluded middle: everything must either be or not be.

Only in philosophy could you build a reputation on obvious statements like this. However, he also expands on this to produce an elaborate array of 'arguments', some of which he says are 'valid' and some of which are 'invalid'. This, the so-called *Prior Analytics*, is the first recorded system of formal logic, and indeed it remained the only 'logic' until the nineteenth century, when Frege discarded most of it. Aristotle's logic was powerful enough to demonstrate, amongst other things, that if Socrates was a man, and all men are mortal, than Socrates must be mortal too. What Aristotle himself did not seem to see, however, was the conventional nature of the assumptions. In the real world, things can both 'be' and 'not be', and occasionally even fall in between. A rock is both large and small, depending on your point of view, and it may not be a rock anyway, if you look at it closely and see it is made up of earth. Nonetheless, the conceit that the world obeyed rules, and the rules could be stated by men such as Aristotle the Aristocrat, proved a seductive and, many would say, a useful one.

And what of Aristotle's ethics, still much studied in philosophy departments, if nowadays less likely to be read out in church? Many of the doctrines often attributed to him, notably the merit of fulfilling your 'function', of cultivating the 'virtues' (see 'virtue ethics'), and of the 'golden mean' between two undesirable extremes, are all much older. In fact, Plato puts the ideas forward more powerfully and cogently. Nonetheless, important differences between Aristotle and Plato are there in their ethics. Aristotle's views on morality are set out particularly in the *Nicomachean Ethics*, where he starts with a survey of popular opinions on the subject of 'right and wrong', to find out how the terms are used, in the manner of a social anthropologist. Plato makes very clear his contempt for such an approach.

The *Nicomachean Ethics* includes accounts of what the Greeks considered to be the great virtues, exemplified by Aristotle's 'great-souled' or 'magnanimous' man, the human being who, we are told, will speak with a deep voice and level utterance, and be not unduly modest either. The main idea is that the proper end of mankind (or rather aristocrats) is the pursuit of *eudaimonia*, which is Greek for a very particular kind of 'happiness'. "Nothing is more absolutely necessary," he writes in Book 2 of the *Politics*, "than to provide that the highest class, not only when in office, but when out of office, should have leisure and not disgrace themselves in any way." This pursuit has three aspects: as well as mere pleasure, there is political honor, and the rewards of contemplation. Quintessentially, of course, as philosophy (but it might be making lists of animals too).

In the seventeenth century, Thomas Hobbes would later say that it was this method that had led Aristotle astray, as by seeking to ground ethics in the 'appetites of men', he had chosen a measure by which correctly there is no distinction between right and wrong. In fact, in passing, it might be noted that Hobbes considered Aristotle a great fool, protesting repeatedly against the "folly" and "fluttering" of "the Ancients," by whom he meant just one: Aristotle. Which is a kind of tribute.

But back to Theocritus' unkind rhyme. Curiously, the cause of Hermias' (a mercenary and later a despot) departure from this earth was that he had been tortured to death. As he had refused to betray his friends, amongst them Aristotle (who had married Hermias' niece and been generally much favored by him), Aristotle was very grateful. In building a memorial to him, Aristotle belied one of his own quoteworthy dictums, namely that the thing on earth that grows old most quickly is gratitude. This small, self-inflicted injury to his corpus of philosophical knowledge won't have bothered him, as he had, Diogenes estimates, four hundred and forty-five thousand, two hundred and seventy lines more.[1] But as we know now, a lot of this was wrong too. So perhaps we should understand Raphael's gestures as Plato's expression of exasperation at the obtuseness of the great pretender.

Pompous Footnote

1   Diogenes Laertius provides a helpful "list of Aristotle's works" which runs:

Four books on Justice; three books on Poets; three books on Philosophy; [just three? But it depends how you define it . . .] two books of The Statesman; one on Rhetoric, called also the Gryllus; the Nerinthus, one; the Sophist, one; the Menexenus, one; the Erotic, one; the Banquet, one; on Riches, one; the Exhortation, one; on the Soul, one; on Prayer, one; on Nobility of Birth, one; on Pleasure, one; the Alexander, or an Essay on Colonists, one; on Sovereignty, one; on Education, one; on the Good, three; three books on things in the Laws of Plato; two on Political Constitutions; on Economy, one; on Friendship, one; on Suffering, or having Suffered, one; on Sciences, one; on Discussions, two; Solutions of Disputed Points, two; Sophistical Divisions, four; on Contraries, one; on Species and Genera, one; on Property, one; Epicheirematic, or Argumentative Commentaries, three; Propositions relating to Virtue, three; Objections, one; one book on things which are spoken of in various ways, or a Preliminary Essay; one on the Passion of Anger; five on Ethics; three on Elements; one on Science; one on Beginning; seventeen on Divisions; on Divisible Things, one; two books of Questions and Answers; two on Motion; one book of Propositions; four of Contentious Propositions; one of Syllogisms; eight of the First Analytics; two of the second greater Analytics; one on Problems; eight on Method; one on the Better; one on the Idea; Definitions serving as a preamble to the Topics, seven; two books more of Syllogisms; one of Syllogisms and Definitions; one on what is Eligible, and on what is Suitable; the Preface to the Topics, one; Topics relating to the Definitions, two; one on the Passions; one on Divisions; one on Mathematics; thirteen books of Definitions; two of Epicheiremata, or Arguments; one on Pleasure; one of Propositions; on the Voluntary, one; on the Honourable, one; of Epicheirematic or Argumentative Propositions, twenty-five books; of Amatory Propositions, four; of Propositions relating to Friendship, two; of Propositions relating to the Soul, one; on Politics, two; Political Lectures, such as that of Theophrastus, eight; on Just Actions, two; two books entitled, A Collection of Arts; two on the Art of Rhetoric; one on Art; two on other Art; one on Method; one, the Introduction to the Art of Theodectes; two books, being a treatise on the Art of Poetry; one book of Rhetorical Enthymemes on Magnitude; one of Divisions of Enthymemes; on Style, two; on Advice, one; on Collection two; on Nature, three; on Natural Philosophy, one; on the Philosophy of Archytas, three; on the Philosophy of Speusippus and Xenocrates, one; on things taken from the doctrines of Timaeus and the school of Archytas, one; on Doctrines of Melissus, one; on Doctrines of Alcmaeon, one; on the Pythagoreans, one; on the Precepts of Gorgias, one; on the Precepts of Xenophanes, one; on the Precepts of Zeno, one; on the Pythagoreans, one; on Animals, nine; on Anatomy, eight; one book, a Selection of Anatomical Questions; one on Compound Animals; one on Mythological Animals; one on Impotence; one on Plants; one on Physiognomy; two on Medicine; one on the Unit; one on Signs of Storms; one on Astronomy; one on Optics;

one on Motion; one on Music; one on Memory; six on Doubts connected with Homer; one on Poetry; thirty-eight of Natural Philosophy in reference to the First Elements; two of Problems Resolved; two of Encyclica, or General Knowledge; one on Mechanics; two consisting of Problems derived from the writings of Democritus; one on Stone; one book of Comparisons; twelve books of Miscellanies; fourteen books of things explained according to their Genus; one on Rights; one book, the Conquerors at the Olympic Games; one, the Conquerors at the Pythian Games in the Art of Music; one, the Pythian; one, a List of the Victors in the Pythian Games; one, the Victories gained at the Olympic Games; one on Tragedies; one, a List of Plays; one book of Proverbs; one on the Laws of Recommendations; four books of Laws; one of Categories; one on Interpretation; a book containing an account of the Constitutions of a hundred and fifty-eight cities, and also some individual democratic, oligarchic, aristocratic, and tyrannical Constitutions; Letters to Philip; Letters of the Selymbrians; four Letters to Alexander; nine to Antipater; one to Mentor; one to Ariston; One to Olympias; one to Hephaestion; one to Themistagoras; one to Philoxenus; one to Democritus; one book of Poems, beginning: 'Hail! holy, sacred, distant-shooting God'. And a book of Elegies which begins 'Daughter of all-accomplish'd mother'.

II
MORE ANCIENTS

CHAPTER 4
LAO TZU CHANGES INTO NOTHING
(6TH–5TH C. BCE)

In China, Lao Tzu is revered as one of the three great sages, a contemporary of Confucius (sixth to fifth century BCE), and as the author of the classic of Taoism, the *Tao Te Ching*.[1] Yet, funnily enough, he is barely acknowledged in the West. Professor Kwong-loi Shun (of the University of California) tries to explain: "Many modern scholars doubt the existence of Lao Tzu as a historical figure, and regard the text . . . known as the *Tao Te Ching* as composite and datable as late as the third century BC."

The Philosophical Tale

Anyway, whether he existed or not, the story goes that one day Lao Tzu was unhappy with China and wanted to leave it to travel the world. However, at the frontier a guard recognized him and refused to let the Great Sage pass until he had first recorded all his wisdom on parchment.

Despite, or perhaps because of, being indubitably so very wise, Lao Tzu managed to do this in just a few weeks, producing a volume of a little over 5,000 Chinese characters. An early chapter reads:

Something amorphous and consummate existed before Heaven and Earth.
Solitude! Vast! Standing alone, unaltering. Going everywhere, yet unthreatened.
It can be considered the Mother of the World.
I don't know its name, so I designate it, "Tao."
Compelled to consider it, name it "the Great."

Handing the completed text to the guard, Lao Tzu mounted his bull and disappeared off, heading westward. (Images of Lao Tzu riding his bull are still popular in China to this day.)

The earliest manuscript copies known date back to the second century BCE, but for many (like the Bible) the text was assumed to have a divine origin, with Lao Tzu revered not merely as an author, or even as a

FIGURE 4 Handing the completed text to the guard, he disappeared off, heading westward.

prophet, but as an immortal. Yet for those who place Lao Tzu somewhere between immortality and complete non-existence, he was born in the sixth century BCE at Juren in the State of Chu, and was the original author of the *Tao Te Ching*, or the 'Classic of the Way and Its Power'.

And whatever its origins, the *Tao Te Ching* is a repository of enormously powerful ideas. Just one of these is the notion of 'yin' and 'yang'. These are the two aspects of everything in reality. Yin, the feminine aspect, is dark, soft, and yielding. Yang, the masculine aspect, is bright, hard, and inflexible. Everything in the world consists of both elements, and everything is in a state of flux, changing to become more yin or more yang.

> *Human beings are born soft and flexible; yet when they die that are stiff and hard . . .*
> *Plants sprout soft and delicate, yet when they die they are withered and dry . . .*
> *Thus the hard and stiff are disciples of death, the soft and flexible are disciples of life.*
> *Thus an inflexible army is not victorious, an unbending tree will break.*
> *The stiff and massive will be lessened, the soft and fluid will increase.*

Another revelation of the *Tao Te Ching* is that everything follows certain patterns, that is, 'the way'. Human beings should also 'follow the way', and yield to the times and influences. According to Lao Tzu, yielding and effortless inactivity are not only the best way to behave in good times, but the best way to confront problems too. 'Rules', such as those favored by Confucius, are part of the problem. However, the lessons of this are not as passive and negative as many seem to assume.

Judging and 'yielding' to the times is also the theme of the older *I Ching*, or 'Book of Changes', written perhaps in 3000 BCE (which makes it the oldest book in the world). The *I Ching* is a guide to action, a guide to achieving the best outcome in the circumstances. It has been used as a practical manual and guide for action for the last 5,000 years, consulted by farmers and generals as much as by emperors and sages. After all, it is part of the philosophy that the 'way' applies to the very small as much as to the great things.

One of the chapters of the *Tao Te Ching* describes Lao Tzu characteristically "wandering" – amongst people, busy as though at a party, feeling like a "newborn before it learns to smile," and alone, with no true home. It continues:

> *The people have enough and to spare,*
> *Whereas I have nothing,*
> *And my heart is foolish, muddy and cloudy.*
>
> *The people are bright and certain,*
> *Whereas I am dim and confused.*
>
> *The people are clever and wise,*
> *Whereas I am dull and ignorant;*
> *Wandering aimless as a wave in the sea,*
> *Attached to nothing . . .*

So where is "Lousy" today?

Lao Tzu fails to appear, either on his bull or off it, in many of the Western dictionaries and encyclopaedias of philosophy. The *Oxford Companion to Philosophy*, as quoted above, casts doubt on his existence. The *Collins Dictionary of Philosophy* acknowledges him not one whit. Even the overtly internationalist *Routledge Concise Encyclopaedia* offers the section heading "Lao Tzu/Laozi," but under it appears only the advice to see "Daodejing," another spelling of the *Tao Te Ching*. In any case, under that entry

Lao Tzu has disappeared again. Not one old gray hair of him is to be found anywhere.

Pompous Footnote

1 It is said that the two great philosophers once met, but Confucius was mystified by his slightly older companion. And as Confucian scholars wrote the history of Chinese Philosophy, they tended to make sure Lao Tzu emerged only in his shadow.

CHAPTER 5
PYTHAGORAS COUNTS UP TO TEN
(ca. 570–495 BCE)

"Pythagoras is one of the most interesting and puzzling men in history," writes Bertrand Russell, in his *History of Western Philosophy*. "Not only are the traditions concerning him an almost inextricable mixture of truth and falsehood, but even in their barest and least disputable form they present us with a very curious psychology. He may be described, briefly, as a combination of Einstein and Mrs Eddy. He founded a religion, of which the main tenets were the transmigration of souls and the sinfulness of eating beans. His religion was embodied in a religious order, which, here and there, acquired control of the State and established the 'rule of the Saints'."

Russell then says (with unusual generosity) that if Pythagoras' theory that "all things are numbers" is literally nonsense, that "what he meant is not exactly nonsense." And he credits the ancient with useful discoveries such as the mathematical notions of the 'harmonic mean' and 'harmonic progression', and the concept of 'square numbers', as well as ways of 'cubing' them. He then concludes:

> I do not know of any other man who has been as influential as he was in the sphere of thought. I say this because what appears as Platonism is, when analysed, found to be in essence Pythagoreanism. The whole conception of an eternal world, revealed to the intellect but not to the senses, is derived from him. But for him, Christians would not have thought of Christ as the Word: but for him, theologians would not have sought logical proofs of God and immortality.

It's a remarkable tribute. But could it possibly be true?

The Philosophical Tale

Pythagoras seems to have been a mysterious fellow. Like Socrates, he left nothing but footprints behind, nothing written anyway. Some dispute he even existed, pointing out that his name, *pythia* and *agoreuein*, literally means 'words of the oracle'. Yet for a mythical figure, there are plenty of practical details recorded. So let us see if Pythagoras, son of Mnesarchus, is really the true father of Western Philosophy.

The story starts sometime, no one is sure exactly when, in the sixth century BCE. At this point Pythagoras, an islander originally from Samos, returned home after years of apparently traveling the world, including Egypt – where he was initiated by the priests into the secrets of their learning – and the mysterious "East," home to the Persian and Chaldean Magi, and the Brahmins of India.

Samos, though, had fallen under the rule of a tyrant, so it was in Southern Italy, at Crotona, that he settled. The locals at the time were notorious for their self-indulgences and laziness, but far from keeping a low profile as an outsider, Pythagoras set about lecturing them on the merits of the simple life. Soon, youths in the gymnasium, other young men, the town women, and the adults in the senate, at least according to the historian Iamblichus, writing 800 years later, saw the light. Six hundred of them became his disciples and dedicated themselves to the pursuit of wisdom. They were required to live communally and simply. Pythagoras had strict rules and required adherents to live by them. The first rule was silence. "He, Pythagoras, says it" was the only thing they needed to know in their search for wisdom.

According to Iamblichus, writing in the third century, the junior monks were not allowed to see Pythagoras and listened to him talking only from behind a veil. The lectures are supposed to have consisted (again like the advice from the Delphic Oracle) in brief sayings such as:

Do not help to unload a burden but do help to load it up.
Always put the shoe on the right foot first.
Do not speak in the dark.
When making a sacrifice, go barefoot.

Only a few very advanced pupils, after years of patient learning, were allowed to speak and even ask questions.

Amongst other rules of Pythagoreanism, much ridiculed by philosophers subsequently, were:

Abstain from beans;
never touch a white cock;
do not allow swallows to live under your roof;
do not look into a mirror beside a light;
do not stir the fire with iron;

FIGURE 5 "He, Pythagoras, says it" was the only thing they needed to know.

if a pot is removed from a fire, immediately destroy the impression it leaves in the ashes.

Similarly, when rising in the morning, roll the bedclothes together to remove the impression of the body, and finally, do not lose yourself in mirth. Russell adds the following, saying that all Pythagoras' rules are really "primitive tabu-conceptions."

do not pick up what has fallen;
never break bread nor eat from a whole loaf;
do not walk along the highway;
never pluck a garland;
do not eat the hearts of animals;
do not sit upon a quart measure.

In *On Divination*, Cicero adds to the stock of Pythagorean misinformation by explaining that the bean rule was because beans "have a flatulent tendency inimical to the pursuit of mental tranquility." This, however, was probably an unkind joke on the sect, but one now confused with historical fact.

They had to learn sayings, or maxims, and passwords. Iamblichus gives some examples:

What are the isles of the blessed?
The Sun and moon

What is the wisest thing?
Number

What is the Oracle at Delphi?
The song the sirens sing

Pythagoras forbade the harming of animals because he believed the souls of people were trapped in them. Vegetarians today may feel the word "trapped" is unkind to animals, but then Pythagoras, like the Orphic priests, also considered the human body to be a kind of tomb for the soul.[1] Earthly existence was something that had to be suffered before being reincarnated as something better. Maybe as a number – maybe even the number ten!

Music was central to Pythagoreanism. Pythagoreans had found out that certain frequencies of sound, and what's more the ones most pleasing to the human ear, bear simple mathematical relationships to one another. For example, halving the length of a string on a lyre produced a note one octave higher.

The Pythagoreans naturally thought the heavens needed to be in 'harmony' too, and by means of tying weights to the ends of strings which were then strung, identified the mathematical fundamentals of the laws of gravity. (Newton himself acknowledged this, 2,000 years later, in his *Principia Mathematica*.) Armed with this knowledge, they imagined that the stars themselves made a beautiful sound as they circled round the 'central fire'. This fire, incidentally, was not the Sun, but nonetheless, Pythagoras could be counted as the first philosopher to have drawn up a detailed system of the movements of the planets that did not insist that the Earth was fixed at the center.

Pythagoras considered the universe to, in some strange sense, consist ultimately of numbers, which actually existed over and above the objects that 'partook' of them; four chairs, for example, offer a glimpse of the heavenly 'number four'. The number ten was especially important, a kind of triangular object consisting of four lines of four, three, two, and one:

The Tetractys of the Decad.

By contemplating the mathematical elegance of the universe, revealed in the movements of the stars and planets, but also in mysterious mathematical truths, humanity could escape earthly corruption and attain immortality. Another chronicler, Aetius, recalls how the Pythagoreans swore their most binding oath by referring not to the Gods but to mathematical shapes:

> By him that gave to our generation the Tetractys of the Decad, the fount and root of eternal nature!

It is said that Pythagoras invented the word 'philosophy', or love of wisdom, to cover his investigation of the mysteries of the other world of numbers. He is also supposed to have coined the word 'cosmos' (kosmos), meaning 'beautiful ornament', to describe the universe.

In the fifth century, Proclus credits Pythagoras with systematizing the study of mathematics that had previously been merely scattered observations, "examining the principles of the science from the beginning and proving the theories in an immaterial and intellectual manner."

Aristotle offers some rather disorganized reminiscences of Pythagoras' method, saying that it starts with 'one' and that this one represents the 'limit'. The 'unlimited' around it is then "drawn in and limited by the limit . . . from the unlimited there are drawn into it time, breath, and the void that constantly distinguishes the places of the various classes of things." The first thing created is number. The universe that people know consists of things distinguished from one another, that is, things that can now be numbered.

If the rest of the sequence was specified, the information has been lost. Aristotle adds:

> such and such a modification of numbers being justice, and another being soul and reason, another being opportunity – and similarly almost everything being expressible as numbers . . . they supposed the whole of heaven to be a musical scale and a number . . .

Aristotle recalls too the 'Table of Opposites'. As well as odd and even numbers, the limited and the unlimited, there are

one and plurality
right and left
male and female
resting and moving

37

straight and curved
light and darkness
good and bad
square and . . . oblong

(That makes ten.)

Aristotle explains that Pythagoras linked numbers to concepts like justice, which is number four, and marriage, which took the number five as it expressed the linking of the male and female, and the male number is three, and the female number is two – but the theory is in reality more complicated.

The complicated theory[2]

The Pythagorean theory starts with 'unity' or the number one, also known as 'the Monad'. This was described as being both even and odd, also known as even–odd. These are the two opposite powers present in unity which separate and recombine to form the rest of the world. Geometrically, it is a dimensionless point. For the Pythagoreans, it is the source of all things. The number two is imperfect, as it creates the possibility of division. Geometrically, it is a line. The number three was called 'the whole' because it combines one and two, and because it allows for a beginning, middle, and end. Geometrically, three is the first shape – a triangle. The number four, representing the square, was considered perfect; while the number ten, as it can be created from various prime numbers, also contains all musical and arithmetical proportions, and hence represents the world. With the number four, the realm of physical bodies has been reached as a three-dimensional figure (a pyramid) can be constructed from just four points.

The numbers five and six were both called 'marriage' as they combined two and three, considered the male and female numbers, the former by adding them, the latter by factoring them. The number seven was called a 'virgin', as it cannot be created out of any other numbers. The number eight is the first 'cube' number, being $2 \times 2 \times 2$, and the number nine was called the 'horizon' for no better reason than it is the last number before the 'Decad' or number ten. Ten contains all the other numbers and so is counted as 'the universe'. It can be constructed in lots of interesting ways, such as by adding 1, 2, 3, and 4; or by cubing 1 and 3 and putting them together. The Pythagoreans considered it a deity and swore (devoutly of course) by it.

(End of complicated theory, or at least as much as we are going to consider of it.)

Anyway, the story was told that one of the Pythagorean students, Hippasus, was put out to sea to drown after he had given away to the 'uninitiated' the difficult fact that some geometrical qualities (such as the square root of two) could not be expressed at all as whole numbers. This kind of fact was evidently troubling for the Pythagoreans and they preferred to keep it secret.

But despite not being able to work out the square root of two, stories of Pythagoras' strange powers accumulated, as one fragment records:

> he was once seen by many people on the same day and at the same hour in both Metapontum and Croton, and that at Olympia, during the games, he got up in the theatre and revealed that one of his thighs was golden!

Aristotle himself notes that Pythagoras was nicknamed the 'Hyperborean Apollo', the Hyperboreans being mythical people thought to inhabit the regions north of Greece. The word literally means the land beyond the north wind, thought of as a utopia where the climate was mild, the Sun produced two crops a year, and old people happily threw themselves into the sea after they had decided that they had lived a good life.

As if this was not enough, other writers record Pythagoras' extraordinary feats:

> He predicted that an approaching ship would carry a dead body.
> He bit a serpent to death.
> He addressed the river Cosas and it replied 'Hail Pythagoras!'

Not everyone was impressed by such tales. Heraclitus describes Pythagoras as a charlatan, who stole other people's ideas and passed them off to his followers as his own. He calls him a thieving jackdaw, whose craft is not wisdom but deceit.

But much of Pythagoras reappears in Plato. For example, at a time when such thoughts were rare, Pythagoras insisted that men and women were equal, that property should be held in common, and that adherents live and eat communally. All of this reappears in the *Republic* as Plato's recommended lifestyle for the Guardians alongside the Pythagorean doctrines of the heavenly forms and the split between the world of knowl-

edge and the world of matter (of which philosophers must remain aloof).
In addition:

- In the *Meno*, Pythagoras' view of how learning is really recollection appears, as the 'slave boy' recalls the geometrical theorem that bears Pythagoras' name.
- In the *Gorgias*, there is the Pythagorean doctrine that the better one knows something, the more one becomes like it.
- The *Timaeus* is a Pythagorean description of the universe in terms of (musical) harmonies, and matter which is revealed mystically here as being made up of geometrical shapes, notably triangles.
- In the *Phaedo* is the Pythagorean view that philosophy is a preparation for death and immortality.

Philosophy is sometimes said to be a series of footnotes to Plato, which in many ways is true. But mysteriously enough, Plato himself seems on closer examination to consist largely of footnotes to Pythagoras.

Pompous Footnotes

1   Curiously, the noise of a beaten gong was similarly explained by considering it the voice of a trapped demon.
2   There are two main roots to Greek mathematics. The older of the sources is ancient Egypt, around 3100 to 2500 BCE, and was evidently quite sophisticated, as the Pyramids with their secret tunnels, their mathematical proportions, and their positioning with respect to various planetary and solar bodies testify. The other source, around 2000 BCE, is the priests of Mesopotamia, or the 'land between the two rivers' (that is, the Tigris and the Euphrates), who created a body of mathematical knowledge. Their mathematics was practical, for building, for trading, and for astronomers to measure the seasons, yet also mystical.

CHAPTER 6
HERACLITUS CHOOSES THE DARK SIDE OF THE RIVER
(ca. 5TH C. BCE)

Heraclitus was an aristocrat who lived on the Ionian coast of Greece. His preference for composing short, almost paradoxical philosophical epigrams later earned him the sobriquet 'the Dark'. But it is an innocuous-looking dictum about rivers that has made his reputation. Professor Godfrey Vesey recalls in his mini-encyclopaedia that 'Fragment 12' says: "Upon those who step into the same river, there flow different waters in different cases" and adds importantly that this led Plato to deny that we can know the everyday world of the senses, "and hence to the Theory of Forms" itself.

The Philosophical Tale

Heraclitus 'flourished', as it is often put (like some sort of exotic philosophical flower), in Ephesus around 500 BCE. According to later writers, he also buried himself in a pile of dung, but alas, as so often, this seems to be more an apocryphal tale than a historical one. Like all the other 'pre-Socratics', little remains to record his thoughts and ideas, just a few 'fragments'. There are about one hundred; the longest is just fifty-five words.

From these it can be seen that Heraclitus was a riddler. Except, that is, when he was talking of his fellow Ephesians. Then he was quite blunt, saying, for example, that "they would do well to hang themselves, every last one of them." Nor was he shy of disparaging other philosophers, declaring that they showed by their example that the learning of many things did not bring wisdom. Nor were the populace in general any better – they were as unaware of what they were doing when they were awake as they were forgetful of what they were doing in their sleep.

In other more philosophical fragments, Heraclitus can be seen rejecting all mystical notions of the origin of the universe, asserting that it was not created by anyone, but had existed always, and that what was important about it was to be found not through examining its bits, but by studying its arrangement, its structure. He himself thought it was essentially made of fire, which was also the essential ingredient of the soul.

But Heraclitus' most famous fragment is the one about the river:

You cannot step into the same river twice.

Sometimes this is put more precisely as: "The waters that flow over those who step in the same river will be different." Sometimes it is put as: "You cannot step twice into the same river; for fresh waters are ever flowing in upon you."

If we now have four different versions of the phrase since the start of the chapter, that is only natural. After all, the remark has usually been interpreted as a kind of metaphor about the nature of reality in general, and 'Heracliteanism' became a doctrine encapsulated by Plato as the view that "all is flux."

In the last century Heraclitus was reinvented as a kind of early quantum physicist stepping not so much into rivers but into energy fields. Werner Heisenberg, the inventor of the 'uncertainty principle', even thought his views only needed a bit of tweaking to bring them totally up-to-date, writing:

> Modern physics is in some ways extremely near to the doctrines of Heraclitus. If we replace the word 'fire' by the word 'energy' we can repeat this statement word for word from our modern point of view. Energy is in fact the substance from which all elementary particles, all atoms and therefore all things are made, and energy is that which moves. . . . Energy may be called the fundamental cause for all change in the world.

But Plato himself was echoing Cratylus, who had only earlier decided for himself what it was that Heraclitus must have meant. Cratylus' idea that everything was changing all the time was then taken up by Empedocles, who embellished the other Heraclitean notion of a world continually torn between the two evocatively named forces, 'love' and 'strife', in order to reveal its essential character. The world becomes a sphere of perfect love in which strife, like a swirling vortex, has infiltrated.

Whose idea was it, then? Heraclitus', or Cratylus', or . . .? It keeps changing. But in any case, the point about the river seems to have been a more prosaic one to do with the nature of human experience. We encounter things all the time as being different, but behind the appearance of diversity is a more important and more fundamental unity: "cold things

FIGURE 6 The world is a sphere of perfect love in which strife, like a swirling vortex, has infiltrated.

grow hot, the hot cools, the wet dries, the parched moistens." Not that Heraclitus is saying that the senses are deceived, for "whatever comes from sight, hearing, experience, this I privilege," he adds.

Even life and death are as one, Heraclitus continues. "The same living and dead, what is awake and what sleeps, young and old . . . for those changed are those, and those changed around are these." The opposites are united by change: they change into each other. And change is the fundamental reality of the universe. The highest, 'divine' perspective sees all the opposites: "day and night, winter and summer, war and peace, plenty and famine," all are the same. With the divine perspective, even good and evil are the same.

Two thousand years later, Professor Hegel found in Heraclitus' swirling vortex of the unity of opposites the kernel of a new 'world philosophy', the origins of 'speculative logic', and the historical notion of perpetual change. Hegel's battle between thesis and antithesis, searching for synthesis, led directly both to Marx's dialectical materialism and to the fascist ideology of the purifying powers of conflict and war. But then, Heraclitus himself had declared: "You must know that war is common to all things, and strife is justice." It is only the heat of battle that can "prove some to be gods and others to be mere men, by turning the latter into slaves and the former into masters."

43

Actually, there is another way of looking at Heraclitus. At the same time as he was outlining his theory of perpetual, cyclical change, the Chinese sage Lao Tzu was explaining the cyclical nature of the Tao, manifested in the famous interplay of yin and yang.

But that is another story altogether.

CHAPTER 7
HYPATIA HOLDS UP HALF OF THE SKY
(ca. 370–415 CE)

Hypatia, at least according to Lucas Siorvanes in the *Routledge Concise Encyclopedia of Philosophy*, was a Neo-Platonist "famous for her public talks on philosophy and astronomy, and her forthright attitude to sex." She was also "a political animal" with a keen sense of practical virtue, he adds. Presumably as a result of one or other of these, she was killed by a Christian mob, "and has remained since a martyr to the cause of philosophy."

The Philosophical Tale

Perhaps the most famous of the 'lost women philosophers' is Hypatia. She was said to be the preeminent Neo-Platonic philosopher and mathematician of her time. By the age of 30 her reputation had spread as far as Libya and Turkey. The daughter of Theon, a professor of mathematics and astronomy at the Museum of Alexandria, she was considered even more brilliant, and what's more, beautiful and modest as well, which apparently Theon wasn't. At that time, Alexandria, under the Romans, was the literary and scientific center of the world, boasting magnificent palaces, the Alexandrian Library and Museum, and several influential schools of philosophy. Intellectual life flourished even as the ancient city was increasingly buffeted by battles between Christians, Jews, and pagans.

Hypatia herself was a pagan, being a kind of 'Platonist', or as we would say nowadays, a free thinker. Yet even as Alexandria's Roman Christian government persecuted Jews and other pagans, the government honored her with an unprecedented, salaried position as the head of the school of Plotinus. According to one chronicler, Nicephore, this was because she excelled in all disciplines and surpassed by far all the other philosophers, not only of her own time, but of previous ages too. Anyway, for fifteen years she headed the prestigious institution, teaching the subtle arts of geometry, mathematics, the works of Plato, Aristotle, astronomy, and mechanics. Students, both male and female, were said to travel from all

45

FIGURE 7 By the age of 30 her reputation had spread as far as Libya and Turkey . . .

over the region to study under her. Because of her dedication, her honesty, and her seriousness, "everyone respected and revered her," records Nicephore, and it seemed, even in that rigidly male-dominated society, that it was quite natural for her to lead them.

Notwithstanding that, many of her male listeners fell in love with her, one of them so badly that it seemed he was determined to die. Hearing this, she tore open her clothes, revealing her beauty, and said "*Voilà*! Here, is what you are in love with, my friend!" *Voilà* indeed! (In fact, Hypatia both married another philosopher and was a lover of the Emperor Arcadius.)

Otherwise, in her lectures, she concentrated on logic, mathematics, writing treatises on geometry and arithmetic, conic sections, and a guide to constructing an 'astrolabe', whatever that is.[1] In any case, none of her works survive, only other scholars' letters mentioning them. They were apparently very good, one chronicler says they touched the sky, and that Hypatia was the epitome of eloquence and an incomparable star in the firmament of wisdom.

Saint Cyril, the Christian bishop of Alexandria, hearing this, had other ideas though, and ordered her cruel death at the hands of the Nitrian monks, a sect of Christian fanatics. She was dragged from her chariot and taken to the nearest church, to be cut up while still alive with sharpened shells, before being finally burned. If she left little bodily, let alone philosophical, trace, she does at least have a crater on the moon named after her. Not many philosophers can claim that. (Saint Cyril, it may be noted in passing, since he was a man and so does not really belong here, also incited numerous pogroms against the Jewish residents of the ancient City. Despite – or perhaps because of – his gruesome murders, he went on to become a highly respected Christian theologian.)

Actually, much of what is published about Hypatia's life is fiction written in the nineteenth and twentieth centuries. The most creative is the exciting account of Hypatia's educational training and life composed by Elbert Hubbard in 1908, who made up most of it to compensate for the lack of historical evidence. He even invented quotations that he attributed to Hypatia, and had a suitably 'ancient'-looking picture of her in profile drawn to illustrate the piece.

This suitably enough brings us to an important point about the history of philosophy – much of it is made up. The teachings of most ancient philosophers were left only in the minds and memories of their listeners, and even if they were then committed to 'paper', that was only papyrus, which is fragile and disintegrates when it becomes at all damp. For that reason, even written records are by and large 'copies of copies', with all the little errors that creep in so easily. Add in that much philosophical writing has been translated between languages – Greek philosophy might well be transmitted through Arabic, on to Latin, translated back into Greek before eventually ending up in the various modern languages.

The invention of paper, and indeed the Internet, has not helped much – errors are merely much more efficiently propagated. Elbert Hubbard's made-up accounts of Hypatia's life in *Little Journeys to the Homes of Great Teachers* seems really to have been intended for children, but (according to Sarah Greenwald and Edith Prentice Mendez) have been passed on by recent scholars, such as Lynn Osen in *Women in Mathematics* (MIT Press, 1974), not to mention Fordham University's 'Medieval History course' proudly available on the web. In such places, we learn that as part of his plan for his daughter's education, Theon established a regimen of physical training ("fishing, horseback riding, and rowing": very unreliable-source, *Hypatia: Her Story*, by D. Anne Love) to ensure that her body would be as healthy as her well-trained mind. We nod in agreement as we learn that she was instructed by her father not to let any rigid system of religion take possession of her life and exclude the discovery of new scientific truths.

It is good to hear that Hypatia discovered that "All formal dogmatic religions are fallacious and must never be accepted by self-respecting persons as final," and of Theon's advice to his daugher, to "reserve your right to think, for even to think wrongly is better than not to think at all." It is not surprising to find that, as a result of her father's influence, Hypatia became an outspoken supporter of Greek scientific rational thought, traveling to Italy and Athens where she was a student at the school of Plutarch the Younger. Her loyalty to this school of thought, however, would eventually lead to her death, Hubbard and others note. No wonder Hypatia once said, "Life is an unfoldment, and the further we travel the more truth we can comprehend. To understand the things that are at our door is the best preparation for understanding those that lie beyond." Hubbard recalls her words too that:

> Fables should be taught as fables, myths as myths, and miracles as poetic fancies. To teach superstitions as truths is a most terrible thing. The child's mind accepts and believes them, and only through great pain and perhaps tragedy can he be in after years relieved of them. In fact, men will fight for a superstition quite as quickly as for a living truth – often more so, since a superstition is so intangible you cannot get at it to refute it, but truth is a point of view, and so is changeable.

On the other hand, everyone must reserve their right to think, "for even to think wrongly is better than not to think at all."

These are fine thoughts, and most befitting to the Queen of Alexandrian mathematics. It is only slightly a shame, then, that she never said any of it. The quotes are all inventions. As is much of the screenplay. She never left Alexandria, as far as anyone knows, and the elegant portrait of her that has become something of a standard was devised by Hubbard just for his book.

The one contemporaneous citation of Hypatia's mathematical work is Theon's introduction to a commentary on Ptolemy's Book III of the *Almagest*. Theon describes the edition as "having been prepared by the philosopher, my daughter Hypatia." The other report of Hypatia's mathematics comes from Hesychius in the sixth century who tells us that: "She wrote a commentary on Diophantus, the Canon of Astronomy, and a commentary on the Conics of Apollonius."

Apollonius of Perga lived in the third century BCE and studied in Alexandria. The names of the mathematical curves, 'parabola, ellipse, and hyperbola', are his and the ideas influenced not only Ptolemy in his studies of planetary orbits, but also Descartes and Fermat in the seventeenth century in their development of analytical geometry. Hypatia's role in advancing the geometry could be one of her lost achievements.

The ghastly circumstances of her death, which sound so implausible, are actually recorded relatively reliably by one Socrates Scholasticus, a fifth-century Christian historian (who has no reason to invent a story that puts the Church in such a poor light), who also notes afterwards her high achievements in science and philosophy, surpassing all the other philosophers of her time.

Letters attributed to one of her students, Synesius of Cyrene, also speak of her teaching and philosophy. These do not mention her mathematics, but are rather addressed to Hypatia as "the Philosopher" and "the most holy revered philosopher." And that is good enough reason for her to be included here.

Pompous Footnote

1 An astrolabe is a very ancient astronomical computer, typically made of a series of engraved brass circular plates, for solving problems relating to time and the position of the Sun and stars in the sky. It is quite possible that Hypatia was responsible for a crucial stage in its development that took place around 400 CE.

III
MEDIEVAL PHILOSOPHY

CHAPTER 8
AUGUSTINE THE HIPPOCRITE
(354–430 CE)

"The influence of Augustine on Western Philosophy is exceeded in duration, extent and variety only by that of Plato and Aristotle," writes Mark Jordan in the *Routledge Encyclopaedia of Philosophy*. "Augustine was an authority not just for the early Middle Ages, when he was often the lone authority, but well into modern times."

An authority on what, though? Indisputably, it is on sinning. And learned scholars believe that Saint Augustine's preoccupation with original sin, or with what the Puritans called our "innate depravity," stemmed from his embarrassment at the changes of puberty revealed to the world while bathing, naked (as was the habit of the times), in the Public Baths. That's what Freudian psychology scholars think, anyway. Not so much maybe the theological ones, who think instead Augustine's interests had something to do with talking directly to God. Even if he didn't really do this, philosophers, noting Augustine's early version of Descartes's 'cogito', and his discussion of time and free will, have tended to side with the theologians against the psychologists, and treat Augustine as a Very Important Philosopher.

The Philosophical Tale

In his main work, the celebrated autobiographical *Confessions*, Augustine starts by discussing his evil nature and describes how in his sixteenth year, while away from school ("a season of idleness being interposed through the narrowness of my parents' fortunes"), the "briars of unclean desires grew rank over my head, and there was no hand to root them out."

He then delicately introduces the unwholesome topic of, ah . . . unwanted erections.

> When that my father saw me at the baths, now growing towards manhood, and endued with a restless youthfulness, he, as already hence anticipating his descendants, gladly told it to my mother; rejoicing in that tumult of the senses wherein the world forgetteth Thee its Creator, and becometh

enamoured of Thy creature, instead of Thyself, through the fumes of that invisible wine of its self-will, turning aside and bowing down to the very basest things.

Fortunately, his mother, Monica, a devout Catholic unlike the rest of the sinful family, was less content. Saint Monica (as she would later become):

was startled with a holy fear and trembling; and though I was not as yet baptised, feared for me those crooked ways in which they walk who turn their back to Thee, and not their face. Woe is me! and dare I say that Thou heldest Thy peace, O my God, while I wandered further from Thee? Didst Thou then indeed hold Thy peace to me? And whose but Thine were these words which by my mother, Thy faithful one, Thou sangest in my ears? Nothing whereof sunk into my heart, so as to do it. For she wished, and I remember in private with great anxiety warned me, "not to commit fornication; but especially never to defile another man's wife."

Alas, as one recent commentator writes disapprovingly: "At the age of sixteen, he failed to contain his lust and sinned. The name of the woman involved is not known." Put another way, Augustine, who was born in Tagaste, a provincial Roman city in North Africa, had a relationship with a young woman that he met in Carthage, where he was studying. She bore his child and would be his concubine for over a decade (until Monica found him someone better).

By the age of 30, Augustine had become the expert in rhetoric at the Holy Roman Emperor's court in Milan, at a time when such posts translated into political power. However, he disliked court life with all its intrigues and politicking, lamenting one day as he rode in his carriage to deliver some rhetoric (a grand speech) to the emperor, that "a drunken beggar on the street had a less careworn existence than he." To make up, Monica, who had accompanied him to Milan, now arranged a society marriage, the sole condition for which was he had to abandon his concubine. However, as it was to be two years before his fiancée came of age, he took up in the meantime with another woman. It is from this period that his famous prayer *da mihi castitatem et continentiam, sed noli modo* comes. "Grant me chastity and continence – but not yet."

Then one day, not long after, while sitting with a friend, Alipius, he heard a voice, like that of a child, repeating, "Augustine! Augustine! Take up the Bible and read!" He realized this was a divine exhortation to open the Scriptures and read the first passage he happened to see. The book fell open at Romans 13:13–14. And there he read:

> take part not in revelry and drunkenness, not in debauchery and licentiousness, not in quarreling and jealousy. But put on the Lord Jesus Christ, and make no provision for the flesh, to gratify its desires.

It is surprising what you find if you open books at random. Anyway, Augustine was impressed. Now aged 32 years, as part of his reform, he received baptism by Bishop Ambrose on Easter Eve (along with his son and Alipius). Monica was greatly moved by this, witnessing her prayers being finally answered. She then promptly died.

A few years later, Augustine returned to North Africa, but now as an assistant to the archbishop of Hippo, who in due course he eventually succeeded. It was soon after this that he began writing the *Confessions*, the *City of God*, and numerous other works, which together became the official policy statements of the Church. Running through them all is the challenge of sexual attraction.

For Augustine and his mother, the connection between sexual desire and committing a sin is a natural, nay, an inevitable one. In *Marriage and Concupiscence*, Augustine makes it clear that, in his view, lust is the vehicle for 'original sin', a term for the 'first sin' committed in the Garden of Eden, originally coined by Tertullian (appropriately enough) of Carthage in the second century. Mind you, for Tertullian procreation in itself is good. But for Augustine:

> whenever it comes to the actual process of generation, the very embrace which is lawful and honourable cannot be effected without the ardour of lust. . . . [This] is the daughter of sin, as it were; and whenever it yields assent to the commission of shameful deeds, it becomes also the mother of many sins. Now from this *concupiscence* whatever comes into being by natural birth is bound by original sin.

Yes, Adam and Eve *could* have had sex without lust, he reproves, but they chose instead to have it with lust. Just as a carpenter can perform his actions without lust, so too could people in sexual intercourse. But they choose not to. Mind you, their ability to choose is rather limited in that human beings are free only in the sense of being "free to sin," as Augustine explains in "Of Corruption and Grace" (*De Correptione et Gratia*). God is good, but as we are all born evil, it follows that even someone (like himself) capable of doing good, can do so only thanks to God. Everyone else is a *massa damnata*, an ugly mass of the damned. Of these, God, in His inscrutable manner, has chosen only a small number to be saved and it is only these few that can act without sinning.

For these, the minority saved by unmerited grace, Augustine writes in *The City of God* (*De Civitate Dei*), "there is the vision of God, a joy we can only dimly discern at the moment." For the rest, "there is the second death wherein their resurrected bodies will be subject to eternal torment by flames that will inflict pain without consuming the body." Assuredly, the degree of torment is proportional to the extent of sin, and worse! "Although the duration is equal in all cases: they must suffer without end, for to suffer any less would be to contradict scripture and undermine our confidence in the eternal blessedness of the small number God has saved" (*De Civitate Dei*, Book XXI, section 23, for those who want to read it out in church). Woe indeed! to use one of Augustine's characteristic phrases.

Saint Augustine was also a strong advocate of the morality of slavery, which he traced back to "righteous" Noah who "branded the sin of his son" with that name, and established the principle that the good were entitled to use the sinful. He explains in *The City of God*: "The prime cause, then, of slavery is sin, which brings man under the dominion of his fellow – that which does not happen save by the judgment of God, with whom is no unrighteousness, and who knows how to award fit punishments to every variety of offence." During the Flood, all but a handful of human-kind were swept away as sinners.

But how did Augustine know all this? It is not in the Bible, after all. It does not matter that the Bible never mentions 'original sin' as such, and indeed Augustine's idea that present generations can be held responsible for Adam's 'Fall' is in direct contradiction to some passages, such as that at Ezekiel 18, where it is stated that only the sinner will die and their children are innocent. In fact, like Tertullian, Augustine's authority is God Himself. Augustine considered "revelations" to be true even if apparently in direct contradiction of the Bible. "Divine revelation, not reason, is the source of all truth." Truly heavenly ethical standards are not formulated by reason alone, but revealed by God. Christian truth did not rest on theoretical excellence or logical consistency; it was true because its source was God. And, like Bishop Origen before him, Augustine interpreted Scripture allegorically. The Bible, he believed, had been veiled by God in order to weed out the worthy from the unworthy amongst those seeking Him. Any ambiguities merely provided new facets of truth to be discovered.

Instead, it is a Christian sect, called the Manichees, who were the authorities that Augustine had found to consult. As a youth, Augustine had been an enthusiastic supporter of the Manichees, even if in later life he became their sworn enemy, writing at length on their wicked errors. The Manichees, who (like Augustine) were influenced by Plato, thought there was a perpetual struggle between two eternal principles of Light and Darkness and that our souls were particles of Light which had become trapped in the Darkness of the physical world. Their lesson for Augustine was that all creation (flesh) was evil. Sex, in particular, even that in marriage resulting in the birth of children, was sinful. They even advised anyone who had a baby to at once put it out on the hillsides so that it might perish. But, Augustine now realized, they were not seeing far enough. It is not enough to just eschew sex, for are not sin and selfishness evident already in the infant – who grasps jealously at the breast? "I have personally watched and studied a jealous baby," Augustine writes.

> He could not yet speak and, pale with jealousy and bitterness, glared at his brother sharing his mother's milk . . . it can hardly be innocence, when the source of milk is flowing richly and abundantly, not to endure a share going to one's blood brother, who is in profound need, dependent for life exclusively on that one food. (*Confessions*, Book I, vii)

Or recall, as Augustine does at length, the incident with the pear tree. This was the time in his carefree youth when Augustine and his friends stole pears from a neighbor's garden. Since the pears were in fact rotten, he was not hungry, and in any case, he had better pears at home, he could not explain the deed at first other than that, evidently, "Foul was the evil, and I loved it. . . . I sought nothing from the shameful deed but shame itself." It seemed to be nothing more or less than an act of sheer willfulness, reflecting (as Hannah Arendt would say many years later of the Nazi concentration camps) the "banality" of evil all the more clearly in its apparent insignificance. But then Augustine – in a flash of insight – realizes that by himself he would not have been interested in stealing the pears at all. He did it because he was with his friends. "*O friendship too unfriendly!*" It is friendship – the "unfathomable *seducer* of the mind" – that is the true source of the wickedness.

For there is a deceptive appeal in fraternity, in the camaraderie of the gang itself. "The friendship of men, bound together by a loving tie, is sweet because of the unity that it fashions among many souls." Yet by embracing this lower good, "the soul commits *fornication* when it is

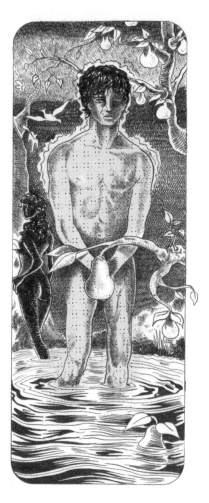

FIGURE 8 Alas, the human race is, more than any other species, social by nature. "O friendship too unfriendly!"

turned away from Thou and, apart from Thou, seeks such pure, clean things as it does not find except when it returns to Thou." By himself, Augustine would "not have committed that theft in which what pleased me was not what I stole but the fact that I stole. This would have pleased me not at all if I had done it alone."

Yet this social fornication is hard to root out. Even by Book 10 and many hundreds of confessions later, and after sorting out the tolerable from the sinful uses of things such as food and music, Augustine is still unable to decide the place of conversation and the company of friends. "For other types of temptation I have some kind of ability for self-examination, but for this scarcely any." His sorrow at the death of his mother and later of a friend reminds him how far he remains from God. Worse! Once jolted by the death of a friend, he would always anticipate the death of others, grasping at passing friendship ever more tenaciously, sensing the loss ever earlier, descending still further into self-centeredness, and down and down. Woe! The fable of human society, the illusion of self-transcendence, "is what we love in our friends."

And so the *Confessions* describes friendships as an "adulterous fondling," declaring *"all* human relationships, even the noblest of friendships, are capable of transmitting original sin." It seems harsh, but then (as Augustine reminds his readers in *The City of God*) lust, or "carnal concupiscence," resides in the soul, and not the body. When a soul is attracted – perversely or otherwise – to another's body or soul or both, then a social relationship, a social transaction, is involved. "Friendly concupiscence" is a dark drive to control, to appropriate, and to turn to one's private ends, all the good things that have been created by God.

Alas, the human race is, "more than any other species," social by nature. Further, since we are a dying race from birth, there is no way to steel ourselves against despair and remain sane without embracing the proud and massive "fable" of societal greatness and immortality.

So what can we do?

Fortunately, there is a way out. For Augustine is able to announce that righteousness now comes by dying. Joy! "It was then said to man, 'You will die if you sin.' Now it is said to the martyrs, 'Die, rather than sin.'"

Even at the time, some Christian intellectuals complained that Augustine made it seem as if the devil were the maker of humanity. They found it absurd to claim that infants were already cursed by guilt in the wombs of their mothers, and they believed that this contradicted God's love of justice. Some complained of the Manichee influence in Augustine's descriptions of evil and the fleshy world. A Welsh monk called Morgan, but known as Pelagius, argued that as sin was something of the soul and not the body, it could not be transmitted sexually and passed from generation to generation. He insisted that people could make choices between good and evil, and that rather than being born sinful, people had no excuse for sinful behavior. He also wanted to reform the Church and criticized Augustine for favoring the wealthy, asserting that a rich man was surely damned. Augustine was alarmed at his undermining of the rite of baptism, and the prospect of the rich (who evidently were made so by God's favor) ruining themselves by distributing their wealth amongst the fornicating masses, instead of leaving their land to Catholic monasteries. So he persuaded the Pope, albeit with difficulty, to "excommunicate" Pelagius. The monk was obliged to return to Britain and stay there for the rest of his life. Woe indeed!

CHAPTER 9
ST. THOMAS AQUINAS DISPUTES THE EXISTENCE OF GOD
(1225–1274)

Thomas Aquinas was very overweight, suffered from dropsy, and had one large eye and one small eye which made him look lopsided. As a child he was silent most of the time and, when he did speak, it was often unrelated to the conversation. So, he decided to become a philosopher-monk. And, as such, he was very successful.

Indeed, in 1323 Thomas was canonized (proclaimed a saint) by Pope John XXII, and in 1567 (better) he was recognized as a 'doctor of the Church', officially to be known as the 'Angelic Doctor'. In 1879, at the Council of Trent, when the Church faced the skepticism of the industrial revolution, it was Thomas's writings that they turned to, alongside the Bible. Afterwards, Pope Leo XIII commended Aquinas to believers as their safest guide to Christian beliefs, and essential reading for all students of theology. Yet Thomas's saintly path was not entirely without obstacles. First of all, on his way to enroll at the monastery, two of his brothers jumped out of the bushes and kidnapped him, before imprisoning him in a castle and plying him with temptations. Worse still, in 1277 the archbishop of Paris tried to have Thomas formally condemned as a heretic.

From heretic in 1277 to saint in 1323 is quite a resurrection . . . But which one was the real Thomas?

The Philosophical Tale

Of all Thomas's essential writings, none is more essential than his *Summa Theologica*, or 'summary of theology'. This is a *magnum opus* of a work consisting of 518 questions and 2,652 responses. The Angelic Doctor worked on this for seven years from 1266 through 1273. The *Summa* is written in the style of the times in the form of 'challenges'. Medieval people, and not just their philosophers, loved these formal disputes (known as *obligationes*) in which opponents were *obliged* to either assent, dissent, or doubt statements. The first person to end up contradicting himself lost. One celebrated dispute involved Aristotle's theory that things like lances would fall bemusedly straight to the ground on being thrown, were it not for the 'pressure' of the air rushing in behind them. In this case, the Aristotelian was considered to have lost when he had to consider whether sharpening the handle of the lance (as opposed to the point) would make any difference. But for Aquinas this is trivial stuff. The first dispute in the *Summa Theologica* is instead over the nature of theology while the second is over God's existence.

Philosophers, not to mention the Church, have tended to emphasize Aquinas's arguments *for*, rather than his excellent, bona-fide, knock-down arguments *against*, the existence of God. In tackling the issue, he was probably hoping to improve on that other Saint Thomas's arguments some two centuries earlier. In 1077, after much thought, Thomas Anselm had laid out his proof of God's existence known as the Ontological Argument. This argument, which was in the form of a prayer to God, begins with a description of Him as "something than which nothing greater can be thought."

The logic of it is that since everyone accepts that – by definition – God is the greatest possible being, and secondly that God does at least exist in our having this concept of Him (that is, He exists "in the understanding"), we only need to take a small step further to realize that God exists in 'reality' as well. And this step is provided by the third, clever, premise of the argument which states that something that exists in reality, as well as in theory, is greater than something that exists in just the understanding. Since God is the Greatest, he must exists in reality as well as in the understanding. The monks considered this demonstration of God's existence a triumph. But the weakness with it was that it still left God existing only by definition. Aquinas thought he could do better.

Aquinas's arguments for the non-existence of God

As part of his investigation headed "Whether God exists," Aquinas notes that it seems that God does not exist, for if one of two contrary things were infinite, its opposite would be completely destroyed. Since by 'God' we mean some infinite good, it follows that, if God existed, evil would not. However, evil does exist in the world. Therefore God does not exist.

Secondly, he adds briskly, "one should not needlessly multiply elements in an explanation." It seems that we can account for everything we see in this world on the assumption that God does not exist. All natural effects can be traced to natural causes, and all contrived effects can be traced to human reason and will. Thus there is no need to suppose that God exists.

Reflecting on possible weaknesses in these arguments, Aquinas's rebuttal of the first point is very half-hearted. He recalls merely that Saint Augustine remarked that "since God is the supreme good he would permit no evil in his works unless he were so omnipotent and good that he could produce good even out of evil." Aquinas may not say so, but it is all too clear that this does not even begin to address the problem. Clearly, an all-good, all-powerful God both could and would prefer "to make good out of good." Why bring in evil?

Aquinas's discussion of arguments against God's existence is rather more detailed. "It must be said that God's existence can be proved in five ways," he starts briskly (or perhaps it may have been wearily) enough. "The first and most obvious way is based on the existence of motion. It is certain and in fact evident to our senses that some things in the world are moved. Everything that is moved, however, is moved by something else, for a thing cannot be moved unless that movement is potentially within it." This is his first point. It is, alas, wrong: Aristotle's mistake being repeated down the centuries. Perhaps that's why Aquinas's schoolmates called him the 'Dumb Ox'.

Now, he brays loudly. A fire, he asserts, which is actually hot, causes the change or motion whereby wood, which is potentially hot, becomes actually hot. "Now it is impossible that something should be potentially and actually the same thing at the same time, although it could be potentially and actually different things," he obfuscates. For example, what is actually hot cannot at the same moment be actually cold, although it could be actually hot and potentially cold. On the other hand, it is impossible that a thing could move itself, for that would involve simultaneously moving and being moved. Thus whatever is moved must be moved by something else, and so on. This cannot go on to infinity, however, for if it did there would be no first mover and consequently no other movers, because these other movers are such only insofar as they are moved by a first mover . . . Thus it is necessary to proceed back to some 'prime mover' which is moved by nothing else, and this is what everyone means by 'God'. Ta da!

Aquinas's argument is simplistic and rather unconvincing, by comparison not so much with today's science as with that of the ancients, notably Zeno and the subtleties of his paradoxes of motion (such as the arrow which appears to need to both move and be stationary at the same time).

A second proof of God's existence also supposes a chain of effects, but this time expands on the notion of 'possibility and necessity', which is a theme dear to Aquinas. But again, the Ox soon seems to stumble. "If it is possible for every particular thing not to exist, there must have been a time when nothing at all existed," he brays inconsequentially. "If this were true, however, then nothing would exist now, for something that does not exist can begin to do so only through something that already exists. If, therefore, there had been a time when nothing existed, then nothing could ever have begun to exist, and thus there would be nothing now, which is clearly false. . . . Thus we must posit the existence of something which is necessary and owes its necessity to no cause outside itself." And again, this is what everyone calls 'God'. Yet, we might ask, before the universe was created, there was no time, and what does it mean to say "before there was time"?

Clearly realizing this was going nowhere, Thomas's next argument adopts a more Platonic flavor. For things to be true, great, noble, *or whatever*, he says, something else must exist which is the "truest, greatest, noblest, *et cetera*"; "for, as Aristotle says, the truest things are most fully in being. . . . Thus there is something which is the cause of being, goodness, and every other perfection in all things, and . . ."

Finally, he considers the idea, again Aristotelian, that things are designed, and appear to have a function or 'end', just as an arrow flies in a certain direction because the archer sent it that way. "We see that some things lacking cognition, such as natural bodies, work toward an end, as is seen from the fact that they always (or at least usually) act the same way and not accidentally, but by design. Things without knowledge tend toward a goal, however, only if they are guided in that direction by some knowing, understanding being, as is the case with an arrow and archer." Therefore, there is some intelligent being by whom all natural things are ordered to their end, and we call this being 'God'.

As has often been observed, if one argument works, you don't need a second, and if you do produce one, it tends to undermine the first. Aquinas comes up with five. Perhaps that is why Martin Luther called the *Summa Theologica* "the fountain and original soup of all heresy, error, and Gospel havoc."

However, many contemporary religious commentators do still rate Aquinas very highly. Take this one on the Internet, at something called "Trinity Communications," recently. For this anonymous expert, Thomas "ranks among the greatest writers and theologians of all time," and his

Summa Theologica continues to set the standard even today. What is most remarkable, though, is that despite his great fame, Thomas:

> nevertheless remained modest, a perfect model of childlike simplicity and goodness. He was mild in word and kind in deed. . . . When someone sinned through weakness, Thomas bemoaned the sin as if it were his own. The goodness of his heart shone in his face, no one could look upon him and remain disconsolate. How he suffered with the poor and the needy was most inspiring. Whatever clothing or other items he could give away, he gladly did. He kept nothing superfluous in his efforts to alleviate the needs of others. After he died his lifelong companion and confessor testified, "I have always known him to be as innocent as a five-year-old child. Never did a carnal temptation soil his soul, never did he consent to a mortal sin."

But this is jumping ahead. Let us return to Thomas's humble beginnings. Aquinas, in fact, came from a very well-off Italian family, and had a large number of brothers, all of whom were groomed for great things. He himself was offered a sinecure as the Head of a Benedictine Abbey that his father had recently taken by force and plundered. However, Thomas refused, saying he wanted to become a Dominican, that is, a 'begging monk' of the kind that forsook earthly wealth instead. So, on his way to the Dominican monastery, two of his brothers, brothers who have since become as sinister as any since Cain and Abel, kidnapped him, dragged him along the road, and imprisoned him in a castle. There, they tried to 'defrock' him of his monk's habit, but Aquinas refused, and they settled instead on locking him in a cell. But as monks welcome any opportunity for quiet reflection, this had little discernible effect.

G. K. Chesterton, the twentieth-century novelist and part-time philosopher, grandly takes up the story.

> He accepted the imprisonment itself with his customary composure, and probably did not mind very much whether he was left to philosophise in a dungeon or in a cell. Indeed there is something in the way the whole tale is told, which suggests that through a great part of that strange abduction, he had been carried about like a lumbering stone statue. Only one tale told of his captivity shows him merely in anger; and that shows him angrier than he ever was before or after.

And this was when his brothers introduced into his room a "specially gorgeous and painted courtesan," with the idea of tempting him into a scandal. GKC enthusiastically relates what happened next:

In this one flash alone we see that huge unwieldy figure in an attitude of activity, or even animation; and he was very animated indeed. He sprang from his seat and snatched a brand out of the fire, and stood brandishing it like a flaming sword. The woman not unnaturally shrieked and fled, which was all that he wanted; but it is quaint to think of what she must have thought of that madman of monstrous stature juggling with flames and apparently threatening to burn down the house. All he did, however, was to stride after her to the door and bang and bar it behind her; and then, with a sort of impulse of violent ritual, he rammed the burning brand into the door, blackening and blistering it with one big black sign of the cross. Then he returned, and dropped it again into the fire; and sat down on that seat of sedentary scholarship, that chair of philosophy, that secret throne of contemplation, from which he never rose again.

This is a fine account, albeit one detail seems to have been left out. Notably that: "After he drove away the temptress, two angels came to him and fastened a chastity belt around his waist." Or so at least embellishes our other theological expert at Trinity Communications on the Internet, along with advice to readers to "Buy or fashion your own chastity belt, easy to make from braided yarn or thin, soft rope." (Adding that "St. Joseph chastity belts are available at some Catholic shops," which Aquinas would not have approved of, being against shops and trading generally.) But at least there is agreement on Aquinas's good character, albeit it still remains a challenge for people who think that sex is that bad to work out how to continue existing once the present batch has died out.

Anyway, when Thomas finally escaped, or more precisely, when his family gave up all hope of changing his mind and let him go, he went off to study Aristotelian philosophy at Cologne, under the famous Dominican friar Albert Graf von Bollstadt, also known as Albertus Magnus, or 'Doctor Universalis', as he became after being canonized. Albertus is counted as the Father of Scholasticism, responsible for the successful union of Christian theology and Aristotelian philosophy. And Aquinas was his star pupil.

Doctor Universalis gave Thomas small jobs to do, of annotation or exposition, and he persuaded him to become less bashful so as to take part in debates. GKC recounts fondly what happened after Albertus learned with amusement that this dunce had been nicknamed the Dumb Ox by his school-fellows. "The great Albert broke silence with his famous cry and prophecy; 'You call him a Dumb Ox: I tell you this Dumb Ox shall bellow so loud that his bellowings will fill the world!'"

FIGURE 9 His brothers introduced into his room "some specially gorgeous and painted courtesan," with the idea of tempting him into a scandal . . .

This was a time when new translations of Aristotle from the Arabic were circulating and causing evangelical chaos. They had been used to provide a philosophical basis for Islam, by theologians such as Idn Rushd, Farabi, and Ibn Sina, and for Judaism by Rabbi Moses ben Maimon, better known as Maimonides. Now Albertus Magnus and Thomas undertook to do the same for Christianity. Armed with translations directly from the Greek produced for him by his fellow Dominican, William of Moerbeck, Aquinas proceeded to standardize the terms of the debate and to tackle heresies. When he was not doing this, or studying a holy text, he walked round and round the cloisters very fast, pacing furiously.

Typical of Aquinas's opinions is that he issued concerning 'Just Wars'. This we might grace with the special title of the 'Argument from Tautology', as it supposes elements of justice in deciding which wars are 'Just'.

He starts firmly enough by saying that a war is just when it is started and controlled by the authority of state or ruler, but then says: "There must be a just cause," and that "The war must be for good, or against evil." In recent years, perhaps sensing a weakness in the Angelic Doctor's work here, or perhaps concerned as it opens the way to rather a lot of wars, two more rules were added by the Catholic Church. These were that the war must be a last resort and that the war must be fought proportionally.

Aquinas also ruled on the status of slaves, which, as we have seen, many philosophers (following Aristotle) considered to be quite justifiable. He concurs, arguing that some men belonged to others, in the sense that sons belong to their fathers (but not, of course, their mothers). Furthermore, he adds, "men of outstanding intelligence naturally take command, while those who are less intelligent but of more robust physique, seem intended by nature to act as servants."

If additional evidence of this were needed, he points out the hierarchical nature of heaven, where some angels are known to be superior to others. Graciously, however, Aquinas adds that slaves, like sons, have some restricted rights, "in so far as each of them is a man."

On the other hand, moneylending, he ruled (following Aristotle) was *unnatural*, and indeed Aquinas sticks his neck out further, saying that trade in general has a certain "inhonestas" about it. "Inhonestas" does not exactly mean dishonesty, it means 'something unworthy', or perhaps 'something not quite handsome'. In this painstaking way, Aquinas also ruled on many issues, major or minor alike. Given the circumstances of the thirteenth century, he left evidence of a surprisingly active letter-writing career, responding to queries from complete strangers – often rather ridiculous questions. When somebody, for instance, asked him whether the names of all the blessed were written on a scroll exhibited in heaven, he wrote back: "So far as I can see, this is not the case; but there is no harm in saying so."

As to the more weighty issue of "Whether heretics ought to be tolerated," his answer in the *Summa* (second part of the second part, dispute 11, article 3, under the same heading) is less reassuring.

> With regard to heretics two points must be observed: one, on their own side; the other, on the side of the Church. On their own side there is the sin, whereby they deserve not only to be separated from the Church by excommunication, but also to be severed from the world by death. For it is a much graver matter to corrupt the faith which quickens the soul, than to forge money, which supports temporal life. Wherefore if forgers of money and other evil-doers are forthwith condemned to death by the secular authority, much more reason is there for heretics, as soon as they are convicted of heresy, to be not only excommunicated but even put to death.

His reputation for tolerance comes from the following qualification to the verdict, however, where he suggests that as the Church "looks to the conversion of the wanderer," it should condemn not at once but only "after the first and second admonition." After this, if the offender is stubborn, the Church looks to the salvation of others, "by excommunicating him and separating him from the Church, and furthermore delivers him to the secular tribunal to be exterminated thereby from the world by death." As Saint Jerome says: "Cut off the decayed flesh, expel the mangy sheep from the fold, lest the whole house, the whole paste, the whole body, the whole flock, burn, perish, rot, die." Aquinas is credited for prescribing instead a process giving chances for repentance.

Even on the ability of good Christians to avoid eternal damnation, Aquinas, like Augustine, was not reassuring. He recalls that in the time of Noah, the entire human race was submerged by the Deluge, and only eight people were saved in the Ark. The Ark is the Church and the eight people who were saved signify that very few Christians are saved, "because there are very few who sincerely renounce the world, and those who renounce it only in words do not belong to the mystery represented by that ark."

So the Angelic Doctor himself, after weighing all the reasons, pro and con, in his immense erudition, finally concludes that the great majority of Catholics (let alone anyone else) are damned. This is because "eternal beatitude surpasses the natural state."

If that left most of his companions in the monastery facing all eternity without hope of mercy or relief from worms, unbearable heat, unbearable thirst, *et cetera et cetera*, Saint Thomas offers them some consolation in ruling that only one form of torture would be used on their way there – the pain of fire. For those not going to hell, there is an additional reward, as in order "that the saints may enjoy their beatitude and the grace of God more abundantly," they are permitted to see the punishment of the damned in hell. On this important matter, Aquinas rules that:

> Nothing should be denied the blessed that belongs to the perfection of their beatitude. Now everything is known the more for being compared with its contrary, because when contraries are placed beside one another they become more conspicuous. Wherefore in order that the happiness of the saints may be more delightful to them and that they may render more copious thanks to God for it, they are allowed to see perfectly the sufferings of the damned.

Squeamish people many not want to see others being tortured, but such people lack proper meal zeal. Those suffering have, after all, earned their punishments many times for doing things like . . . er . . . having sex, or opening shops and selling goods. The baker, the butcher (assuredly), and the candlestick maker – all of those deserve to be there.

Some have puzzled whether Hell and Purgatory are actually in the same location. St. Thomas Aquinas quotes Gregory the Great (who himself draws on Saint Augustine): "Even as in the same fire gold glistens and straw smokes, so in the same fire the sinner burns and the elect is cleansed." Aquinas concludes that there are probably two Purgatory locations: one is inside the Earth and is close to Hell so that they can share the same fire. The other location is above the Earth, between us and God. This is philosophical deduction at its purest and most powerful.

Yet, even if Aquinas's medieval warnings let alone his Aristotelian arguments look dated today, his method remains impressive, a return to the style of Socrates and the open philosophical examination of great issues. If (like Kierkegaard centuries later) he insists that there are things about God we must accept by faith alone, he also insists that they cannot be opposed to reason but merely beyond reason. Arguments, he writes, should be based not "on documents of faith, but on the reasons and statements of the philosophers themselves." He continues:

> If then there be anyone who, boastfully taking pride in his supposed wisdom, wishes to challenge what we have written, let him not do it in some corner nor before children who are powerless to decide on such difficult matters. Let him reply openly if he dare. He shall find me then confronting him, and not only my negligible self, but many another whose study is truth. We shall do battle with his errors or bring a cure to his ignorance.

For Aquinas, religious and scientific or philosophical truths, far from being contradictory, are just different sides of the same truth, indeed, they complement each other. Both sensation and thought are needed to understand the universe, and revelation to understand the divine. That said, "If the only way open to use for the knowledge of God were solely that of reason, the human race would remain in the blackest shadows of ignorance."

Dante awarded Doctor Angelicus a pinnacle in paradise, a little higher than Aristotle, and called him a flame of heavenly wisdom. Alas, as Colin Kirk, has recently put it, "Tolerance is incompatible with divinely inspired truth expressed in terms of Aristotelian logic."

As one of Thomas's final acts, he was called upon by the Church authorities to defend the status of religious knowledge against Siger of Brabant's claim that something could be true in theology even if demonstrably false in science and philosophy. Aquinas was concerned to win the argument, in order to prevent the Church becoming irrelevant in matters of knowledge. After the debate, his followers hailed a most surpassing victory and called it a crowning achievement of which he could be proud. Yet, instead, Aquinas suddenly stopped writing. What had happened, it seems, was this. On December 6, 1273, whilst saying mass, the philosopher experienced a heavenly vision. And when urged to take up his pen again, he now replied, "Such things have been revealed to me that all that I have written seems to me as so much straw. Now I await the end of my days."

And although still not quite 50 years old, he died just three months later.

IV
MODERN PHILOSOPHY

CHAPTER 10
DESCARTES THE DILETTANTE
(1596–1650)

And then there is Descartes, with whom, we are authoritatively told, 'real' philosophy comes into being. "Here we finally reach home," Hegel wrote in his magisterial *History of Philosophy*, "like a mariner after a long voyage in a tempestuous sea, we can shout 'Land ho!', for with Descartes the culture and thought of modern times really begin."

So hats off, please, to Descartes, "Father of Modern Philosophy," soldier, scientist, geometer, philosopher. But "How is he to proceed?" asks Professor F. E. Sutcliffe, before quickly answering himself.

> By rejecting [he says] as being absolutely false everything of which he should have the slightest cause to doubt, and then to see if there remained anything which was entirely indubitable. . . . But whereas Montaigne had concluded that the Sceptics had been right in asserting that the human mind is incapable of reaching any certainty, Descartes, at the moment when all issue appears closed, brings forward dramatically his proposition "I think, therefore I am."

The Philosophical Tale

But Descartes is a historical individual as well as a philosophical legend. And the work of the military gentleman who wrote the *Meditations* and the *Discourse on Philosophical Method* can also be understood when seen as the product of an egotist, as well as the work of a 'genius'. So it was that Descartes can be found at the age of 23 confidently predicting that he had discovered an "entirely new science," and announcing his intention to reveal all in a book. But then, ever wary of possible ridicule, he could not bear to commit himself and this book, after years of revisions, fell by the wayside. The same fate awaited his next project, the thirty-six "Rules for the direction of the Mind," and indeed the one after that, "Elements of Metaphysics." In fact, by the middle of his life, Descartes had published nothing and the whispers said that he was as a *celebris promissor* – a great promiser – who boasted everything but produced nothing.

However, Descartes was not finished yet. In a letter to his monkish friend, Marin Mersenne, he wrote that while previous works had of necessity had to be modified, abandoned, and restarted as he gained new knowledge, he had now a new work that would at last be beyond modification, "whatever new knowledge that I may require in the future."

Somewhat ironically perhaps, this was the work which would in due course be heralded as introducing the 'method of doubt'. What had happened, in fact, was that as he approached the ominous human milestone of age 40, Descartes had decided to cobble together – perhaps we best say 'prepare' – a 'collection' of all his unpublished works, to be entitled "The Project for a Universal Science, suited to Raise our Nature to the Highest Level of Perfection." It was at this point that he decided that perhaps it would be better if most of the essentially self-serving first-person references were removed. Except, that was, in the preface, which instead became almost autobiographical in its account of 'the method', or more precisely, of how he had cleverly discovered these many things. In time, though, his affection for this part soon led him to downgrade the much more lengthy scientific writings to an appendix with the apologetic words that he abhors publication as it "interferes with his freedom to think," but wishes to allow the reader to inspect some recent work . . . The 'Preface' then became the main dish of the book, which now requiring a new title became the "Discourse on the Method for the Correct Use of Reason and for Seeking the Truth in Science."

But to the modern eye, it is the mark of the democrat, the 'modern', that has Descartes writing in the first person. Not only as he mused in his oven room over the possibility of the Devil deceiving him or recalling his impressions of the wax as it melted and disappeared, but also in the original scientific writings on light and geometry – throughout them all at center stage is the young Descartes, holding forth on his discoveries.

This, then, was part of the charm of Descartes's highly personal style of philosophy – but even so, the novelty was less than it seems to those of us unfamiliar with the seventeenth-century French traditions. Descartes was in fact also mimicking the highly popular writings of Montaigne, whose *Essays*, consisting of carefully self-deprecating rambling observations, had delighted French aristocrats for a good fifty years already. Descartes even opens the *Discourse* with a crafty reference to his predecessor, when he says that "good sense" is "the most evenly distributed thing in the world." Montaigne went on to say, however, that this is only because it seems no one is dissatisfied with their own share of it. Descartes offers no such humorous note.

But Montaigne is not Descartes's only unacknowledged source. As befits one educated under the most stern and orthodox Jesuit masters, Descartes repeats many of St. Augustine's credos in his philosophy. The 'method of doubt' crucially does not include doubting those opinions that appear particularly plausible. St. Augustine himself referred to the assistance of "divine revelation" in coping with the uncertainties of human knowledge; this is recast as "natural light" by Descartes, saying that all that appears obvious to us – "everything perceived clearly and distinctly" – must be true. Alas, it leaves open the possibility for others to see by the natural light truths that we ourselves want to doubt. Nonetheless, deduction in Descartes's new Geometry of Knowledge is based on identifying such certainties, labeling them as clear truths, and then enlarging and expanding on them. So, for example, having discovered it to be "impossible" to doubt the existence of his thoughts but entirely possible to imagine the non-existence of his body, Descartes concludes that the "thing that thinks" is a separate substance, entirely independent of the body. And expanding on this he concludes that animals have no souls but are unconscious brutes, mere machines.

For Descartes, investigating now the realm of physics, the essence of the everyday, observable world is "extension," that is, height, length, width, place. And these attributes he makes literally universal: all matter must be the same everywhere in the universe. He thus offered science an apparently sturdy foundation for building on, although even with modest testing, the structure often began to shake. One example is his 'law of collision', which Leibniz soon refuted.

Descartes's law of collision stated that when a smaller object hits a larger one (like a rock thrown at a wall), it bounces straight back with equal speed, but when a larger object collides with a smaller one (like a rolling boulder squashing a fly), they move off together in a way that conserves the total quantity of motion. So far, so apparently obvious, but consider a collision in which a ball strikes an ever-so-fractionally larger ball. In this case, according to Descartes's law, the first ball must bounce back at the same speed as it approached, while the other remains unmoved. Now, Leibniz says, suppose a tiny wafer is shaved off the second ball so that it becomes now fractionally the smaller of the two – what do we imagine happening if the experiment is re-run then?

According to Descartes's theory, if the collision is re-run, the first ball which previously bounced off the other at full tilt will this time combine with it, and the two roll off together in the same direction at half-speed. Leibniz thinks it implausible that such a tiny change could have such a dramatic effect, and hence that there is a need for Descartes to doubt his own law. And many of Descartes's other notions, including those of the impossibility of 'empty space' and the nature of 'motion', let alone the relation of the mind to the body, were also rather hard to explain. Gabrielle-Émilie Le Tonnelier de Breteuil, who translated Newton's *Principia* into French, and who we may remember more easily as Voltaire's lover ("a great man whose only fault was being a woman," he wrote of her), said of Cartesianism: "It is a house collapsing into ruins, propped up on every side. . . . I think it would be prudent to leave." But the inventor of the method of doubt eschewed the approach for himself. After all, in the opening summary for the *Meditations* he had written:

> The whole of the errors that arise from our senses are brought under review, while the means of avoiding them are pointed out, and finally all the grounds are adduced from which the existence of material objects may be inferred. Not, however, because I deemed them of great utility in establishing what they prove, *viz.*, that there is in reality a world, that human beings are possessed of bodies and so on – the truth of which no one of sound mind ever seriously doubted; but because, from close consideration of them, it is perceived that they are neither so strong nor clear as the reasoning which conduct us to the knowledge of our mind and of God . . .

More Des Cartes

If the *Discourse on Method* was originally a collection of practical writings on scientific matters, not really philosophy at all, the *Meditations* was equally clothed grandly as a collection of "famous people" talking about a new essay – the *Meditationes de Prima Philosophia* by 'Renatus Des Cartes' (as he now wished in Latinate style to sign himself). Amongst these objections is one, lightly brushed off, from Thomas Hobbes disputing the notion of "doubting" everything. This objection is dismissed as irrelevant since (Des Cartes explains tersely) he had only mentioned the "disease" of doubt in the spirit of a medical writer intending a moment later to demonstrate how to cure it. (But perhaps mindful of the comments received, the preface to the *Meditations* explains that the book is not intended to be suitable for "weaker intellects.")

Montaigne constantly referred to himself as a way of both ridiculing and excusing his views. Des Cartes uses the same device to distance himself from anticipated criticism, and also to create the dramatic story of the author's 'enlightenment' after some six days reflecting on the nature of the world in a warm oven room. But it is only a device; the process of enlightenment seems to have taken as many years as the six days described in the book. Of course, if the whole enlightenment process has religious (Jesuit) undertones, so very particularly does the choice of six days.

On the first day, Renatus enters the terrifying world of nothingness by allowing everything to be unknown and uncertain . . .

On the second day, he calms his fears by reflecting that at least he knows one thing, that he is a doubting, fearing, thinking thing: "What am I? A thing that thinks, what is that? A thing that doubts, understands, affirms, denies, is willing, is unwilling and also imagines and has sensory perceptions . . ."

On the third day, he proves to himself that the existence of God is certain . . .

On the fourth day, he teaches himself some ways to avoid error . . .

On the fifth day, he furnishes himself with a superior proof of God's existence, and . . .

On the sixth and final day, he throws aside any doubts and prepares to reenter the world equipped with a new science for understanding it, a science that applies more carefully the very tools of sense perception originally jettisoned on day one.

The famous words *cogito ergo sum* (which render themselves so elegantly in English as "I think, therefore I am") never appear in the original version of the *Meditations*, only in a later and indeed rather casual translation. The actual words used are better translated as: "let the Demon deceive me as much as he may, he will never bring it about that I am nothing so long as I think I am something. So, after considering everything very thoroughly, I must conclude that this proposition, *I am, I exist*, is necessarily true, every time that I say it, or conceive it in my mind."[1]

Des Cartes after all was clear to emphasize the difference between "I think" and "there are thoughts," a distinction that has got lost many times along the way ever since. And there are Augustine's saintly footprints all over the '*cogito*' too. The Saint had taught that: "He who is not can certainly not be deceived; therefore, if I am deceived, I am."

So what makes Renatus Des Cartes so 'modern'?

Descartes said his intention was to create a "geometry of metaphysics" – but one built up not by putting one brick upon another in mental sequence,

FIGURE 10 *". . . this proposition, I am, I exist, is necessarily true, every time that I say it."*

but by analysis of the various parts of the intellectual edifice, to see if they agree and can hold together. The whole logical approach, as with the philosophical narrative itself, was of necessity to rest on the delayed effect of "what is not yet known."

His greatest works, the *Discourse* and *Meditations*, were in many ways afterthoughts – egotistical appendages intended to flatter the author, and not the attempt to overturn the fusty standards of French philosophy, let alone Church authority, in a kind of iconoclastic "counter-thrust" as they are sometimes reinvented as today. The 'method of doubt' is a mere device, speedily replaced by the author's ability to directly obtain true knowledge.

The tale told by Descartes of how he split the world into two separate parts, mind and matter, certainly ushers in the modern world, of machines and dispassionate science, as well as sidelining mystery, feeling, and compassion. Yet Plato too has it that there are two kinds of substance, and strongly favors the separate existence of the soul (which made his works popular with Church Fathers like Augustine, and Descartes was brought up as an Augustinian). In Plato's dialogue, the *Euthyrpro*, featuring Socrates in his condemned cell about to drink the hemlock, the case is set out for the separation of the soul from the body, firmly predicting that it alone will go to heaven. When Socrates is challenged to justify his faith in the soul's immortality, he uses the same sort of examples later used so effectively by Des Cartes – of the perishable world of substance and appearance, as opposed to the unchanging world of pure knowledge.

Descartes died only a few years after publication of the *Meditations*, in Sweden, that "land of bears between rocks and ice," as he describes it unfondly. He was intent on his writings to the last – but not (as might be assumed by those reared on the Cartesian legend) great philosophical treatises, rather on finishing a comedy and a ballet for the queen and her courtiers' amusement.

Pompous Footnote

1   *Ego sum, ego existo, quoties a me profertur, vel mente concipitur, necessario esse verum* is the original Latin text of 1641, for purists. The French version of the principle in the *Discourses* is superficially nearer to "I think, therefore I am," being "Je pense, donc je suis," but an accurate translation of this is not "I think, therefore I am," but "I am thinking, therefore I exist." Anyway, the '*cogito*' does not refer to this text but to the argument in the *Meditations*. So that's clear.

CHAPTER 11
HOBBES SQUARES THE CIRCLE
(1588–1679)

Despite his humble origins as the son of an unemployed vicar in back-country England (his father disappeared shortly after quarreling with another pastor at the church door – indeed, "blows had been exchanged"), Thomas Hobbes somehow managed to rise to the top of the English social hierarchy, hobnobbing with dukes and living off a personal income courtesy of the king himself.

But then, by the time he had left school at age 14, he had already translated Euripides' *Medea* from Greek into Latin iambics, a feat which continues to impress philosophical commentators today (perhaps rather more than it should do). Now leaving his uncle's care to become a scholar at Oxford, he started to move in increasingly aristocratic circles. After finishing at Oxford, he took up a post with the Earl of Devonshire, and traveled Europe, even meeting the celebrated Italian astronomer Galileo in 1636.

Hobbes was impressed by Galileo's descriptions of the mountains on the Moon, the phases of Venus, and the movements of the planets, as well as by biological discoveries such as that of the circulation of the blood by Harvey, all of which tended to challenge established opinion. In fact, the most striking aspect of Hobbes's political philosophy is that, at a time of elaborate and obligatory respect for the various authorities of God, the Pope, the high-born, or whoever, it is resolutely rational in its approach. His arguments are based on clearly set-out grounds, his reasoning shown in clear step-by-step terms with no waffle or "fluttering," as he derisively describes the efforts of other philosophers:

> When men write whole volumes of the stuff, are they not Mad, or intend to make others so? . . . So that this kind of Absurdity, may rightly be numbered amongst the many sorts of Madness; and all the time that guided by clear Thoughts of their worldly lust, they forbear disputing, or writing thus, but Lucid intervals. And thus much of the Virtues and Defects Intellectual.

As Tom Sorell put it, in the *Routledge Encyclopedia of Philosophy*, by the time Hobbes had finished visiting Europe, he had "succeeded in making a name for himself, particularly as a figure who managed to bring geometrical demonstration into the field of ethics and politics." But not, assuredly, as one capable of bringing philosophy into mathematics.

The Philosophical Tale

In fact, it is because of his contempt for the conventional assumptions of philosophy that the influence of Hobbes's own work has been so great. Modern societies today reflect and accept his view that people are motivated by self-interest and, left to their own devices, they always come into conflict. Hobbes explains that the "human machine" is programmed to direct its energies selfishly and he doubts if it is ever possible for human beings to act altruistically, as even apparently benevolent action is actually self-serving, perhaps an attempt to make people feel good about themselves. Rather, in human beings, the primary motion is towards power. In the first place, he writes, "I put for a general inclination of all mankind, a perpetual and restless desire of Power after power, that ceaseth only in Death." Because of this, an *absolute* power is required to control them.

> The final Cause, End or Design of men, (who naturally love Liberty, and Dominion over others,) in the introduction of that restraint upon themselves . . . is the foresight of their own preservation and of a more contented life thereby; that is to say, of getting themselves out from that miserable condition of War, which is necessarily consequent . . . to the natural Passions of men, when there is no visible Power to keep them in awe, and tie them by fear of punishment to the performance of their Covenants . . . Covenants without the Sword are but Words.

Yet, despite favoring one absolute authority, Hobbes dismantled the claims of kings to divine favor, and for doing this (amongst other reasons) he was considered by many of his contemporaries to be, if not actually an atheist, certainly a dangerous heretic. After the Great Plague of 1666, when 60,000 Londoners died, followed by the Great Fire straight afterwards, a parliamentary committee was set up to investigate whether his writings might have brought the two disasters on the realm. As a result of its findings, he was forbidden to write any more books about matters relating to "human conduct" and so had to publish his work abroad instead.

All Hobbes's books are a strange mixture of jurisprudence, religious enthusiasm, and political iconoclasm. The legal points are innovative and perceptive, even if sometimes rather dodgy in the logic of their argument. Starting from a single supposed "fundamental right," that of self-preservation, individual rights are deduced and derived. In his most famous account of the workings of society, the *Leviathan*, Hobbes determined the direction of political theory, social ethics, and international law. These are big achievements. But perhaps his greatest achievement is not often appreciated. Thomas Hobbes managed to square the circle.

How to do it

Buried deep in his book *De Corpore* ('On the Body'), which is part of what was supposed to be a trilogy, moving on to 'the Man' and 'the Citizen', was Hobbes's solution to a 3,000-year-old mathematical problem – squaring the circle. The ancient riddle, which had perplexed Plato, had been whether a square could be constructed, using only a straight edge and a pair of compasses, that had *exactly* the same area as a given circle. The problem had probably started as a practical one to do with measuring land. But in the seventeenth century, 'squaring the circle' was the object of more general interest amongst the common people – perhaps the first mathematical puzzle to become so. There were even contests open to "all members of the publick" and the topic cropped up regularly in polite conversation. A report in the *Journal des Savants* of March 4, 1686, records that one young lady had refused "a perfectly eligible suitor" because "he had been unable, within a given time, to produce any new idea about squaring the circle."

In the view of both Plato and Hobbes, only the two traditional tools could be used as implements in geometry. Any constructions using other devices were considered vulgar and taboo. To square the circle you should start with a straight line and, using this line as a radius, draw a circle. Then, it seems that, still using only a straight edge and compasses, it should be possible to measure out and construct, using a finite number of steps, a square that has the same area as the circle. Only that despite 2,000 years of trying, no one had managed it.

But since, whatever way you look at it, the problem had nothing to do with the subject of his book, Hobbes's solution, other than being in his opinion excellent, did not really fit in with the rest of *De Corpore*. Worse still, Hobbes's friends soon pointed out an error in it. Hobbes was reluctant to remove the "proof" but instead retitled it: "From a false hypothesis, a false quadrature." A bit later on he added a second proof but this too he had to change, this time explaining, rather feebly, that it was "an approximate quadrature." A third "exact" proof was then added,

FIGURE 11 Hobbes imagined that his proof of the squaring of the circle would establish his authority in all matters . . .

but when the book was being printed he realized that this too was wrong. By now it was too late to remove the offending text, so he added, at the end of the chapter, "the reader should take those things that are said to be found exactly of the dimension of the circle . . . as instead said problematically."

Hobbes imagined that his proof of the squaring of the circle would establish his authority in all matters, not merely mathematics. By solving the problem discussed by Plato, the Babylonians, Hindus, Arabs, and the ancient Chinese for thousands of years to no avail,[1] he hoped to rise aloofly above the controversy caused by his political writings. He was tired of being the "Monster of Malmesbury," the "Bugbear of the Nation," the "Apostle of Infidelity," the "Insipid Venerator of a Material God," and the "Panderer to Bestiality." But he reckoned without the Savilian Professor of Geometry at Oxford. Here, amongst his readers, was one of the foremost mathematicians of the time, who had invented the symbols for infinity, for "greater" and "less than," and a substantial part of calculus itself. A former "Roundhead" opponent of the king, a strict Presbyterian, John Wallis had come to his post after decoding a military message for Oliver Cromwell's revolutionary army during the Civil War. Fiercely opposed to Hobbes, and all he stood for, he now decided to take apart the whole of Hobbes's mathematical work revealed in *De Corpore*.

In a letter dated January 1, 1659, to the Dutch physicist and astronomer Christiaan Huygens, Wallis outlines his plan.

Our Leviathan is furiously attacking and destroying our universities, . . . and especially ministers and the clergy and all religion . . . as though men could not understand religion if they did not understand philosophy, nor philosophy unless they knew mathematics. Hence, it has seemed necessary that some mathematician should show him, by the reverse process of reasoning, how little he understands the mathematics from which he takes his courage; nor should we be deterred from doing this by his arrogance which we know will vomit poisonous filth against us.

The first broadside, intended to sink Hobbes in one swift blow, came in the form of a pamphlet called *Elenchus Geometriae Hobbianae* ("An Elenchus of the Geometry of Hobbes," an 'elenchus' being the popular method of cross-examination that Socrates uses in all Plato's dialogues and which sometimes takes the name 'Socratic method'). In this conversational format, Wallis went systematically, one by one, through Hobbes's definitions as well as his methods, pushing over and collapsing each claim in turn, combining both effortless mathematical skill and mocking words. He didn't even stop short of making fun of Hobbes's name, calling him a *hobgoblin*.

The "hobgoblin" bit doubtless hurt, but the mathematical insults mattered more because Hobbes, like many both before and since, had attempted to reduce philosophy to mathematics. Indeed, reasoning, he had claimed, was "nothing else but the addition and subtraction of name," and "true propositions" were "not about the nature of things, but about the names of things." Worse still, it is knowledge of geometry that he had placed at the center of understanding.

Seeing then that *truth* consisteth in the right ordering of names in our affirmations, a man that seeketh precise *truth* had need to remember what every name he uses stand for, and to place it accordingly, or else he will find himself entangled in words: as a bird in lime twigs, the more he struggles the more belimed. And therefore in geometry (which is the only science that it hath pleased God hitherto to bestow on mankind) men begin at settling the significations of their words; which settling of significations they call *definitions*, and place them in the beginning of their reckoning.

Indeed, geometry, Hobbes remarks elsewhere, "hath in it something like wine." Certainly it did for him. Such was its appeal that he was known to often make geometrical drawings on his thighs and bed-sheets when paper was not to hand.

Historians think that Hobbes's love affair with geometry had begun during his 'Grand Tour' of Europe with the Duke of Devonshire. He had by chance come across Euclid's *Elements* lying open temptingly at Pythagoras' theorem in a foreign gentleman's library. Euclid would remain always his inspiration, even if, in characteristic style, he later would not hesitate to rewrite Euclid's definitions, changing that of a point, for example, to make it more like a particle in motion. Hobbes, following Galileo, Robert Boyle, and others of the time, considered that mechanical motions were the way to understand the universe.

And now his beloved geometrical proofs were being shredded before his eyes! But if Hobbes's father had fled from the church pastor, Hobbes Junior was made of sterner stuff. He responded with a frenzy of new pamphlets. First off was *Marks of the Absurd Geometry, Rural Language, Scottish Church Politics, and Barbarisms of John Wallis*. This was followed by six rather unappealing 'dialogues', in the spring of 1660, under the title *Examinatio et Emendatio Mathematicae Hodiernae* (1660), with the last consisting unintelligibly of seventy or more propositions "on the circle and cycloid."

Returning to *De Corpore* itself, he added an appendix to the English edition entitled: "Six Lessons to the Professors of the Mathematics, one of Geometry, the other of Astronomy." This takes on not only the *Elenchus* but also two of Wallis's other works, *De sectionibus conicis* (1655), a highly respected book about the properties of cones, and *Arithematica Infinitorum* (1656), on the arithmetic of the infinitesimally small, a book that would influence Newton and perhaps Leibniz in the development of calculus. Actually, this also explored matters related to the "squaring of the circle" as it set out a new method for determining the area of a circle, and therefore pi, using algebra. The value of his formula is recorded in the fact that it bears his name to this day: the Wallis formula.

However, Hobbes splendidly dismisses Wallis's *Arithematica Infinitorum* with the words: "I verily believe that since the beginning of the world, there has not been, nor ever shall be, so much absurdity written in geometry."

But his most cunning riposte was to publish a new solution to another ancient problem, the problem of the "duplication of the cube," anonymously in French. Hobbes was pretty sure that this time his solution was right, but even so, when Wallis took the bait and wrote a response, Hobbes was ready. After the Savilian Professor had pointed out the weaknesses, Hobbes republished the proof under his own name but this time incorporating Wallis's points as if they were his own ideas!

And so, throughout the 1660s, even as thousands of his countrymen were perishing in the Great Plague, Hobbes was concerned only to score points off the "geometrical professors." Wallis's algebraic methods he dismissed as "mere ignorance and gibberish"; his books were "scurvy" and "so covered with the scab of symbols" that it looked "as if a hen had been scraping there." In 1666, as London burned, he published *De principiis et ratiocinatione geometrarum* ("Principles of Geometry"), followed three years later by *Quadratura circuli, Cubatio sphaerae, Duplicitio cubii* (squaring the circle, cubing the sphere, and doubling the volume of a cube), all intended as a grand statement of his mathematical achievements. Alas, they were all refuted immediately by Wallis, and the two men entered into a vicious cycle of publication and refutation through numerous other papers seemingly without end.

Typical of this exchange was the pamphlet printed by Wallis entitled *Due Corrections for Mr. Hobbes,* or *School Discipline for not saying his lessons Aright,* which focused on Hobbes's misuse of technical language and in particular on the word "point," and Hobbes's angry response with an equally ridiculous title: *Marks of the Absurd Geometry, Rural Language, Scottish Church Politics and Barbarisms of John Wallis, &c.,* mentioned earlier.

Over time, Wallis seems to have grown tired of the "warre," but Hobbes defended his mathematical works to the end of his life. Even at age 91, shortly before his death, he was working on yet another book on squaring the circle. The introduction explains:

> And so, after I had given sufficient attention to the problem by different methods, which were not understood by the professors of geometry, I added this newest one.

Pompous Footnote

1   In 1882 the German mathematician Ferdinand Lindemann produced a fairly compelling proof that it is *not possible* to "square the circle." The reason is because the length of a side of the square would be some number multiplied by pi, and pi is what's called a transcendental number, that is, it is a number with an infinite number of decimal places.

CHAPTER 12
SPINOZA GRINDS HIMSELF AWAY . . .
(1632–1677)

"Spinoza is the noblest and most humble of the great philosophers," declares Bertrand Russell in the *History of Western Philosophy*. "Intellectually, others surpassed him, but ethically he is supreme." Russell thinks this great goodness must explain why he was generally considered "a man of appalling wickedness" both during his life and for centuries afterwards. *But there could have been other reasons.*

The Philosophical Tale

Spinoza's life seemed innocuous enough. He spent his days making optical and scientific lens in Amsterdam. He could have taken up a Chair in Philosophy at Heidelberg but preferred to continue his polishing and grinding. Only in his spare time did he write, coming to the conclusion that everything must be essentially one thing and that mind and body were two aspects of this same thing, a something which has many aspects including that of being rocks, being animals, and being God.

He only published two books in his lifetime. The first was *The Principles of Descartes's Philosophy*, with a foreword noting that he disagreed with most of it (he did not think that there were two distinct things, mind and matter, but that they were two 'aspects' of the same thing, nor that human beings have 'free will', nor that there is anything beyond human understanding). The second was the *Tractatus Theologico-Politicus* (*A Theologico-Political Treatise*). This contained many skeptical comments on the Christian Scriptures, although praise for the "moral message" of the Bible as a whole. From the vantage point of today it looks like a devotional work, but he was sufficiently concerned about being accused of heresy to falsify the book details in a bid to remain anonymous. Indeed, the *Tractatus Theologico-Politicus* was immediately controversial and when Spinoza was 'unmasked' as the author, he became much reviled. So much so that even after his death, when his other writings

FIGURE 12 Sometimes, to "rest his mind," he put flies into a spider's web, "and then watched the battle with so much enjoyment that he burst out laughing."

were published by his friends, they chose to conceal his authorship by crediting the books, including his 'masterpiece', the *Ethics*, to 'B.D.S.' Thus one of the foundational 'modern' texts of Western Philosophy, "Ethics demonstrated in Geometrical Order," had to be published, in effect, anonymously.

The *Ethics*, like Descartes's *Meditations*, is concerned to provide a logical basis for believing in God, a strategy which today seems harmless enough. But since Spinoza's God is stripped of so many attributes (such as having wishes, ideas, or preferences), for many at the time it was considered to be atheism by another name, and to substantiate the worst things that his countrymen had said about him.

No one knows now exactly what he was accused of, but one of his early biographers, Colerus, describes how Spinoza, relaxed by smoking a pipe, or when he wanted to "rest his mind" rather longer, looked for some spiders which had gotten into a fight with one another, or (failing that) he put flies into a spider's web, "and then watched the battle with so much enjoyment that he sometimes burst out laughing."

Such diversions there were before there was telly.

90

Are such people born – or made?

Spinoza was born, in Amsterdam, plain Baruch Ben Michael (he only later Latinized his name to Benedictus de Spinoza). His parents had fled to the Netherlands from Spain, then being terrorized by the Spanish Inquisition and its hunt for heretics. His mother died while he was an infant, and his father, who was a respected figure in the Amsterdam business and Jewish communities, died when Baruch was 22.

The Ben Michael family had been Jewish, and then for several generations, officially at least, a kind of Catholic derisively known as 'Marrano', before subsequently becoming Jewish again. (The term was used to describe the kind of Jews who "ate pork," this being strictly forbidden in the Jewish religion.) But whether Jewish or 'Marrano Catholic', religion placed them at odds with the strongly Calvinist Netherlands, then a young Republic. Spinoza himself refused to identify with any of the cultural or religious associations of his day, accepting only one affiliation, the most secular one. He regarded himself as a citizen of the Netherlands Republic, which he referred to proudly as his "homeland."

Mind you, like many Dutch immigrants before and since, he could hardly speak its language. As a child he had been brought up on Spanish and Portuguese, and later, for scholarly purposes, Latin and Hebrew. But no Dutch. This he only seems to have picked up incidentally and imperfectly, by 'osmosis', as it were.

Baruch was sent to a strict ultra-traditional Rabbinical school, which dwelt obsessively on the great religious texts of the Jewish religion, the Talmud, the Old Testament, as well as occasionally more 'philosophical' commentaries, such as those by the medieval philosopher Maimonides.

Maimonides clearly had a great influence on Spinoza. In his *Guide to the Perplexed*, he raises a number of problems for believers, and then answers them confidently. Spinoza, always a quick learner, soon began to see problems in the texts for himself, but was less good at finding the solutions. In fact, he decided there weren't any. This was because the texts were flawed human constructs, with several authors, not divine at all!

For example, he had been taught at school that the Pentateuch, the first five books in the Old Testament, were divine as they had been written entirely by Moses. But Spinoza wondered how, in that case (as had other scholars), could the section that describes the death of Moses and the subsequent events have been written by him?

Spinoza eventually decided that conventional religions were a mixture of superstition and deceit, and useful only in as much as they guided the unphilosophical masses towards basic moral principles. Spinoza's alternative God, unlike the Jewish one, does not have views or preferences, and certainly does not select between people or tribes. Loving Spinoza's God seems to involve oneness with 'nature'. *"Deus sive Natura"* – God and Nature are one. At the age of 18 he began to learn about this kind of God when he studied with a Dutch teacher who taught him Latin and introduced him to a new world of the 'scientists', Copernicus, Galileo, Kepler, Huygens – and Descartes.

By 1656, when Spinoza was 24 years old, the elders of his synagogue had had enough. They excommunicated him from the Jewish community:

> having failed to make him mend his wicked ways, and, on the contrary, daily receiving more and more serious information about the abominable heresies which he practiced and taught and about his *monstrous deeds*, they have decided that the said Spinoza should be excommunicated and expelled from the people of Israel. By decree of the angels and by the command of the holy men, *we excommunicate, expel, curse and damn Baruch de Spinoza*, with the consent of God (Blessed be He) . . . Cursed be he by day and cursed be he by night; cursed be he when he lies down and cursed be he when he rises up. Cursed be he when he goes out and cursed be he when he comes in.

As if not sure this was enough, they add: "The Lord will not spare him, but then the anger of the Lord and his jealousy shall smoke against that man, and all the curses that are written in this book shall lie upon him, *and the Lord shall blot out his name from under heaven.*"

However, although the official decree, or 'cherem' as it is known, speaks of "evil opinions and acts," "abominable heresies," and "monstrous deeds," no specific deeds are recorded and so philosophers have speculated ever since about what occasioned such hostility.

One theory is that he offended the Jewish community in Amsterdam by reviving a vicious dispute that had troubled it during the 1630s. This had been over what happened to the soul after death, and had only finally been laid to rest after appealing to the Jewish community in Venice for guidance. One of the views on the matter, sometimes attributed to Maimonides, is that the only thing that is left after death is 'knowledge', or more precisely knowledge of God. Spinoza's views seem to be similar. On the other hand, perhaps because of the controversial nature of the topic, commentators complain that he expresses them in a particularly complex and confusing way. So much so that some have concluded that they are meaningless – "rubbish that causes others to write rubbish," as the contemporary British philosopher, Jonathan Bennett, put it unkindly.

But let us judge for ourselves. In Part V of the *Ethics*, Spinoza says that the human mind "cannot be absolutely destroyed with the body but something of it remains which is eternal." This eternal part is an "idea which expresses the essence of the human body, *sub specie aeternitatis*, and which pertains to the essence of the human mind." Rubbish? Perhaps. But classy rubbish. Anyway, Spinoza has proof. "And though it is impossible that we should recollect that we existed before the body – since there cannot be any traces of this in the body, and eternity can neither be defined by time nor have any relation to time – still, we feel and know by experience that we are eternal."

Or it could simply have been that, rather than arguing any particular position, but simply by advocating a 'critical reading' approach to religious texts, he had already made himself unpopular. Anyway, excommunication was scarcely going to worry someone operating within Spinoza's religious system. It served on the contrary only to reinforce his political convictions that society requires a secular regime to keep the various religious authorities in check. In his political theory, Spinoza adopted much of his contemporary and correspondent Thomas Hobbes's views of human nature and the need for strong central government, but unlike Hobbes, he favored political toleration. Natural enough, in his personal circumstances, but he also argued that toleration was essential to retain the consent of the citizens to being governed.

By the age of 30 his fame was considerable and there was a society dedicated to discussing and promoting his views. But it was only some years later, in 1670, that he published the *Tractatus Theologico-Politicus*, setting them out more publicly. The book is intended to examine the role of religion in the context of society and politics. It says things like:

> So God revealed himself to the Apostles through Christ's mind, as formerly he had revealed himself to Moses through the heavenly voice. And therefore, Christ's voice, like the one Moses heard, can be called the voice of God. And in this sense we can also say that God's Wisdom, that is, a Wisdom surpassing human wisdom, assumed a human nature in Christ.

But the method Spinoza was developing (and showcases in his *Ethics*) was much more mathematical. To investigate questions, he identifies underly-

93

ing 'axioms' and proceeds to draw conclusions only through sound demonstrations. It all impressed the elders of the University of Heidelberg enough for them to offer him the Chair of Philosophy there in 1673, but he declined it. He preferred instead to stay in the Netherlands, prepare publication of the *Ethics*, and work as a grinder of lens – not only for spectacles but for scientific instruments – supported also by money from his philosophical admirers.

In consequence of his quest for rigor, the 'mathematical' part of his philosophy is impressively unreadable. Only little bits not couched in mathematical style, often as footnotes, offer more insights. One such, stemming from an excess of rationalism, is that it is "irrational" to be more worried about a future disaster than one that had already happened. For instance, it is illogical to be more worried about being tortured to death by the Spanish Inquisition tomorrow, for example, than about the "Exodus" from Palestine a thousand years or so ago. To the response that "well, yes, the Exodus may have involved much suffering but we can do nothing about that, whereas what happens tomorrow we *can* affect," he replies that to God all events are already planned and only human ignorance makes us think that we can control events.

Then there is his "remedy" against the emotions. "Blessedness," he writes, "is not the reward of virtue, but is virtue itself," adding, "we do not delight in blessedness because we restrain our lusts, but on the contrary, because we delight in it, therefore we are able to restrain them."

And the closing section of the *Ethics*, much quoted within philosophy circles, optimistic and friendly in tone, says:

> I have finished everything I wanted to explain about the power of the mind over its emotions and about its liberty. From what has been said we see in what the strength of the wise man consists and see how much he surpasses the ignorant who is driven on by lust alone. For the ignorant man is not only agitated in many ways by external causes and never enjoys true peace of soul, but also lives ignorant, as it were, both of God and of things, and as soon as he ceases to suffer ceases also to be. On the other hand, the wise man, insofar as he is considered as such, is scarcely ever moved in his mind, but being conscious by a certain external necessity for himself, of God and of things, never ceases to be and always enjoys true peace of soul.

This, then, is Spinoza's kind of immortality: the individual shares in an idea which outlasts him. In the same way, if someone discovers a mathematical formula (say, Pythagoras' one) and writes it on a piece of paper, the formula continues to exist long after the piece of paper, as long as the idea is remembered or considered. Spinoza then concludes his *magnum opus* with the words:

> If the way which, as I have shown, leads to this seems very difficult, it can nevertheless be found. It must indeed be difficult since it is so seldom found. For if salvation lay ready to hand and could be discovered without great labour, how could almost everyone neglect it? But all excellent things are as difficult as they are rare.

Spinoza is truly the "philosophers' philosopher." Things are difficult and only philosophers can understand them. But the reassuring message he offers to the common man is that because God is perfect, God, and the world, is unable to be any other way. This position, or at least the version Spinoza's contemporary Leibniz promulgated, is ridiculed very amusingly by Voltaire in *Candide*, where Dr. Pangloss goes through life encountering disaster after disaster, all the time insisting that "everything is for the best in this best of all possible worlds" – but here is what Spinoza himself says:

> That things should be different from what they are would involve a change in the will of God, and the will of God cannot change (as we have most clearly shown from the perfection of God): therefore things could not be otherwise than as they are. (*Ethics*, Part I, note 2 to proposition XXXIII)

In consequence, a 'free man' thinks of "nothing less than of death; and his wisdom is a meditation not of death, but of life," Spinoza concludes enthusiastically. Everything is already determined, and people are 'free' only in the limited sense that they are free to accept events rather than just suffer them. A bit like the fly caught in the web. Ha ha ha!

V
ENLIGHTENED PHILOSOPHY

CHAPTER 13
JOHN LOCKE INVENTS
THE SLAVE TRADE
(1632–1704)

John Locke was born in a quiet Somerset village into a Puritan trading family, and into a not at all quiet period of Civil War between Parliament and Royalists. Tall and thin, with a long nose like a horse, and what one biographer has called "soft, melancholy eyes," his 1689 *Essay Concerning Human Understanding* soothingly described knowledge as nothing more than "the perception of the connexion and agreement" of ideas. Since this rules out the possibility of innate knowledge, his philosophy was seen as an antidote to Descartes'. And in describing how the mind might take in "simple or complex ideas" via the senses, before assembling them to create knowledge, he also reflected the mechanistic science of the time.

However, it is his political theory, set out in the *Two Treatises on Civil Government* (1690), that became the more influential. It is credited with inspiring both the American and the French Revolutions in the name of fundamental rights and freedoms. Locke's influence is there in the American Declaration of Independence, in their constitutional separation of powers, and the Bill of Rights. It is there too in the doctrine of natural rights that appears at the outset of the French Revolution, and in the Declaration of the Rights of Man, "All being equal and independent, no one ought to harm another in his life, health, liberty, or possessions," declares Locke, firmly.

Everyone, that is, except slaves. Because, curiously, the philosopher whose name inspired others to demand "liberty" had another more sinister side.

The Philosophical Tale

Many notable contemporaries thought highly of Locke. The brilliant mathematician and physicist Sir Isaac Newton, who otherwise shunned company, cherished Locke's thoughts. The celebrated English physician Dr. Thomas Sydenham worked with him on many medical explorations, declaring that this was "a man whom, in the acuteness of his intellect, in the steadiness of his judgement . . . I confidently declare to have, amongst the men of our time, few equals and no superiors." The French philosopher Voltaire called Locke a man of the greatest wisdom, adding: "What he has not seen clearly, I despair of ever seeing." A generation later, in America, Locke's reputation had risen still higher. Benjamin Franklin thanked him for his "self-education"; Thomas Paine spread his radical ideas about revolution, and Thomas Jefferson credited him as one of the greatest philosophers of liberty of all time.

The ascent to this giddy status started with one of the grand English schools, followed by a scholarship to Oxford. Locke first appeared in print there whilst still an undergraduate. These early works were four poems written to celebrate special occasions between 1654 and 1668, a period which offered plenty of opportunities for commemorative poems. He could have written, for instance, about the Bubonic Plague of 1665 or the Great Fire of London in 1666, not to mention a possible retrospective on the beheading of the king in 1649. But Locke's poems were instead written to mark more mundane occasions. There was one to introduce his friend Thomas Sydenham's (the celebrated doctor's) book on fevers, and another to mark a victory of Oliver Cromwell's Republican army against the Dutch monarchy. Eight years later, with Cromwell now gone and a Dutch prince restored to the English throne, Locke contributed to another collection, this time celebrating the new king's marriage to Catharine of Braganza. "Our prayers are heard," penned Locke, just as he had earlier hailed Cromwell with the opening stanza "You, mighty Prince!"

Actually, owing to a well-placed desire to avoid not merely publicity but being executed, nothing else apart from those poems would appear in public by Locke until he was nearly 60. Such timidity was reinforced when, in 1683, the Oxford University authorities ordered all the books that they considered dangerous to be burned, an event which prompted Locke to travel to Holland shortly afterwards. Here he would stay for the next five years, passing much time in the pavement cafés, while, back in London, the government prepared a warrant for his extradition to face capital charges . . .

But back to 1660, when John Locke, then aged 28, had just been appointed as a junior tutor in Greek at Oxford. The appointment required that he take Holy Orders, but he declined, and was unusually granted an exception in 1666. After this tussle with authority, albeit satisfactorily resolved, Locke started to write two essays, one in English, one in Latin, on the power of the magistrate in matters of religious practice, Even so, being a cautious sort of chap, he might well have kept this work secret and stuck in public to his poems and respectable medical and scientific studies (in collaboration with figures of high repute such as Robert Boyle and Sydenham) had it not been for a chance encounter in the summer of 1666.

It was then, whilst working as secretary to a diplomat, that he met Lord Anthony Ashley Cooper. The noble lord was charmed by Locke's wit and learning, and immediately invited him to join his household as his personal physician-cum-philosopher. Ashley, later to become the First Earl of Shaftesbury, was a key player in English political life and under his influence Locke soon started work, alongside the *Essay Concerning Human Understanding*, on drafts for more controversial studies, such as his *Essay Concerning Toleration* and the *Two Treatises of Government* itself. The celebrated latter work reflects his patron's interest in trade and the colonies and his view, as Lord Chancellor of England, that both were crucial to the strength of the country.

Life, liberty, and the pursuit of wealth

Shaftesbury was also one of the leaders of the Lords Proprietors of the Carolinas, a company that had been granted the Royal Charter to found a colony in what is now North and South Carolina, in the 'New World'. Locke became the secretary to the Lords Proprietors (1668–71), as well as secretary to the Council of Trade and Plantations (1673–4), and lastly member of the Board of Trade (1696–1700). In fact, Locke was one of just half a dozen men, during 'the Restoration', who created and supervised both the colonies and their iniquitous systems of servitude. And one of his most important jobs involved writing a constitution for the new colony, thus putting his philosophical principles into practice.

The preamble to the Constitution for Locke's mini-state states specifically that in order to "avoid erecting a numerous democracy," eight Lords Proprietors (including Earl Shaftesbury himself) would become a hereditary nobility, with absolute control over the citizens. These would be treated as feudal serfs, or what Locke calls "leet-men."

Article XIX explains that: "Any lord of a manor may alienate, sell, or dispose to any other person and his heirs forever, his manor, all entirely together, with all the privileges and leet-men there unto belonging. . . ."

And Article XXII notes further that all the "leet-men" shall be "under the jurisdiction of the respective lords of the said signory, barony, or manor, without appeal from him. Nor shall any leet-man, or leet-woman, have liberty to go off from the land of their particular lord, and live anywhere else, without license from their said lord, under hand and seal."

FIGURE 13 In his constitution for a mini-state, Locke declared that no one should "have liberty to go off from the land of their particular lord, and live anywhere else, without license from their said lord, under hand and seal."

If elsewhere in Locke's philosophy all men are created "equal and independent," in the Carolinas the leet-men are unequal and dependent on their masters. What's more, "All the children of leet-men shall be leet-men, and so to all generations" (Article XXIII).

As for the Africans (arriving there in chains), each colonist is given "absolute power over his Negro slaves." This privilege, Locke adds with a nod to egalitarianism, applies to colonists "of what opinion or religion soever" (Article CX).

The trans-Atlantic slave trade was just beginning as Locke wrote this. In time it would become one of the largest involuntary migrations of peoples in the modern era. During the three and a half centuries of the trade, nearly nine million black Africans would be transported to the Americas – and that's not even counting those who died along the way.

The bulk of the slaves were transported between 1700 and 1850 and the British set the pace, counting for at least a quarter of all the slave ships.

If Locke, like Shaftesbury, had public responsibilities to fulfill, he also had his views in private. In 1671 he bought shares in the profitable slave traders, the Royal Africa Company (which used to brand each of its slaves with the letters RAC) and, one year later, the Bahama Adventurers.

For sure, slavery had existed in Africa prior to the colonization of America. Plenty of accounts record that slaves used to be sent across the North African desert to the Berber kingdom, along with gold. These were people generally enslaved following their capture in wars, or "sold" to settle debts – occasionally even to amend for crimes such as murder or sorcery. However, historians consider that the practice was originally not only on a much smaller scale, but also much less malevolent. These African slaves might be treated as part of the family of the person to whom they were enslaved. Their owner might work alongside them and share the same food and shelter. In the Americas, by contrast, the trade represented what has been called a new "industrial slavery." Huge anonymous gangs of slaves were kept in camps and used to produce labor-intensive crops such as sugar cane, tobacco, and cotton. Their owners did not work alongside them, but lived in mansions and employed overseers with whips to force the slaves to work "until they dropped." Conditions were inhumane and horrific in the plantations of the New World.

Conditions on the way there in the slave ships were pretty bad too. Once picked up in the ports of the western coast of Africa, the prisoners were crowded together in chains below decks and held in unsanitary and inhumane conditions for long weeks. Their ship followed a long route dictated by what has come to be known as "the triangular trade." This typically involved sailing from British ports, such as Liverpool or Bristol, to the western coast of Africa carrying the products of the new industries, such as ironware or cotton goods, which were then exchanged for the slaves. Once these were on board, the ships would reset sail for the West Indies or other ports in the Americas – the second side of the triangle. On arrival, the surviving slaves would be sold, and products such as sugar cane, rum, or tobacco would be taken on board for the third and final leg of the trip back to England. No wonder that in 1723 John Houstoun described the slave trade as "hinge on which all of the trade of the globe moves."

Astonishingly, by 1820, there were more slaves in America than 'colonists' – five times more! (Not for nothing was George Washington himself a slave owner.) The indigenous Indians had, of course, been largely exterminated too (by wars, by eviction from their territories, and by disease). But both in cruelty and bureaucratic attention to details and cost, the only parallel to the slave trade is with the transportation of the Jews and the other 'inferior races' by the Nazis during the 1930s and 1940s to the concentration camps.

Europeans greatly expanded the already existing African slave trade by offering money and other commodities for larger and larger numbers of slaves. These inducements led Africans to go on raids to capture other Africans to sell. The raids themselves also added to destitution, thus encouraging people to sell their children into slavery (perhaps ignorant of the full consequences) to buy food for the remaining members of the family.

Locke's *Second Treatise of Civil Government* contains a special discussion of slavery. Chapters 4 and 16 give an account of the "state of slavery"; this explanation in turn depends on his account of the "state of nature" in Chapter 2 and of the "state of war" which makes up Chapter 3.

Why does Locke dwell at such length on the topic? After all, it seems to sit uncomfortably with much of his other writings, in praise of equal rights and freedoms. But there is a long tradition of philosophers favoring the division of society into slaves and owners. Philosophers since Aristotle and Plato had emphasized an elite's ability to think rationally – to command – and these thinkers needed someone to command, people to be denied the power to think for themselves.

For Aristotle in particular, the domestic slave was defined as the possession and property, or, as it were, the "separable part of the master," even if he or she were supposed to be used not merely according to the owner's interest or caprice but for the general good, and according "to reason." Likewise, Aristotle defined the slave as a person "naturally" fitted to be such, writing:

> Those men, therefore, whose powers are chiefly confined to the body, and whose principal excellence consists in affording bodily service; those, I say, are naturally slaves, because it is their interest to be so. They can obey reason, though they are unable to exercise it; and though different from tame animals, who are disciplined by means merely of their own sensations and appetites, they perform nearly the same tasks, and become the property of other men, because their safety requires it.

In the *Second Treatise*, Locke updates this:

there is another sort of servants, which by a peculiar name we call slaves, who being captives taken in a just war, are by the right of nature subjected to the absolute dominion and arbitrary power of their masters. These men having, as I say, forfeited their lives, and with it their liberties, and lost their estates; and being in the state of slavery, not capable of any property, cannot in that state be considered as any part of civil society; the chief end whereof is the preservation of property.

But apart from the philosophical interest of the discussion, Locke may have had more specific reasons to include it at length in his political writings. One hypothesis is that Locke thought he needed an account of 'legitimate' slavery to show that the English royal family were illegitimately attempting to enslave the English people. As one of the aims of his political philosophy is to distinguish between legitimate and illegitimate civil government, the account of slavery may be simply a variation on this theme.

A second reason, in line with Shaftesbury, may have been that Locke considered it his patriotic duty to explain and justify an activity so profitable and useful to the national power of England.

Or a third reason may simply have been that Locke, like Aristotle and so many others before him, simply considered some people to be naturally greatly inferior and so any theory of natural rights need not apply to them.

Nowadays philosophers don't talk much about Locke's view of slaves. But that does not mean the subject was an irrelevance. Because in Locke's philosophy, property is the key to 'civil' society, and the key to property is labor. Indeed, as morality for him starts with the institution of property, slavery is a very peculiar but significant case. In the *Two Treatises*, he says that "initially the earth, and all inferior creatures on it" belong to everyone in common – with one important exception. Each individual does own one thing; they have property in their own person. In the "original state," nobody has any right to this but himself. Locke adds: "It is only this property that gives individuals freedom." But Locke crucially adds a new requirement to being able to be free. The freedom of someone to follow his own will is now "grounded on his having reason which is able to instruct him in that law he is to govern himself by."

In the *Essay Concerning the True Original, Extent, and End of Civil Government*, Locke urges that slavery is "so vile and miserable an Estate of Man" and "so directly opposed to the benevolent temper and spirit of the nation" that it was "hardly to be conceived that any Englishman, much less a Gentleman, should plead for't." The natural liberty of man here represents an inalienable freedom from absolute, arbitrary power. However, in order to justify the economics of slavery, it seemed to become necessary to strip some people of their reason and thus their freedom. The problem for Locke was that he thought that "man's natural state is one of equality, wherein all the Power and Jurisdiction is reciprocal, no one having more than another."

Mutatis mutandis, as Locke might say in one of his Latin poems (things being changed that have to be changed), both in private life as an investor in the Royal African Company and in public life as draftsman of the Constitution of the Carolinas, Locke's position on liberty is, let us say, ambiguous. In fact, it was only by creating new concepts of cultural and intellectual inferiority, and locating slaves outside the social contract, that Locke could reconcile his belief in man's inalienable rights over his person to the grim reality of his day.

CHAPTER 14
THE MANY FACES OF DAVID HUME
(1711–1776)

In the introduction to his epic work, the *Treatise of Human Nature*, David Hume advises readers to be wary of philosophers who "insinuate the praise of their own systems, by decrying all those, which have been advanced before them." Then he proceeds to denounce the weak foundations of everyone else's philosophical systems, replete with "incoherencies" which are "a disgrace upon philosophy itself," and instead to propose "a compleat system of the sciences" of his own.

Thus operates David Hume, whose lazy style, as much as his plump and expressionless face, belies a cunning and determination that Rousseau described as quite simply terrifying. Religion has no place and no role in his philosophy. Knowledge, ethics, and God are all obliged to return to earth for Hume's scrutiny. In so doing, as Bertrand Russell says, "he hoped for vehement attacks, which he would meet with brilliant retorts." Yet he was to be disappointed. The *Treatise* fell, famously, "dead-born" from the press. Later revisions of it, the two "Enquiries," the first *Concerning Human Understanding* (1748) and the other *Concerning the Principles of Morals* (1751), also failed to receive the attention that he thought they really deserved, with the describing of "the Passions" faring particularly badly despite being, in many ways, the most original part. But then, Hume's philosophy, as Bertrand Russell also observed, is a dead-end. "In his direction it is impossible to go further."

The Philosophical Tale

David Hume is admirably frank about his aims and ambitions in life. These consisted of just two things: a literary reputation and a comfortable income. And so it is perhaps fitting that history records in the account of David Hume not a grand philosophical declaration but a much more practical observation on the sales of his first book. "Never literary attempt," says Hume, "was more unfortunate than my *Treatise of Human Nature*. It fell dead-born from the press, without reaching such distinction, as even to excite a murmur among the zealots."

Actually, this was not quite true. The book did "excite" a small murmur, including a review in a London publication called *The Works of the Learned*. The reviewer concluded that the book

> bears, indeed, incontestable marks of a great capacity, of a soaring genius, but young, and not yet thoroughly practised. The subject is vast and noble, as any that can exercise the understanding; but it requires a very mature judgement to handle it as becomes its dignity and importance; the utmost prudence, tenderness, and delicacy, are requisite to this desirable issue. Time and use may ripen these qualities in our author; and we shall probably have reason to consider this, compared with his later productions, in the same light as we view the *juvenile* works of *Milton* or the first manner of a *Raphael*.

Authors have to take the rough with the smooth. But it seems that to mild-mannered, gentlemanly Hume this review went just a bit too far. Indeed, on reading it, he "flew in a violent rage to demand satisfaction of Jacob Robinson, the publisher, whom he kept, during the paroxysm of his anger, at his swords point, trembling behind the counter."

No one has since been able to confirm this shocking episode, described in Dr. Kendrick's *London Review*, and certainly Hume himself gives no mention of it. Rather, he says of the reception of the *Treatise* in general that "being naturally of a cheerful and sanguine temper, I very soon recovered the blow, and prosecuted with great ardour my studies in the country."

Such sanguinity befits a philosopher. But the paroxysm of rage is more the mark of a literary man. And in order to make sense of Hume, counted by some at least as the greatest philosopher writing in the English language, we need to decide which of the two, literary professional or gentleman philosopher, David Hume really was.

Who was whom?

Unlike most philosophers, Hume took the opportunity (albeit the rather late and final one of being confined to his deathbed) to write his own autobiography, or what one commentator called "that curious memoir," which he entitled "THE LIFE OF DAVID HUME, ESQ. WRITTEN *BY HIMSELF.*"

Augustine had pioneered the genre, with his *Confessions*, and Hume's contemporary, Rousseau, had told him of his plans to write one, also entitled "the Confessions." But Hume's is no confessional account, rather a shrewd attempt to dictate the terms by which posterity would record, interpret, and understand him. It starts by offering a sketch of his youth. He remarks:

> I passed through the ordinary course of education with success, and was seized very early with a passion for literature, which has been the ruling passion of my life, and the great source of my enjoyments; my studious disposition, my sobriety, and my industry, gave my family a notion that the law was a proper profession for me: but I found an insurmountable aversion to every thing but the pursuits of philosophy and general learning; and while they fancied I was poring upon Voet and Vinnius, Cicero and Virgil were the authors I was secretly devouring.

So immediately there *is* some juicy stuff. But then such secrets could scarcely be hidden forever. Anyway, it was shortly after this, Hume says, that he settled upon "that plan of life which I have steadily and successfully pursued. I resolved to make a very rigid frugality supply my deficiency of fortune, to maintain unimpaired my independency, and to regard every object as contemptible, except the improvement of my talents in literature." Naturally, the first step would be publication of a book.

This landmark came not many years later, towards the end of 1738, with the publication of the *Treatise*. It had been written while he was renting rooms in Descartes's old stamping-ground of La Flèche, in Anjou, in the heart of France. And still in his mid-twenties, it is a youthful charge at all philosophy, inspired by the French Master's own 'method of doubt'. (Not that Descartes gets many mentions here.) On the opening page, he says it is "an attempt to introduce the experimental method of reasoning into moral subjects." But it is the character of the experimental method that dominates the book, and that in due course would waken Kant "from his dogmatic slumbers." Because (Hume announces) there are only the two kinds of genuine knowledge: that born from experience and experiment, and that born from rationally examining relationships. The rest of it needs to be doubted. Indeed, Hume puts it rather more strongly:

> If we take in our hand any volume of divinity or school metaphysics, for instance; let us ask, Does it contain any abstract reasoning concerning quantity or number? No. Does it contain any experimental reasoning concerning matter of fact and existence? No. *Commit it then to the flames*: for it can contain nothing but sophistry and illusion.

In passing, Hume dismisses science and ethics and points out that no amount of past experiences can provide information about the future, just as no amount of factual evidence can decide an ethical issue. An 'is' can never imply an 'ought', as he elegantly puts it.

Rather later, in introducing a new version, Hume explained his aims more generally as to enquire whether anything "can be *ascertained*" in philosophy. It is, he says, not merely "the same system of doubt" as that of Robert Boyle and others (which "merely went to show the uncertainty of the conclusions attending particular species of argument"), but "a sweeping argument to show that by the structure of the understanding, the result of all investigations, on all subjects, must ever be doubt."

In a very distinctive passage, reminiscent of the *Meditations*, where Descartes warns of the effects of jettisoning even temporarily all his conventional assumptions, Hume speaks of his restless philosophy, and of the feelings it produces in his mind.

> I am first affrighted and confounded with that forlorn solitude in which I am placed in my philosophy, and fancy myself some strange uncouth monster, who, not being able to mingle and unite in society, has been expelled all human commerce, and left utterly abandoned and disconsolate. Fain would I run into the crowd for shelter and warmth, but cannot prevail with myself to mix with such deformity. I call upon others to join me, in order to make a company apart, but no one will hearken to me. Every one keeps at a distance, and dreads that storm which beats upon me from every side. I have exposed myself to the enmity of all metaphysicians, logicians, mathematicians, and even theologians; and can I wonder at the insults I must suffer? I have declared my disapprobation of their systems; and can I be surprised if they should express a hatred of mine and of my person? When I look abroad, I foresee on every side dispute, contradiction, anger, calumny, and detraction. When I turn my eye inward, I find nothing but doubt and ignorance. All the world conspires to oppose and contradict me: though such is my weakness, that I feel all my opinions loosen and fall of themselves, when unsupported by the approbation of others. Every step I take is with hesitation, and every new reflection makes me dread an error and absurdity in my reasoning.

It is a brave philosopher who takes such a lonely path. And Hume scholars today count the *Treatise* as a great work, "in some ways the most important work of philosophy in the English language," as one, Professor Selbe-Bigge, puts it, brushing aside the two later "Enquiries" as having left out the "best bits."

Alas Hume himself later denounced his "juvenile work," saying that continuing attention by scholars was not fair to him, a "practice very contrary to all the rules of candour and fair-dealing, and a strong instance of polemical artifices, which a bigoted zeal thinks itself authorised to employ." Evidently a different Hume from the one who had written in 1740 to Francis Hutcheson, one of the most eminent philosophers of his day (and whose post at Edinburgh University he coveted), claiming to be eager to correct his errors in the work and begging to discover more of "the particulars wherein I have fail'd."

It is the first Hume who, in a letter to John Stewart, Professor of Natural Philosophy at Edinburgh, confesses:

> I shall acknowledge (what is infinitely more material) a very great mistake in conduct; viz., my publishing at all the *Treatise of Human Nature*, a book which pretended to innovate in all the sublimest parts of philosophy, and which I composed before I was five and twenty. Above all, the positive air which pervades that book, and which may be imputed to the ardour of youth, so much displeases me, that I have not patience to review it.

Although, actually, there is a detailed review, called "An Abstract" of the work, that was published shortly after, and turned out to have been written by Hume himself. Or one of them anyway. But we can respect his wishes and leave the summarizing instead to his Church opponents. These were numerous, including well-known figures such as William Warburton, who had written public-mindedly to Hume's publisher to say:

> You have often told me of this man's moral virtues. He may have many, for aught I know; but let me observe to you, there are vices of the mind as well as of the body: and I think a wickeder mind, and one more obstinately bent on mischief, I never knew.

Similarly, James Beattie saw in his writings "the vile effusion of a hard and stupid heart, that mistakes its own restlessness for the activity of genius, and its own captiousness for sagacity," while Samuel Johnson roundly declared Hume a "blockhead" and a "rogue" that lied. But it was not until 1756 that his opponents organized themselves enough to present a summary of the *Treatise* to the Edinburgh Church court.

A close reading showed, they said, that Hume believed:

> *First*, that all distinction between virtue and vice is merely imaginary.
> *Second*, that justice has no foundation farther than it contributes to public advantage.
> *Third*, that adultery is very lawful, but sometimes not expedient.

Fourth, that religion and its ministers are prejudicial to mankind, and will always be found either to run into the heights of superstition or enthusiasm.

Fifth, that Christianity has no evidence of its being a divine revelation.

Sixth, that of all the modes of Christianity, popery is the best, and the reformation from thence was only the work of madmen and enthusiasts.

Their wrath was all the greater because Hume was actually less of a disbeliever than a deviant believer, an agnostic more than an atheist. Indeed, years later, Hume declared at one of his beloved soirées in Paris that he had never met an atheist and questioned whether they really existed. His host, the Baron d'Holbach, replied firmly that he was dining with seventeen of them.

Anyway, and alas, at least given Hume's thirst for literary controversy, the Church at the time had had enough of such trials, and the authorities declined to pursue "so abstruse and metaphysical a subject," ruling that it "would be more for the purposes of edification to dismiss the process."

If they hoped to deprive their fellow-townsman of publicity, they were to be disappointed, for Hume was now well into his next publishing project, an epic six-volume *History of England*. This started to appear in 1754 and by 1762 had become one of the eighteenth century's bestsellers, bringing in enough money to make Hume feel for the first time financially independent. The *History* would, in due course, go through more than a hundred editions and still be in use at the end of the nineteenth century.

By the time the final volume had been published, Hume had received enough royalties to move up a bit, relocating to a posher part of Edinburgh, as he recorded in a letter to Dr. Clephane.

> About seven months ago, I got a house of my own, and completed a regular family, consisting of a head, viz., myself, and two inferior members, a maid and a cat. My sister has since joined me, and keeps me company. With frugality, I can reach, I find, cleanliness, warmth, light, plenty, and contentment. What would you have more? Independence? I have it in a supreme degree. Honour? That is not altogether wanting. Grace? That will come in time. A wife? That is none of the indispensable requisites of life. Books? That is one of them; and I have more than I can use. In short, I cannot find any pleasure of consequence which I am not possessed of in a greater or less degree: and, without any great effort of philosophy, I may be easy and satisfied.

For his admirers, such as the anonymous writer – and anonymous writers, as today in Amazon reviews (at least the positive ones), were often either the authors themselves or their close friends – of an article in the *Weekly Magazine, or Edinburgh Amusement*, the work shows Hume turning his back on the prevailing style of history writing "as a sequence of dates, names and glorifications," instead "brilliantly combining character studies with an analysis of the broad sweep of underlying forces."

Others read it differently. One Mr. Fox complained of Hume, saying, "He was an excellent man, and of great powers of mind; but his partiality to kings and princes is intolerable. Nay, it is, in my opinion, quite ridiculous: and is more like the foolish admiration which women and children sometimes have for kings, than the opinion, right or wrong, of a philosopher."

John Stuart Mill, writing a history review some time after Hume had departed this earth and could no longer be offended, commented favorably on Hume's intellect, but deplored his honesty, saying that:

> He reasoned with surprising acuteness; but the object of his reasoning was not to obtain truth, but to show that it is unattainable. His mind too was completely enslaved by a taste for literature; not those kinds of literature which teach mankind to know the causes of their happiness and misery, that they may seek the one and avoid the other; but that literature which without regard for truth or utility, seeks only to excite emotion.

But the views of Anon carried the day. "His History of the House of Stuart requires only to be read to be admired . . . taken as a whole, it may be considered as one of the most excellent productions of the human genius, and is certainly the greatest historical work of modern times." Anon adds that in the hands of Mr. Millar, then at the head of the London booksellers, it soon became "a favourite performance" among "the higher class of people."

Nonetheless, at least at first, Hume was disappointed with his book's reception. The "banks of the Thames," he complained, were "inhabited by barbarians." "I was, I own," says the author with reference to the first volume, "sanguine in my expectations of the success of this work. I thought that I was the only historian that had at once neglected present power, interest, and authority, and the cry of popular prejudices; and as the subject was suited to every capacity, I expected proportional applause. But miserable was my disappointment; I was assailed by one cry of reproach, disapprobation, and even detestation."

The final humiliation came in June 1763, when Lord Bute, who was at the time the Scottish prime minister, appointed another Scottish historian, William Robertson, to be Historiographer Royal for Scotland. Lord Bute offered Hume instead a pension.

A pension! For the greatest writer of the century! Preposterous! And so Hume went back to France.

In France, Mr. Hume was indeed counted very highly, a *cause célèbre*. He was universally fêted. Great nobles and their ladies showered him with invitations, not content unless *le gros David* was to be seen at their receptions, and in their theater boxes. Another visiting Briton, Lord Charlemont, recalls how he invariably would come across him at the opera, "his broad unmeaning face" usually seen *"entre deux jolis minois."*

For if in Edinburgh Hume had only a maid and cat for company, in Paris he was surrounded by admirers. The hosts of all the literary circles, the so-called "Republic of Letters," the unique French Enlightenment phenomenon of salons governed by talented women competed for his favor. One such, Madame d'Épinay, who called him the *grand et gros historiographe d'Angleterre*, describes a curious occasion when once their entertainers asked the famous philosopher to act the part of a sultan, endeavoring to seduce by his eloquence two beautiful female slaves. Hume was accordingly whiskered, turbaned, and blackened, and placed on a sofa between two of the most celebrated beauties of Paris. Following the instructions he had received:

> he bent his knees, and struck his breast, (or as Madame has it, "le ventre,") but his tongue could not be brought to assist his actions further than by uttering "Eh bien! Mes demoiselles. Eh bien! Vous voilà donc. Eh bien! Vous voilà . . . voulez-vous voilà, ici?" exclamations which he repeated until he had exhausted the patience of those he was expected to entertain. (*Mémoires et Correspondance de Madame d'Épinay*)

Hume himself remembered the times more rosily, writing to a fellow historian that:

> I can only say that I eat nothing but ambrosia, drink nothing but nectar, breathe nothing but incense, and tread on nothing but flowers. Every man I meet, and still more every lady, would think they were wanting in the most indispensable duty, if they did not make to me a long and elaborate harangue in my praise.

In the salons, Hume was introduced to the critics, writers, scientists, artists, and philosophers who powered the French Enlightenment, the *philosophes*. One hostess was the beautiful, intelligent, and virtuous Madame de Boufflers, in whose salon, hung with huge dazzling mirrors,

FIGURE 14 He bent his knees, and struck his breast, but his tongue could not be brought to assist his actions further than by uttering "Eh bien! Mes demoiselles. Eh bien! Vous voilà donc!"

Mozart had once performed. And the correspondence between Hume and Madame de Boufflers likewise shimmers with false reflections. She flatters him for his genius, declaring that meeting Hume makes her "disgusted with the bulk of the people I have to live with," while he gushes in reply: "Alas! Why am I not near you so that I could see you for at least half an hour a day!"

Indeed, Hume particularly appreciated the French acceptance of him as a person, of his character as *le bon David*, and of his personal principles, the cause of so much scandal nearer to home. "What gave me chief pleasure was to find that most of the elogiums bestowed on me, turned on my personal character; my naivety & simplicity of manners, the candour and mildness of my disposition *et cetera*." This was the origin of his French sobriquet, *le bon David*. Yet even at the zenith of his happiness, a cloud was stealing across the sun.

The affair is one of the most famous philosophical tales of them all, widely discussed both at the time and indeed more recently, in books like the popular and impressively detailed *Rousseau's Dog*. Here, David Edmonds and John Eidinow observe that Hume considered the affair to show him as the innocent, indeed somewhat tragic victim of the ungrateful French philosopher's paranoia. But the reality is a little more complicated than that.

The main events are clear enough. When the ambassador, Lord Hertford, was replaced, Hume's holiday in paradise came abruptly to an end. He would have to go back to Britain. This was a blow. But what in fact was far more unfortunate was an apparently innocuous request, by his favorite lady host Madame de Boufflers, for his help with the case of a needy writer. This was in fact none other than the iconoclastic French philosopher, Rousseau. The two had never met, but had several times exchanged mutual congratulations with each other by letter, and now Hume was asked if he could possibly help Rousseau find political refuge in England. How could *le bon David* possibly say no? The two philosophers finally met in Paris in December 1765. Rousseau was ecstatic, writing of Hume: "Your great views, your astonishing impartiality, your genius, would lift you far above the rest of mankind, if you were less attached to them by the goodness of your heart." Hume too penned rather more stately compliments to a friend in the Church of Scotland comparing Rousseau to Socrates.

A sour note, however, was struck even the night before Hume and Rousseau set out for England. Hume had gone to visit Baron d'Holbach for a final farewell. Apologizing if he might be puncturing his illusions, the Baron warned him against Rousseau, saying: "You don't know your man. I will tell you plainly, you're warming a viper in your bosom"!

Yet, at first, all went well. Arriving in London, Rousseau was acclaimed not only as a great novelist but as a celebrated radical as well! The London papers congratulated both themselves and their readers on this display of English hospitality, tolerance, and fair-mindedness, in sharp contrast, they sniggered, to the bigoted, autocratic French.

Yet it must have been galling for Hume, hailed in Paris, reduced now, in the shrewd observation of an intimate friend, William Rouet (Edinburgh's Professor of Ecclesiastical and Civil History), to being "the show-er of the lion." The lion stood out in his bizarre Armenian outfit, complete with gown and cap with tassels, and was almost everywhere accompanied by his small brown and white dog, Sultan. Hume, by contrast, cut a ridiculous figure.

Lord Charlemont, who (we recall) attended many of the same parties as Hume, has left the best description of him, saying:

> His face was broad and fat, his mouth wide, and without any other expression than that of imbecility. His eyes vacant and spiritless; and the corpulence of his whole person were far better fitted to communicate the idea of a turtle-eating alderman than of a refined philosopher. His speech in

English was rendered ridiculous by the broadest Scottish accent, and his French, was, if possible, still more laughable; so that wisdom, most certainly, never disguised herself before in so uncouth a garb. Though now near fifty years old,[1] he was healthy and strong; but his health and strength, far from being advantageous to his figure, instead of manly comeliness, had only the appearance of rusticity. His wearing a uniform added greatly to his natural awkwardness, for he wore it like a grocer of the train-bands. (Hardy's *Life of Charlemont*)

And the sad contrast does not seem to have escaped Hume. Even while he was professing to his French friends his undying love for Rousseau, writing "I have never known a man more amiable and more virtuous than he appears to me; he is mild, gentle, modest, affectionate, disinterested; and above all, endowed with a sensibility of heart in a supreme degree," he was telling his fellow Scots and relatives a very different story. Only a week after he had returned to London, he wrote to his cousin John Home, the "Scottish Shakespeare," calling Rousseau a philosopher "who allowed himself to be ruled equally by his dog and his mistress."

Hume went on to predict that Rousseau would be unhappy living in the English countryside, "as he has indeed been always in all situations."

He will be entirely without occupation, without company, and almost without amusement of any kind. He has read very little during the course of his life, and has now totally renounced all reading: He has seen very little, and has no manner of curiosity to see or remark; He has reflected, properly speaking, and studied very little; and has not indeed much knowledge: he has only felt, during the whole course of his life; and in this respect, his sensibility rises to a pitch beyond what I have seen any example of: but it still gives him a more acute feeling of pain than of pleasure. He is like a man . . . stripped not only of his clothes, but of his skin.

Actually, Rousseau read avidly and widely, and was writing too – his *Confessions*, which would become one of the most influential works in European literature. And, of course, he loved the countryside. Indeed, once he was in his new house, he soon met and made friends with the collector and botanist the Duchess of Portland, and together they went on many happy plant-hunting expeditions in the Peak District. Far from his being "stripped of his skin," Rousseau's creativity burnt as fiercely as ever, whilst Hume struggled for ideas.

But initially Rousseau had to lodge in London with two Scottish landladies near the Strand, and as London was at the peak of its industrialization Rousseau certainly found it "full of black vapours." Fortunately, this was only a temporary arrangement. Soon, Hume found for Rousseau a cottage in the village of Chiswick with "an honest grocer," James Pullein. Then, in March 1766, the offer of a country house came from an English gentleman, Richard Davenport, with an empty Staffordshire mansion, Wootton Hall.

On the surface, then, all seemed to be going well, when Rousseau stopped off in London on his way to his new home in Staffordshire to see his friend. Yet already Rousseau was torn between feelings of gratitude to Hume for his help and suspicion of the Scot. The evening ended disastrously after Rousseau accused Hume of lying to him about his supposedly opportune discovery of a convenient "post-chaise" to carry Rousseau safely, and at small expense, to his retreat.

Indeed, the "discovery" was an artifice, supposedly to spare Rousseau from feeling too indebted. But as an "anonymous" account (again probably either the work of Hume or one of his friends) of the time continues, the trick stirred up all Rousseau's doubts.

> Rousseau suspected the benevolent artifice, and accused Mr. Hume of being an accomplice in it. Mr. Hume protested his innocence, and endeavoured to shift the subject. After a sarcastical reply, Rousseau sat for some time in seeming melancholy, then sprung up, walked two or three times across the room, and at last threw his arms about the neck of his brother philosopher, bathing the astonished David's face with tears, and crying like a child. "My dear friend," said he, as soon as he was able to speak, "will you ever forgive me this extravagance? After all the pains which you have taken to serve me, after the numberless proofs of your friendship, is it possible that I can thus repay your kindness with spleen and abuse! But in pardoning me you will give me a new mark of your regard, and I hope when you know me better, you will find that I am not unworthy of it."

Yet Rousseau had some grounds for feeling suspicious even if history has often been content to conclude that he was simply "paranoid." Bertrand Russell, for example, says in his *History* that after their "unfortunate quarrel," Hume behaved with "admirable forbearance, but Rousseau, who had a persecution mania, insisted upon a violent breach." Yet, if so, like many others, Rousseau had his reasons. He was correct in his suspicion that his letters were being intercepted and read by others, and he had already found out that cruel and mocking accounts of him and his exile were circulating widely, both in Britain and at home in France.

The most hurtful of these was a satirical letter purporting to be from the King of Prussia, mocking the rootless Swiss refugee by offering him sanctuary, adding caustically: "If you want new misfortunes, I am a king and can make you as miserable as you can wish." The "King of Prussia" letter made its way into the London press and even to Rousseau's refuge in Staffordshire. He was very upset. Hume maintained he was totally ignorant of the spoof. But, according to Edmonds and Eidinow, he was present at a dinner where the joke started, as well as at two dinners where Walpole read the letter aloud, and he probably contributed some of the letter's most wounding thrusts.

And behind Rousseau's back, Hume had been conducting an intrusive investigation into Rousseau's finances. He had asked various French contacts to make inquiries on his behalf – concealing from each that he had also asked the others. Madame de Boufflers was put out to learn that Hume had set both her and Baron d'Holbach on the same errand. "To what purpose?" she demanded of Hume. "You will not become his denunciator, after having been his protector." Yet it seemed that was exactly the intention. There was no possibility of Hume's seeking the information to help Rousseau. Rather, Hume himself makes clear that it was Rousseau's character that he was investigating: he was trying to determine whether Rousseau was a rich fraud professing to a pauper! As to the truth of that, history records that by the time Rousseau came to leave England in May 1767, he was obliged to sell his cutlery to pay his fare.

By now Rousseau thought he had seen through to the heart of the plot, and that at the center of the web, like a malevolent spider, was his supposed ally, Hume.

On June 23, 1766, he wrote to declare his suspicions: "You have badly concealed yourself. I understand you, Sir, and you well know it." And he spelled out the essence of the plot: "You brought me to England, apparently to procure a refuge for me, and in reality to dishonour me. You applied yourself to this noble endeavour with a zeal worthy of your heart and with an art worthy of your talents." Hume was appalled, and perhaps a little scared. He appealed to friends for support against "the monstrous ingratitude, ferocity, and frenzy of the man."

Worryingly, from Hume's point of view, was the potential damage to his own reputation as a writer. After all, his accuser was one of the most celebrated writers in Europe, an author whose books, it was said, were rented out by the hour in the shops in Paris! "You know," he wrote to another Edinburgh friend, the Professor of Rhetoric, Hugh Blair, "how dangerous any controversy on a disputable point would be with a man of his talents."

Hume's initial response to Rousseau's letter describing "the plot" had been to ask that Rousseau identify his accuser and provide evidence of the plot. Rousseau's reply to the first question was short and to the point: "That accuser, Sir, is the only man in the world whose testimony I should admit against you: it is yourself." As to the question of his "evidence," on July 10, 1766, Rousseau supplied a mini-indictment of sixty-three paragraphs containing the "incidents" that had brought him to his conclusion.

The indictment is scarcely legally compelling, but rather shows a novelist's love for drama. Central amongst the accusations is Rousseau's claim that on the fateful trip from Paris to England together he had heard Hume mutter in his sleep, *"Je tiens J. J. Rousseau"* – "I hold J. J. Rousseau." Rousseau plays with what he calls these "four terrifying words." "Not a night passes but I think I hear, 'I hold you J. J. Rousseau' ring in my ears, as if he had just pronounced them. Yes, Mr. Hume, you hold me, I know, but only by those things that are external to me . . . You hold me by my reputation, and perhaps my security . . . Yes, Mr. Hume, you hold me by all the ties of this life, but you do not hold me by my virtue or my courage."

Hume always lacked Rousseau's style. Instead he laboriously went through the indictment, incident by incident, writing "lye," "lye," "lye" in the margins as he went along. This he eventually used as the basis for his own account.

Particularly in France, where his reputation as *le bon David* had stood so high, he feared the consequences of public attention. So Hume conducted an increasingly bitter and desperate campaign of defamation against Rousseau. His first denunciations were made in a booklet called the "Concise and Genuine Account of the Dispute between Mr. Hume and Mr. Rousseau," published in French (edited by Rousseau's long-standing enemies) and sent to his friends in Paris. Hume avoided direct contact with Madame de Boufflers, suspecting she would, as indeed she eventually did, counsel against such attacks and urge instead "generous pity." Far from that: Hume's descriptions of Rousseau as a treacherous villain, "noir, black, and a coquin, knave," were splashed enthusiastically across the newspapers and became the staple topics of the fashionable drawing rooms and coffee houses.

Letters reveal Hume's hostility and desperation. Rousseau, according to Hume, was exposed as "surely the blackest and most atrocious villain, beyond comparison, that now exists in the world." In a letter to D'Alembert, he attacked Rousseau in such foul terms that D'Alembert destroyed the letter and replied counseling the "man of moderation" to remain moderate.

In fact, even in Britain, press coverage of what the *Monthly Review* called the "quarrel between these two celebrated geniuses" was not entirely in Hume's favor. If Rousseau was condemned for lack of gratitude, the *Review* was not alone in urging "compassion towards an unfortunate man, whose peculiar temper and constitution of mind must, we fear, render him unhappy in every situation." When Voltaire, Rousseau's perennial enemy, asked Frederick the Great to support Hume against Rousseau, Frederick replied: "You ask me what I think of Rousseau? I think he is unhappy and to be pitied," adding reprovingly that "only depraved souls kick a man when he is down." This even-handed treatment was not what Hume had expected, and not the version he gave Madame de Boufflers, writing that there had been "a great deal of raillery on the incident, thrown out in the public papers, but all against that unhappy man."

Edmonds and Eidinow, having examined the matter in considerable, indeed indefatigable, detail, conclude that Hume's handling of the affair was "full of malevolence." His letters, they say, were "flush with half-truths and lies," such as that Rousseau had called him the blackest of men; that he had proof that Rousseau had plotted for two months to dishonor him, and that King George III was "very much prejudiced" against Rousseau. After Rousseau returned to France to live under the protection of Madame de Boufflers, Hume even wrote to Madame to suggest that "for his own sake" Rousseau would best be locked away as a madman.

Commentators have been quick to quip that in all this, *le bon David* allowed reason to become a slave to his passions. But although this sounds suitably disdainful, of course Hume had written that reason is, and ought to be, just that. If much of his life he hid behind stratagems and pseudonyms, here at least he cannot be faulted for inconsistency.

And so what of Hume himself? Should he really be remembered as a great philosopher or, as he puts it himself, as "a literary man"? (A judgment still viciously fought over by contemporary philosophers.) He claimed to be an expert on ethics, but as a moral individual, was he the plotter and the tormentor of Rousseau, as his letters seem to show, or the saintly figure that Adam Smith described to William Strathern after his death?

His temper, indeed, seemed to be more happily balanced, if I may be allowed such an expression, than that perhaps of any other man I have ever known. Even in the lowest state of his fortune, his great and necessary frugality never hindered him from exercising, upon proper occasions, acts both of charity and generosity. . . . The extreme gentleness of his nature never weakened either the firmness of his mind, or the steadiness of his resolutions. His constant pleasantry was the genuine effusion of good-nature and good-humour, tempered with delicacy and modesty, and without even the slightest tincture of malignity, so frequently the disagreeable source of what is called wit in other men. . . . And that gaiety of temper . . . attended with the most severe application, the most extensive learning, the greatest depth of thought, and a capacity in every respect the most comprehensive. Upon the whole, I have always considered him, both in his lifetime, and since his death, as approaching as nearly to the idea of a perfectly wise and virtuous man, as perhaps the nature of human frailty will admit.

Clearly not that. Smith's picture is kindly but not insightful. Perhaps Smith felt bad (as well he might) after blocking Hume's chance to be appointed Professor of Philosophy at Edinburgh, and this was some small way to make up. But neither is he, perhaps, the other, more vindictive Hume either. Probably the answer is more psychologically interesting, and after all, Hume was in his own terms a scholar of human nature, pointing to the complex ways in which we construct the world in our minds to suit ourselves – and then proclaim it is really, "objectively" out there. Hume could have been both a cold-hearted plotter and an emotional and good man; both an iconoclast and a conservative; both an original thinker and a superficial one. Perhaps the final word on Hume should go to himself, or at least his youthful self, in the *Treatise*. It is here he writes:

The mind is a kind of theatre, where several perceptions successively make their appearance – pass, repass, glide away, and mingle in an infinite variety of postures and situations. There is properly no *simplicity* in it at one time, nor *identity* in different, whatever natural propension we may have to imagine that simplicity and identity . . .

Pompous Footnote

1   Actually, at the time Lord Charlemont was writing, Hume may have looked 50 but was only in his late thirties. And, by the time Hume brought Rousseau to London, he was well into his fifties, and so could be excused for looking a bit faded. Nonetheless, the dashing Rousseau was only a year younger.

CHAPTER 15
ROUSSEAU THE ROGUE
(1712–1778)

One of the most interesting essays in Bertrand Russell's monumental *History* is that on Rousseau. Indeed, Russell seems to have been quite a Rousseau expert. This despite insisting that, as he puts it, Rousseau is not "what we would nowadays call a *philosopher*." A *philosophe* perhaps, but assuredly not a philosopher. Even so (Russell regrets), despite this, Rousseau had "a powerful influence on philosophy" and whatever may be "our opinion of his merits as a thinker, we must recognise his immense importance as a social force." This, Russell speedily sums up, is inventing the political philosophy of "pseudo-democratic dictatorships" which led directly to Hitler. And to think others associate Rousseau with *liberté*, *égalité*, and *fraternité*!

Nietzsche, Hitler's favorite philosopher, certainly did. In his notebook for autumn 1887, otherwise preoccupied with lamenting the abolition of slavery and the new propaganda in favor of treating people as "equal," Nietzsche speaks of his struggle against Rousseau and his notion of natural man as good. It is a philosophy born, Nietzsche declares fiercely, "out of a hatred of aristocratic culture." Russell, by contrast, instead associates Rousseau with *sensibilité* – the way of living that elevates feeling over mere calculation. *Sensibilité* is what makes Rousseau the founding figure of Romanticism, the movement in poetry, the arts, and indeed philosophy which praises grand gestures over shrewd calculation, celebrates the fierce, splendid, and really rather unnecessary tiger, as it were, over the dull but useful cow.

The Philosophical Tale

Fortunately for historians, if not serious philosophers, Rousseau's story is very well told by the man himself in his *Confessions*. This account is not particularly accurate, but at least (unlike so many others who record their memoirs) it is interesting. Indeed, some of the most interesting aspects are exaggerations of how wicked a man he was. Not in the strange navel-regarding way of Saint Augustine who laboriously seeks to find evil in the minutiae of his everyday existence (the theft of the pears, feeling sad when his friend died, *et cetera, et cetera*), but rather in shockingly selfish acts such as his "faked" conversion to Catholicism (to obtain a household to live in), his lying denunciation of the family servant (to hide his own theft), and the abandonment of not merely one (which is happenstance), or two (which is becoming rather careless), but five of his children to foundling homes.

Each act of wickedness he acknowledges freely – indeed, with some fascination. The fake conversion (a process he repeated at various stages of his life, and always for mercenary reasons) came about when he fled his native Geneva, then the center of rigid Calvinism, to avoid being made an apprentice to his uncle. Finding a gullible Catholic priest, he recalls he uttered any holy words required, while feeling himself to be participating in "at bottom the act of a bandit."

The denunciation of the poor servant girl came shortly after he was sent away by the Catholic priest and had managed to inveigle himself instead into the household of a rich aristocratic lady, from whom he stole a ribbon with a pretty silver medallion on it. He finds his reaction to being found out particularly interesting, in a psychological sense, writing:

> Never was wickedness further from me then at this cruel moment; and when I accused the poor girl, it is contradictory and yet it is true that my affection for her was the cause of what I did. She was present to my mind, and I threw the blame from myself on the first object that presented itself.

Rousseau explains the story in all its distasteful detail. His hostess having died, he had helped himself to the pretty thing imagining no one would notice. However:

> such was the fidelity of the domestics, and the vigilance of Monsieur and Madame Lorenzy, that no article of the inventory was found wanting; in short, nothing was missing but a pink and silver ribbon, which had been worn, and belonged to Mademoiselle Pontal. Though several things of more value were in my reach, this ribbon alone tempted me, and accordingly I stole it. As I took no great pains to conceal the bauble, it was soon discovered; they immediately insisted on knowing from whence I had taken it; this perplexed me – I hesitated, and at length said, with confusion, that Marion gave it me.

He continues, describing Marion, a young Mauriennese girl, who had worked in the kitchens making "a fine broth."

Marion was not only pretty, but had that freshness of colour only to be found among the mountains, and above all, an air of modesty and sweetness, which made it impossible to see her without affection; she was besides a good girl, virtuous, and of such strict fidelity, that every one was surprised at hearing her named. They had not less confidence in me, and judged it necessary to certify which of us was the thief. Marion was sent for; a great number of people were present, among whom was the Count de la Roque: she arrives; they show her the ribbon; I accuse her boldly; she remains confused and speechless, casting a look on me that would have disarmed a demon, but which my barbarous heart resisted.

Rousseau, like Augustine, wallows in his wickedness.

At length, she denied it with firmness, but without anger, exhorting me to return to myself, and not injure an innocent girl who had never wronged me. With infernal impudence, I confirmed my accusation, and to her face maintained she had given me the ribbon: on which, the poor girl, bursting into tears, said these words – "Oh, Rousseau! I thought you had a good disposition – now you render me very unhappy – yet still I would not be in your situation."

Her moderation, Rousseau notes, "did her an injury; as it did not appear natural to suppose, on one side such diabolical assurance; on the other, such angelic mildness." The end result was that the count sent them both packing, saying brusquely that "the conscience of the guilty would revenge the innocent," but Rousseau imagines she would have been forever under "an imputation cruel to her character in every respect." She would be suspected not only of having been a thief, but of having as her motive the seduction of Rousseau, and the disgrace of failing to admit it when exposed.

I do not even look on the misery and disgrace in which I plunged her as the greatest evil [says Rousseau egotistically], who knows, at her age, whither contempt and disregarded innocence might have led her? Alas! if remorse for having made her unhappy is insupportable, what must I have suffered at the thought of rendering her even worse than myself. The cruel remembrance of this transaction, sometimes so troubles and disorders me, that, in my disturbed slumbers, I imagine I see this poor girl enter and reproach me with my crime, as though I had committed it but yesterday.

Other than that, of course, Rousseau did not suffer too badly. For fortunately the world is full of rich aristocratic women willing to befriend

FIGURE 15 Sometimes in his slumbers, he imagined he could see the poor girl enter his bedroom and reproach him with his crime.

handsome young rogues, and Rousseau spent the next ten years in the household of Madame de Savoy, becoming in due course her lover, this even while her original (older) partner still lived with her. In fact, all three got on very well together: Rousseau called Madame "Maman" and looked forward, as he writes, to the day when he would inherit the older lover's clothes.

In 1743, again playing the card of his aristocratic connections, he obtained his first proper job, as secretary to the French ambassador to Venice. Two years later he met Thérèse le Vasseur, a servant in a hotel in Paris that he sometimes stayed at. Russell says that no one has ever understood what attracted him to her, noting that everyone agrees she was "ugly and ignorant," but here Russell surely reveals more about himself than Rousseau. Love at least should not have to follow the dictates of rational calculation. Nonetheless, Russell has support from Rousseau himself, who writes that he never had a spark of love for his lifelong partner; that although he taught her to write a few words she was too stupid to ever learn to read; that her mother and her family used him simply as a source of easy money; and finally that she was not even faithful to him, running after "stable boys," particularly in later life. Scarcely, it would seem, the appropriate relationship for the founder of Romanticism.

Of some relevance here is the story told that when James Boswell volunteered to bring Rousseau his mistress over from France to join him in England, *en route* he took the opportunity to seduce Thérèse – not once but thirteen times – before arriving at their destination. This reflects poorly upon the English gentleman[1] and perhaps contributes to Rousseau's suspicions about Hume's help in his refuge (see "The Many Faces of David Hume," above), but at least Boswell was suitably admonished afterwards by Thérèse. She told him that his lovemaking was unsophisticated – albeit she then offered to give him lessons.

So far, then, so trivial. But at age 38, rather late by the standards of many *philosophes*, let alone philosophers, Rousseau underwent a profound period of sudden insights. The catalyst for this was seeing an advertisement offered by the Academy of Dijon for a prize essay on the subject "Have the arts and sciences benefited mankind?"

A flurry of ideas came to him pell-mell. Rousseau wrote them down furiously in his little room: science, literature, art were all "bad": the acid that eats into morals, not the foundation. They contribute to a culture of acquisition, of unsatisfied desires, which leads in due course to conflict, slavery, and subjugation. Every strand of knowledge is derived from a sin: geometry comes from avarice; physics from vanity and empty curiosity; astronomy from superstition. Ethics itself is rooted in pride.

Scientists, far from being our saviors, are ruining the world, and any notion of progress is an illusion that spreads even as we move further and further away from the healthy, simple, and balanced lives of the past. Instead, the *Discourse on Sciences* salutes the kind of society advocated by Plato, two millennia earlier, indeed the "simple life" of ancient Sparta.

The essay was like a breath of fresh air in the stale debates of the time, and what is rather more surprising, Rousseau won the prize. Propelled thus from obscurity to celebrity, he began to adopt new patterns of behavior more fitting to his essayist views: he developed a love for long walks and quiet contemplation of the countryside; he eschewed all sophistication and technology. He even sold his watch, saying he no longer needed to know the time.

He wrote a follow-up essay, entitled a *Discourse on Inequality*, but this, alas, failed to win a prize, despite being every bit as controversial. It explained that "man is naturally good, and only by institutions is he made bad," a view that could be expected to displease the all-powerful Church, in all its Catholic and Protestant hues. Here, like Thomas Hobbes, he uses an imaginary 'state of nature' to infer certain 'natural laws', only upon which can the State establish its own order. Like Hobbes too, he says that men are essentially equal, even accepting evident differences due to health, intelligence, strength, and so on. But the differences seen in society

> the extreme inequality of our ways of life, the excess of idleness among some and the excess of toil among others, the ease of stimulating and gratifying our appetites and senses, the over-elaborate foods of the rich, which inflame and overwhelm them with indigestion, the bad food of the poor which they often go without altogether, so that they over-eat greedily when they have the opportunity; those late nights, excesses of all kinds, immoderate transports of every passion, fatigue, exhaustion of the mind, the innumerable sorrows and anxiety that people in all classes suffer, and by which the human soul is constantly tormented

– have another origin, an unnatural one. Inequality stems from the institution of private property. In a famous phrase, he says that the "first man who, having enclosed a piece of land, thought of saying 'this is mine', and found people simple enough to believe him, was the real founder of civil society." Another memorable quote, borrowed by Marx to front the *Communist Manifesto*, comes from Rousseau's book the *Social Contract*: "Man is born free, and everywhere he is in chains."

Better, Rousseau says, that people be measured not by their social position, nor by their possessions, but by the shared divine spark that he sees in them all: the immortal soul of 'Natural Man'.

In both the *Social Contract* and the *Discourse on Inequality*, Rousseau argues that man in his natural state, far from being greedy, or fearful, as described by Hobbes, is in fact living in a peaceful, contented state, truly free. This is a freedom with three elements. The first is free will, the second is freedom from the rule of law (as there are no laws), and the third is personal freedom. It is this last that is the most important.

Rousseau says that the first people lived like animals. He says this not in any derogatory sense, merely in the sense that the original people sought only simple fulfillment of their physical needs. They would have had no need of speech, nor concepts, and certainly not property. Rousseau points out that much of the imagery in both Hobbes and Locke belongs to a property-owning society, not the supposed natural state prior to the invention of property rights. By realizing this, we are not obliged "to make a man a philosopher before we can make him a man." The first time people would have had a sense of property (he thinks) is when they settled in one location, when they built huts to live in. Even sexual union, Rousseau notes pragmatically, as well as reflecting on his own experience, is unlikely to have implied any exclusivity, being more likely to have been just a lustful episode no sooner experienced than forgotten, least of all in terms of the children.

This primitive state is for him, if not for Voltaire (who complained of being required to "walk on all fours"), superior to those which followed it. Rousseau explains the change by the development of self-consciousness, and with it the desire for private property. According to Rousseau, at this point agreeing with Hobbes's famous assertion of "war of all on all," society necessarily leads people to hate each other – in accordance with their different economic interest. But Hobbes's so-called social contract is, he says, in fact made by the rich, as a way of doing down the poor. Actually, not even the rich benefit from it, as they warp themselves and become increasingly out of touch with nature's harmony, raised needlessly above their own proper state, just as the poor are pushed below theirs.

Rousseau offers instead just two laws, or principles, that could be said to precede the arrival of reason. The first is a powerful interest in self-preservation and our own well-being; the second is a natural aversion to seeing any other sentient being perish or suffer, especially if it is one of our own kind. His own life amply reflects the truth of the first principle. To illustrate the second, he recalls romantically the "mournful lowing" of cattle on entering the slaughter-house, and the "shudders" of animals as they hurry past the corpse of one of their kind. The only time natural man would hurt another is when his own well-being requires it.

Rousseau paints a mocking portrait of the social contract offered by the rich man, seeking to protect his gains by pretending concern for his victims. Let us unite, says his rich man, to protect the weak from oppression, to ensure for each that which he owns, and create a system of justice and peace that all shall be bound to, without exception. Rousseau thinks this explanation of civil law is more convincing than those offered by philosophers who suppose some other sort of universal social contract, for, as he puts it, the poor have only one good – their freedom – and to voluntarily strip themselves of that without gaining anything in exchange would appear to be absolute folly. The rich, on the other hand, have much to gain.

In fact, human society leads people to hate each other in proportion to the extent that their interests conflict. People pretend to do each other services whilst actually trying to exploit them and do them down. We must attribute to the institution of property, and hence to society, murders, poisonings, highway robbery, and, indeed, the punishments of those crimes. That is at the individual level. On the national scale, inequality, being almost non-existent in the state of nature, "becomes fixed and legitimated through the institution of property and laws." When society has, as it inevitably will, degenerated into tyranny and all are slaves again, the circle is complete, for all individuals become equal again when they are nothing. And all the time civil man torments himself constantly in search of ever more laborious occupations, working himself to death, "renouncing life in order to achieve immortality." Civil society is, in fact, a society of people who nearly all complain and several of whom indeed deprive themselves of their existence. This is the logic of property owner- ship and capitalism.

There is only one way around this conflict, only one way that the sovereign and the people can have a single and identical interest and ensure that all the "movements of the civil machine" tend to promote the common happiness, and that is for them to be one and the same. The people must be sovereign.

Rousseau thus marks a radical shift in philosophy, away from the perennial philosophical search for authority towards the uncertainties of 'freedom' instead. As the eighteenth century drew to an end and new ways of looking at the world were needed, Rousseau, despite his personal aristocratic pretensions, seemed in his writings to offer a complete rever- sal of the values of the time. Many were entranced and inspired. His views were also, of course, anathema to many. Dr. Johnson said of Rous- seau and his supporters that "Truth is a cow that will yield them no more milk, so they have gone to milk the bull." After receiving a copy especially from the author, asking for his comments, Voltaire speedily wrote back:

> I have received your new book against the human race, and thank you for it. Never was such cleverness used in the design of making us all look stupid. One longs, in reading your book, to walk on all fours. But as I have

lost that habit for more than sixty years, I feel unhappily the impossibility of resuming it.

In 1754, having become famous, Rousseau was invited to return to his native Geneva and become a 'citizen' of the then tiny independent state once again. Rousseau was very pleased to do this, and had himself reconverted to Calvinism. Both the *Discourse on Inequality* and the *Social Contract* are dedicated to his "fellow free citizens of Geneva, and to the Magnificent and Most Honoured Lords" who governed the mini-state.

But relations with the unappreciative burghers of Geneva soon soured, partly because of Voltaire, who lived there himself, despite almost all cultural activities being forbidden on Puritan grounds. When Voltaire tried to have the ban on performing plays lifted, Rousseau (despite having written a much admired opera himself, *Le Devin du village*, while living in Paris) weighed in on the City's behalf to condemn theater as contrary to nature and virtue. But sauce for the goose is also sauce for the gander. Accused equally of corrupting public morals, the *Social Contract* was publicly burned in the City Square of Geneva in 1762, along with Rousseau's idealistic work on education, *Émile*.

Rousseau died in 1778, the same year as his critic, Voltaire, possibly by his own hand, and certainly in sad and lonely circumstances. But as Goethe commented: with Voltaire an age ended, and with Rousseau, a new one began.

Pompous Footnote

1   Boswell it was who wrote (in Volume 2 of the *Life of Johnson*): "Most vices may be committed very genteelly: a man may debauch his friend's wife genteelly: he may cheat at cards genteelly." However, it is not clear that he achieved this standard here.

CHAPTER 16
IMMANUEL KANT, THE CHINAMAN OF KÖNIGSBURG
(1724–1804)

Ted Honderich, in his weighty capacity as editor of the *Oxford Companion to Philosophy*, considers Kant to be "the most important European Philosopher of modern times," so important, indeed, that he writes the entry on him himself. In this we learn that Johann Herder describes him (Kant, that is, not Honderich, though doubtless it is true for both) as:

> having a broad forehead, the seat of an imperturbable cheerfulness and joy. Speech, the richest in thought, flowed from his lips. Playfulness, wit and humour were at his command. . . . No cabal, no sect, no prejudice, no desire for fame could ever tempt him in the slightest way from broadening and illuminating the truth. He incited and forced others to think for themselves; despotism was foreign to his mind.

Thomas de Quincey, writing in *Blackwood's Magazine* in the early nineteenth century, said that Kant's personal life was much more interesting than his philosophy, a view which Professor Bird of Manchester University says "would now be regarded as odd to the point of perversity." Graham Bird thinks instead that Kant's 'transcendental apperception' and 'noumena' are much more interesting, and indeed, he points out, since they inspired Husserl to come up with 'transcendental-phenomenological-reduction' and propelled David Davidson to devise 'anomalous monism', they must also be considered the most *important*.

But we can afford to be a little perverse. For Kant's contribution to philosophy is a set of rules. And rules are also what defined his personal life. So it is entirely appropriate to investigate both.

The Philosophical Tale

One of Kant's important, if not interesting, ideas is that 'space' and 'time' are merely part of our mental apparatus – not really 'out there'. We place events in time, inventing the notion of cause and effect to help order the world. David Hume's revelation that the notion of cause and effect is based on nothing more than lazy habit and blind faith awoke Kant, he wrote in the *Critique of Pure Reason*, from his "dogmatic slumbers" (although Bertrand Russell unkindly adds that, evidently, the awakening was only "temporary and Kant soon invented a soporific that enabled himself to sleep again").[1]

The low philosophical status of cause and effect is important to Kant as he does not want our behavior to be reduced to being merely mechanical, and ourselves to automata following biological and chemical promptings.

Take his own daily routine, so reliable that the people of Königsburg were said to set their clocks by him. This is more than merely an 'amusing' notion, but a record of fact. Such precision! Such triumph over the trivia of human affairs! So at least the philosophers have always thought.

The "Chinaman of Königsburg," as Nietszche dubbed him, obscurely, awoke at 5.00 a.m. each morning, not a minute earlier, and certainly not a minute later. He would then, without pausing for breakfast, begin writing. Philosophy was only a small part of his output. In fact, papers on natural law, mechanics, mineralogy, mathematics, physics, and geography all fell within his remit. When it was morning proper, and the rest of the world woke up, he would deliver lectures. Kant became a professor only in his late forties, so for much of his life he was an hourly paid lecturer and it made sense to have as many strings to his bow as possible.

Lunchtime, in the continental style, was a grand occasion, with Kant leading a number of shrewdly chosen intellectual, but non-academic, friends. There always had to be at least three (the number of Graces) and never more than nine (the number of Muses). The conversation at Kant's table spanned a broad range of topics, and Kant himself was always keenly interested in the latest political, economic, and scientific developments. With his memory for detail, he could also describe at length foreign towns and places, although, of course, having no desire to ever leave Königsburg, he had never visited any of them. Another of Kant's little categorical imperatives concerned his favored drink. Since he considered the oil of coffee beans to be unhealthy, lunch did not finish with a coffee but always with weak tea instead. If the meals were leisurely, and they were, this was, however, Kant's only one of the day.

In the afternoon, Kant would take a long walk along the river, accompanied by his servant, Lampe, carrying an umbrella in case it rained. Kant's rule that everyone must be treated as an end in themselves and never merely as a 'means' to an end ("there can be nothing more dreadful than that the actions of a man should be subject to the will of another") evidently did not apply to servants carrying umbrellas.

FIGURE 16 In the afternoon, Kant would take a long walk, accompanied by his servant, Lampe, carrying an umbrella in case it rained.

On returning home, Kant would get out his books and study until bedtime. This was always at exactly 10.00 p.m. Or nearly always. For, on one occasion, after rashly accepting an invitation to go out for the day, Kant was unable to return home until shortly after 10 o'clock. Following this disruption, he was so shaken with worry that he vowed never to take such a risk again.

Even in bed, the rules had to be followed: Kant had a system for rolling himself up in his sheets so that they fitted tightly around him. Kant, it will be noted, slept for less than seven hours. He wrote a little booklet about health matters, warning against the dangers of too much sleep. He explained that as each person had only a certain amount of sleep in them, if they used it all up by lying in bed, they WOULD DIE EARLY. (My parents should have told me that . . .)

Since Kant's first love was science (his doctorate, completed in 1755, was not on philosophy as such but rather "About Fire"), this warning should be taken seriously. He continued to lecture in physics and geography for all his career, writing a treatise on earthquakes after there was one in Portugal, another one on the rain-bearing winds of the Atlantic, as well as (in the *General Natural History and Theory of the Heavens*, in 1755) setting out a theory about how the solar system itself might have been formed. This theory was taken further by the mathematician Pierre Simon Laplace, and is honored as the Kant–Laplace theory today. Parts of it are, however, now fallen into disuse, such as the bit saying that all the planets in the solar system must have life on them, with the intelligence of the life increasing the further away they are from the Sun.

In the *Critique of Practical Reason* (1786) Kant's thought leaves the physical universe behind to find a proof for the existence of heaven and the afterlife. He points out that since justice is the good flourishing and the wicked being punished, and that this does not happen on Earth, as we can see by looking around us, then it must take place "in the next world." This is sublime reasoning. And so to the less than fully appreciated Kantian treatise on the beautiful and the sublime. Night is sublime, day is beautiful. The sea is sublime, the land is beautiful, men are sublime, women are beautiful – and so on. Lots of professors wrote treatises like that at the time, it was almost compulsory.

Despite his scientific interests, Kant criticizes knowledge obtained by the senses, and suggests that it is better derived by Transcendental Deduction instead. Unfortunately, no one has ever been able to find out what this is. But certainly mind is better than matter, which in any case only takes on the form it does thanks to our looking at it. Old philosophical story though that may be, Kant had the boldness to describe his idea, in the preface to the second edition of the *Critique of Pure Reason* (that is in 1787, the first edition being a good six years earlier), as "a Copernican revolution" in philosophy. Adding, in case it was not clear, "I venture to say that there is not a single metaphysical problem that has not been solved, or for the solution for which the key at least has not been supplied."

A large part of this *Critique*, then, is devoted to exposing the errors that follow from failing to understand the true nature of space and time. This is a bit like Zeno, with his paradoxes, and indeed the most effective part of the 700-odd pages of the *Critique* is the short section of "antinomies" that seeks to demonstrate four examples of paradoxical reasoning. The first paradox is that the world must have had a beginning in both time and space, and that it cannot have done. The second is that everything must be made up of smaller parts, and that everything must be all part of the same thing. The third is that cause and effect are entirely mechanical – and that they are not. The last is that God exists necessarily – and that God does not necessarily exist.

Whatever its borrowings from the debates of Zeno and the ancients, this part of the *Critique* certainly impressed Hegel, who conducted his entire philosophy using the same style of 'thesis' followed by 'antithesis'. Hegel, however, solves the riddles by adding a supposed 'synthesis', whereas Kant, like Zeno, seeks merely to discredit certain ways of thinking.

Kant proceeds further in *Religion Within the Limits of Reason Alone* (1793) to roundly demolish all the popular theories of God's existence, and was forbidden, for his trouble, to do so again by Frederick William III, the then ruler of Prussia. Kant, evidently, 'broke the rules'!

But despite this, it is the 'rules', rigid and inflexible but supposedly the manifestation of reason itself, that make Kant's thinking so distinctive. Of these perhaps the best known is what he calls the categorical imperative:

> Act only according to a maxim by which you can at the same time will that it shall become a general law.

This is a bit like "Do unto others only what you would have them do unto you," which runs through the New Testament like mold through blue cheese. And when Kant's version appears in the *Metaphysic of Morals* (1785), the imperative is also offered to decide all moral issues. Curiously, though, it seems to collapse at the most easy tests. For example, it allows things that surely should be banned, while outlawing things that don't seem to matter very much. A rule, for instance, that all children under 5 who disturb philosophers should be beaten with a stick and have their tongues cut out is approved by the 'rule' since it is universalizable, but borrowing is forbidden, as if everyone borrowed, it would lead to a run on the bank. Kant would have to condemn the charities that make micro-loans to Third World farmers for seeds and shovels, for example, as people of great wickedness.

Kant was implacably opposed to utilitarianism and argued that moral principles are to be followed unconditionally and without regard for the consequences. That is what makes his 'imperative' so categorical. So, for example, it is certainly always necessary to tell the truth, even to the famous madman hunting his victim. On the other hand, someone who never does anything to hurt anyone else is not a good person if their action is prompted merely by fear of going to prison, and trades-people who are always helpful are not good people if they intend by so doing to improve their sales. In a way, this is 'ancient' ethics. By comparison, Adam Smith, writing at the same time, cheerfully constructed his moral system around "enlightened self-interest" operating within a social setting.

Families, let alone societies, need to allow a little space for self-interest, alongside the rules. But then Kant never married, although he did have some discussion of romantic matters with correspondents such as one Maria von Herbert, an admirer.

Maria wrote to Kant, in 1791, to say that she had long been a fan of his, and had recently applied the "truth-telling principle" in her most intimate affections.

"As a believer calls to his God," Maria begins fervently, "I call to you for help, for comfort and for counsel to prepare me for death." It seems that by telling her lover of "a previous affair," she caused him to be offended because of the "long-drawn-out lie." Although "there was no vice in it," she explains, "the lie was enough, and his love has vanished." As an "honorable man," her lover offers to continue as a "friend." "But that inner feeling that once, unbidden, led us to each other is no more – and my heart splinters into a thousand burning pieces!"

So far so tragic. Maria adds that it was only Kant's strictures against committing suicide that had thus far stopped her from taking that way out. Kant wrote back promptly the following spring (this is before email slowed down the rate of correspondence). After a few kindly words on her evident good intentions, he speaks sternly to remind her of her duty. He warns that lies cause contracts to be voided and to lose their force, and that "this is a wrong done to mankind generally." A lie does not need to cause harm directly to be wrong, and even when it appears to do good, it instead must be judged by this general collapse of the truth. "To be truthful in all declarations, therefore, is a sacred and absolutely commanding decree of reason, limited by no expediency."

If such full frankness leads a couple to split asunder, this is because their "affection is more physical than moral" and would soon have disappeared anyway. This, sighs Kant, the confirmed bachelor, is a misfortune often to be encountered in life. Fortunately, the value of life itself, when it depends on the enjoyment we get from people, "is vastly over-rated."

Maria replied a year later, to say that she had now achieved the high level of moral exactitude outlined by Kant, albeit that she now found her life rather empty. Instead, she says, she feels indifferent to everything, and suffers from ill health. Like the best moral philosophers, "Each day interests me only to the extent that it brings me closer to death." She thinks she would like to visit Kant, however, as in his portrait she has discerned "a profound calm there, and moral depth – if not the acuity of which the *Critique of Pure Reason* is proof." She entreats "her God" to "give me something that will get this intolerable emptiness out of my soul."

But for that, apparently, Kant had nothing to offer.

Pompous Footnote

1 Prior to Kant, as Bertrand Russell also notes, philosophers were gentlemen, addressing an audience of amateurs in the language of the everyday. After Kant, philosophy became a dialogue (indeed, often a monologue), conducted in technical language and obscure terms.

VI
THE IDEALISTS

CHAPTER 17
GOTTFRIED LEIBNIZ, THE THINKING MACHINE
(1646–1716)

"I love Leibniz," said Voltaire, "he is surely a great genius, even if he is also a bit of a charlatan . . . add to that, his ideas are always a bit confused."

Leibniz is that rare thing, a philosopher born of a philosopher – his father was a professor of ethics. He himself studied law, although the year that he graduated there were more lawyers than jobs, so he, along with several others, was told to wait a year. He suspected a conspiracy, centered on the Dean's wife, but no one knows what the conspiracy might have been. When he was eventually offered a post at the University of Altdorf he refused it, saying he had "very different things" in mind. But then he always seems to have been very self-assured.

So it was he taught himself Latin from an illustrated book, and by the age of 8 was proficient enough to read the technical accounts in his father's library, or so at least he says in his letters. When still just 15 years old, young Gottfried wrote out his first grand scheme, "On the Art of Combination," being a system by which all reasoning would be reduced to a complicated grid of numbers, sounds, and colors. This was the start of his quest for the "universal language" for which he would later build the first computer.

The Philosophical Tale

All his life Leibniz prided himself on his poetry (written mostly in Latin), and his ability to recite the bulk of Virgil's *Aeneid* by heart. Despite these noteworthy abilities, he never seems to have had any 'close' lady friends, let alone get married.

Fortunately, he fell in love instead with numbers. The affair became serious when, prior to his law course, he spent the summer at the University of Jena. It was here he encountered Pythagoreanism, and the view that numbers are the ultimate reality. Pythagoras believed that the universe as a whole was harmonious, in that it manifested simple mathematical ratios, like those of the basic intervals in music (the "harmony of the spheres"). Leibniz's philosophy reflects both these perspectives.

All the same, the only work that he published in his lifetime was the *Theodicy* (in 1710), which was concerned with the problem of evil. This is the work which advances his view, parodied by Voltaire in *Candide*, that everything that happens in this world happens because it is for the best – because we live in "the best of all possible worlds."

In his essay *The Principles of Nature and Grace, Based on Reason*, he explains:

> It follows from the supreme perfection of God that he chose the best possible plan in producing the universe, a plan in which there is the greatest variety together with the greatest order. . . . The most carefully used plot of ground, place and time, the greatest effect produced by the simplest means; the most power, knowledge, happiness, and goodness in created things that the universe could allow.

Anything that appears bad is, from a divine perspective, not bad at all, as it is necessary in order to create more happiness somewhere else. The present world is the best possible one in that it is, at the same time, "the simplest in hypotheses and the richest in phenomena" (*Discourse on Metaphysics*, §6). There is a reason for everything. This he dubs the 'principle of sufficient reason'.

His argument, of course, has political resonances, and Leibniz was counted as both an aristocrat and a snob. But he saw himself as "a citizen of the world," and indeed his political vision of a single world society was radical enough at the time to create political friction within the European elite, and not merely closer to home, with his employers in the aristocracy of Hanover.

His university thesis on the topic of the 'Principle of Individuation' (that which would later become his 'principle of the identity of indiscernibles') attracted the attention of the Archbishop of Mainz, who took him into his employment. The archbishop had a project for universal peace, based on a shared foundation for Christianity between the Protestant and Catholic factions of Europe.

In pursuit of this, Leibniz was sent on a diplomatic mission to persuade the French king to attack Egypt rather than Germany, but his efforts were rebuffed with the suggestion that holy war against the infidel had gone out of fashion.[1] Of more lasting significance was that, as part of the strategy, he traveled to Paris in 1672 and stayed there for four years drinking in eagerly the full range of new debates and ideas – including that of the new mathematics of the 'infinitesimal', or 'calculus'. On his way back to Germany too, he stayed with the celebrated Dutch philosopher Spinoza, reading with interest an early version of Spinoza's ethics "based on geometry." (In later years, however, when Spinoza was unfashionable, he minimized his visit, saying he had met him just the once and that the Jewish philosopher had told him some political anecdotes.)

While in Paris, Leibniz was also able to explore many of his own technological dreams. One was a watch with two symmetrical balance wheels working in tandem. He demonstrated a model of this to the Paris Academy in April 1675. Another gadget was a device for calculating a ship's position without using a compass or observing the stars, alongside a method for determining the distance of an object from a single observation point. Then there was his design for an aneroid barometer (useful enough to be reinvented by Vidi of Paris in 1843), and various improvements to the design of lenses, not to mention his compressed-air engine for propelling vehicles and projectiles, and plans for a ship which could go under water to escape enemy detection. In his way, Leibniz was a little Leonardo da Vinci, interested not only in all the arts and sciences, but practical enough to want to implement his ideas too.

Ever an admirer of the Chinese, one of his schemes was that the German economy could be rejuvenated through silk production. He himself experimented on it in his own garden, using mulberry trees grown from seeds imported from Italy. It may seem absurd, yet in 1703 he obtained a license to start production in Berlin and Dresden, and it became quite a practical venture. Other schemes included a fire service, steam-powered fountains for the palace gardens, and an isolation hospital for plague victims, to mention just a few.

To his dying day he retained a close interest in alchemy (even discussing it with his doctor on his deathbed), periodically testing out the claims of various alchemists. Around 1676, he generously entered into a legally binding profit-sharing agreement with two practicing alchemists, his side of the bargain being to provide capital and technical advice, theirs merely to share their discoveries. Leibniz's main concern was that with all the easily produced gold, the metal might lose its market value. Fortunately, as it were, this did not happen.

But of all his inventions it was the computer that was the most characteristic (and in its way most impressive) achievement.

In 1673, Leibniz demonstrated his "calculating machine" to the Royal Society in London, which promptly elected him to membership, thereby infuriating Newton. Writing in 1685, Leibniz gives the following account of his moment of inspiration for this invention:

> When, several years ago, I saw for the first time an instrument which, when carried, automatically records the number of steps taken by a pedestrian, it occurred to me at once that the entire arithmetic could be subjected to a similar kind of machinery so that not only counting, but also addition and subtraction, multiplication and division could be accomplished by a suitably arranged machine easily, promptly, and with sure results.

But as with his later wrangle with Dr. Newton over who invented calculus, Leibniz was not the first to think of it. Pascal had made a calculating machine a generation earlier to help his father – a tax inspector – with his tedious sums. It could add five-figure numbers but could not do any other calculations. It was very expensive to manufacture and jammed easily. Fewer than fifteen machines were ever made.

Leibniz's father was not a tax collector, as we have seen, but a moral philosopher, and fittingly Leibniz's machine was designed to automate the dreary task of solving moral problems. It utilized:

> a general method in which all truths of reason would be reduced to a kind of calculation. At the same time, this would be a sort of universal language or script, but infinitely different from all those imagined previously, because its symbols and words would direct the reason, and errors – except those of fact – would be mere mistakes in calculation.

FIGURE 17 Leibniz's machine was designed to automate the dreary task of solving moral problems.

Leibniz later defended his originality, saying that that the "calculating box of Pascal" was not known to him at the time he made his computer, although he acknowledged that when he did hear of it, he had "requested the most distinguished Carcavius by letter to give me an explanation of the work which it is capable of performing."

Generally speaking, in fact, Leibniz was tireless in ferreting facts out of friends, acquaintances, and strangers alike. Once he had gotten all the information he could, he applied himself to going one step further (and claiming all the credit). And so it was with Pascal: once he had understood how it worked, he swiftly set about making one even better. And in this case he did, by developing something called the "Stepped Reckoner." Now the machine could add, subtract, and even (up to a point!) multiply.

Leibniz's machines, which he called his living bank clerks, had two main parts. The first, similar to Pascal's, was a collection of pin wheels which performed the adding. The second part, his own innovation, was a movable carriage that could follow decimal places when multiplying. The two sections were ingeniously linked by cylinders containing ridge-like teeth of different lengths corresponding to the digits 1 through 9. Turning the crank that connected the cylinders engaged smaller gears above the cylinders, which in turn engaged the adding section. Much to Leibniz's disappointment, his machines did not meet his intended excellence. In fact, they were cumbersome, hard to operate, frequently jammed, and inaccurate.

However, Leibniz was often pleased with himself, and this invention he was very proud of. He thought of commemorating it with a medal bearing the motto SUPERIOR TO MAN, and had a machine made for Peter the Great of Russia to send to the emperor of China as an example of superior Western technology.[2]

Indeed, although the implementation was flawed, the principles according to which it worked led the way to the development of the first successful mechanical calculator. This machine used the principle of the motion of teeth on gears. The same design was used in calculators until the twentieth century and is still used today in counters such as kWh-meters (for measuring electricity usage) and speedometers. (An even more elaborate machine that would divide, calculate square roots, and determine the square of numbers was planned but never built – supposedly due to the technology not being advanced enough at the time to manufacture the components.)

Even with its much-vaunted ability to multiply, despite spending a small fortune on the project right up to the end of his life, Leibniz's machine was never capable of carrying completely automatically. In this respect, his advance was less practical and more theoretical.

In 1676, when the archbishop died, Leibniz moved to the service of the court of Hanover, to research the genealogy of the House of Brunswick, of which the Duke of Hanover was a member. In due course, Georg Ludwig (who could hardly speak English) would become George I of England, and this is sometimes said to be due to Leibniz's research. Actually, this seems unlikely, as Leibniz had started the genealogy rather earlier than perhaps his employers expected, dealing at length with fossils and European language traditions. (His assistant, Eckhart, wrote pointedly that with genealogy, as with his study of numbers, Leibniz knew how to extend matters to infinity.) And when Georg Ludwig became King George of England, he left Leibniz behind in Germany less because of (as has been suggested) the controversy over calculus (which had indeed made Leibniz *persona non grata* in the English capital), but because, at the time of his departure, Leibniz was on one of his many long absences pursuing his loosely defined research (and hobnobbing).

Not that Leibniz bothered to pretend that he was pursuing the family history all the time. In 1679 he became interested in ways of harnessing wind power and using it to pump water out of mines. For the next seven years he spent half his time in the mines of the Harz mountains. He designed all sorts of pumps using various techniques ranging from the ancient Archimedes screw method to one that anticipated the rotary pumps of today. He also came up with numerous related inventions – for casting iron and making steel, for separating chemicals, and even for replacing the pit ponies. Remarkably, every single project ended in failure, which Leibniz blamed on everyone else from the workers to the managers.

And all the time he was writing. Not books, but letters. Leibniz was in correspondence with literally hundreds of people at a time on a wide range of topics: science and cosmology; mathematics, law, and politics; economic problems (such as monetary policy, tax reform, and the balance of trade); not to mention religion, philosophy, literature, history, linguistics, numismatics, and anthropology. Over 15,000 letters survive. Some, such as his correspondence with Sophie-Charlotte, the daughter of the previous duke (but evidently also a close and real friend), contain lengthy and clear accounts of his theories, such as that of the transmigration of souls. Philosophy has not been kind to Leibniz's letters. In his *Critical Exposition of the Philosophy of Leibniz* (1900), Bertrand Russell unkindly dismisses them as obsequious panderings to aristocratic patrons. The message has been passed on by recent popularizers of philosophy, such as Richard Osborne, writing in *Philosophy for Beginners*, who says that most of what Leibniz published while alive "was designed to appeal to the Royalty to whom he attached himself, and was reactionary and shallow."

Certainly the two are right that Leibniz's letters had two purposes at least, one of which, no doubt, was social climbing. Here he did remarkably well. By 1712, he had obtained salaried positions in not one but no fewer than five different courts! These were: Hanover, Brunswick-Lüneburg, Berlin, Vienna, and St. Petersburg, each of which, naturally, resented the time he spent serving the others, and periodically suspended his salary until he reappeared. And professionally speaking he did well, too. He was offered the prestigious librarianships of the Vatican (in 1689) and of Paris (in 1698), even if he declined them saying he was not willing to convert formally to Catholicism.

When he was younger he had a reputation as an elegant courtier ("an elegant man in a powdered wig," as one contemporary summed him up), a savant, and wit. He drove around in a carriage flamboyantly painted with pink roses. The Duchess of Orléans remarked of him: "It's so rare for intellectuals to be smartly dressed, and not to smell, and to understand jokes!" His influence in seventeenth-century intellectual circles was enormous, much to the envy of Sir Isaac Newton, his rival for the honor of being first to invent calculus. But, according to Russell, who, as we have seen, dislikes him, Leibniz was very mean. When young ladies of the court at Hanover married, Leibniz used to give them a wedding present consisting of useful maxims, such as not to give up washing now they had found a husband. And in his later years he became an object of ridicule for his old-fashioned and over-ornate clothes, his enormous black wig, and his half-baked schemes.

Typical of this, an alchemist that Leibniz had fallen out with satirized him in a book called *Foolish Wisdom and Wise Folly*. J. J. Becher claimed that Leibniz believed he had invented a coach capable of traveling from Amsterdam to Hanover (nearly 400 kilometers) in six hours, even though the roads at the time were not smooth, but deeply rutted cart tracks. It is known that in 1687 Leibniz had built an experimental coach, but whether or not it managed this speed, alas, the records have now been lost.

But back to those letters. And if they were part of his social climbing, they were also crucial for his *modus operandi*, both philosophical and scientific. It had been in April 1673, for example, when Leibniz had received from Heinrich (Henry) Oldenberg, the secretary of the Royal Society of London, a report drawn up by John Collins on the state of mathematics in England. A prominent part of this report was a list of problems (many involving infinite series) that could be solved by an unspecified method possessed by a secretive man at Cambridge named Isaac Newton. As Leibniz later remembered it, he himself had already had the original inspiration for calculus, prior to seeing any of the reports on the work of Barrow, Gregory, and Newton, and it is true that there was no actual description of calculus in the 1673 report.

In 1675, and on into 1676, there was an exchange of letters between Newton and Leibniz (via Oldenberg) in which Newton, although still very reticent about revealing general methods, gave ever more explicit hints of calculus, including even an anagram stating the inverse relationship between differentiation and integration. Leibniz too dropped important sounding details of his own version of calculus into the exchange. The two men were playing poker with each other, each trying to figure out exactly how much the other knew, without revealing too much of what he himself did.

Actually, the principles of calculus are laughably simple, as all schoolchildren know. (I didn't understand it at school, but clearly everyone else did, so it must have been easy.) Differentiation is a way of working out gradients.[3] The gradient of a road up a hill is the distance it goes up divided by the length of the road. If it goes up 10 meters in a distance of 100 meters, it is 1 : 10, for example. Leibniz and Newton simply saw that the gradients of mathematical curves are equivalent to a series of very small straight lines, all joined imperceptibly together. Thus, any particular point on the curve can be treated as a tiny straight line. The length of the straight line is then divided by the 'height', which depends on the mathematical equation of the line. This is useful, at least in the eyes of math teachers, because the gradient of a curve at a point is the mathematical way of representing, for example, the 'rate of change' at any given moment. Similarly, the area under a curve can be calculated by treating it as the sum of a series of little rectangles also generated by imagining many thin strips under the curve. This is known as 'integration' and is useful for something else (but as I say, I lost the thread of the topic somewhere before this point).

It is perhaps hard to see why anyone should want to be responsible for inventing it. Nonetheless, a long battle with Newton over the right to be known as the true discoverer of calculus ensued. The battle was conducted on Leibniz's side through anonymous letters promoting his case, and if eventually it was his notation that would eventually be adopted internationally,[4] the result was also that Leibniz's name, as the euphemism has it, became "mired in controversy."

But it was not just over calculus that Leibniz was at odds with Newton. The two had different views of how the universe worked. Leibniz considered that Newton was wrong to take phenomena and derive laws to explain them. Instead he thought that philosophers should postulate grand systems capable of reproducing the observed phenomena. Disliking Newton's 'invention' of the 'gravitational force' able to act instantaneously over a distance to explain gravity ("Sir Isaac Newton and his followers have also a very odd opinion concerning the work of God. According to their doctrine, God Almighty wants to wind up His watch from time to time; otherwise it would cease to move . . . !" he sneered.), he told the Royal Society in London of his explanation of planetary motion, which derived ultimately from Descartes and was intended to show how the Sun could force the planets to travel in their orbits simply by means of pushing. Leibniz suggested that space was filled with an ether of extremely fine particles, and that a rotation of the Sun set up circular motions ("vortices") in the ether, which pushed the planets round like boats in a whirlpool.

In a letter to Newton's secretary, Samuel Clarke, he writes:

> To conclude. If the space (which the author fancies) void of all bodies, is not altogether empty; what is it then full of? Is it full of extended spirits perhaps, of material substances, capable of extending and contracting themselves; which over therein, and penetrate each other without inconveniency, as the shadows of two bodies penetrate one another upon the surface of a wall. . . . Nay, some have fancies that man, in the state of innocency, had also the gift of penetration; and that he became solid, opaque, and impenetrable by his fall. Is it not overthrowing our notions of things, to make God have parts, to make spirits have extension? The principle of the want of a sufficient reason does alone drive away these spectres of the imagination. Men easily run into fictions, for want of making a right use of that great principle.

If science was to successfully adopt Newton's mechanical world, that was not necessarily to say that Leibniz lost the theoretical debate. His letter continued:

> I don't say that matter and space are the same thing. I only say, there is no space where there is no matter; and that space in itself is not an absolute reality. Space and matter differ, as time and motion. However, these things, though different, are inseparable.

Likewise, he disparaged Newton's mechanics as it allowed two objects to bounce off each other although, in theory, this also required an infinite series of smaller and smaller movements of particles. To avoid this logical nonsense, Leibniz said matter ultimately consisted of energy fields, anticipating in this way the developments in physics known as 'field theory', as their Italian exponent, Ruggiero Giuseppe Boscovich (1711–87), himself acknowledged. Nonetheless, it was Newton who produced the model capable at the time of advancing scientific knowledge. Even the founder of the 'new physics', Einstein, freely acknowledged that physics in the twentieth century remained established on the formidable achievements of Newton.

But, most of all, Leibniz disagreed with those at the time, like Newton, Boyle, and even Descartes, who explained the world in terms of small particles, or atoms, moving according to certain 'absolute' laws. His point was that even the smallest particle must be capable of being divided further, unless it is no longer something we can consider a particle of matter. Instead of atoms, he built the world out of what he called "a simple substance without parts." These are the monads.

Leibniz's 'monads' are amongst the most mysterious objects in philosophy.[5] Here is how he introduces them:

> The body belonging to a monad (which is the entelechy or soul of that body) together with an entelechy constitutes what may be called a living being and together with the soul constitutes what may be called an animal. Now the body of a living being or an animal is always organised; for, since every monad is a mirror of the universe in its way, and since the universe is regulated in perfect order, there must also be an order in the representing being, that is, in the perceptions of the soul, and consequently in the body in accordance with which the universe is represented.

And he continues with characteristic enthusiasm.

> Thus each organised body of all living beings is a kind of divine machine or natural automaton, which infinitely surpasses all artificial automata. For a machine constructed by man's art is not a machine in each of its parts. For example, the tooth of a brass wheel has parts or fragments which, for us, are no longer artificial things, and no longer have any marks to indicate the machine for whose use the wheel was intended. But natural machines, that is, living bodies, are still machines in their least parts, to infinity. This is the difference between nature and art, that is, between divine art and our art. (*The Monadology*)

150

Leibniz had been very much impressed by the new world of the microscope, through which his contemporary Anton van Leeuwenhoek had revealed a host of tiny living organisms previously unsuspected.

> There is a world of creatures, living beings, animals, substantial forms, souls in the very smallest part of matter. Each bit of matter can be thought of as a garden full of plants or as a pond full of fish – except that every branch of a plant, every part of an animal's body, every drop of the liquids they contain is in its turn another such garden or pond. And although the earth and the air occupying the spaces between the plants in the garden, or the water occupying the space between the fishes in the pond, is not itself a plant or a fish, yet they contain still more of them, only mostly too small to be visible. Thus there is nothing uncultivated, sterile or dead in the universe – no chaos or confusion, except in appearance. It is rather as a pond appears from a distance, when you can see a confused motion and milling around, so to speak, of the fishes in the pond, but without being able to make out the individual fishes themselves. One sees from this how every living body has a dominant substantial form which is the soul in the animal; but the members of this living body are full of other living bodies, plants and animals, each one of which also has its own substantial form, or dominant monad. (Ibid., ¶¶ 66–70)

Leibniz's universe is similarly alive – and conscious. Monads – the ultimate building blocks of the universe – are living centers of energy and activity. However, they can only be found through pure logic, and not through the microscope. In fact, they only need postulating. And the *Rules of Monadology* are simple enough.

1 Each monad is indestructible. (Since a monad has no parts.)
2 Nor can it be created, except by God. (As matter can neither be created nor destroyed.)
3 It is colorless. (It has no physical properties.)
4 It has no windows. (Monads cannot affect other monads.)
5 It is interchangeable with any other monad. (Since the essential character of monads is simply 'activity'.)

Leibniz explains that although the monads do not appear to the senses ("they are colorless"), we need to assume their existence in order to explain reality and the meaningfulness of language. Their main activity is 'perception', or mirroring, as Leibniz puts it, and every monad perceives every other monad – equally. Every physical body is a "colony" of monads, living in "pre-established harmony." However, for some reason to do with supposed grades of "mirroring," Leibniz allows for different types of monads for plants, stones, animals, and human beings. Leibniz tries to explain his colorless monads with the metaphor of the rainbow. It appears to us a bright spectrum of color in the sky but in reality is made up of many millions of tiny droplets of water. And each of these is certainly colorless.

One of the implications of monadology is that even human beings are not that different from rocks, being still collections of monads. Another is that since monads are indestructible and eternal, so are we, albeit that our consciousness varies depending on the arrangement the monads happen to take up. Another is that God must have programmed every monad at the birth of the universe in order that (without needing to interact causally) they could behave exactly as if they were interacting. Leibniz uses the example of a choir to explain how the monads can appear to be interacting, while in fact remaining totally independent. This, the 'principle of preestablished harmony' also tidily explains away that problem between the interaction of the soul and the body that had been left over by Descartes when he split the world into the two kinds of substance. But Leibniz sees his machine very differently from those of his contemporaries (including Descartes).

On the other hand, Leibniz seems to have divided the monads into 'mind monads' and 'material monads', with just one superior sort of 'mind monad' controlling those which make up the human body. In this way, his theory becomes little more than a relabeling of Descartes's, especially by introducing a dominant monad, which he says orders the other monads in the body to move. In doing this, he seems to undermine the elegance of his own theory.

But if Leibniz realized the contradictions and incoherencies in this, the grandest scheme of them all, at least an explanation was already at hand. As part of his original quest for a "universal language" ready for the computation of thinking, he had already realized that existing languages are poorly structured, illogical, and hence quite unsuitable for deep thought. It was for this reason that he had set about creating a new, logical language based on Latin, an enterprise in the spirit of Aristotle himself. (Indeed, Leibniz is sometimes called the Aristotle of the Modern Era.)

A phrase like 'Leibniz invented calculus', for example, he preferred to see expressed as 'Leibniz is (the inventor of calculus)'. In fact, Leibniz had decided, all verbs should be done away with, with the exception of 'is'.

More importantly (for Leibniz anyway), the expression 'All A are B' or 'All Leibniz's are great inventors' should be rewritten as 'Leibniz NOT a great inventor is NOT POSSIBLE' (A ≠ B is not possible).

All this is said to have been a forerunner of the system finally produced by George Boole (1815–64) that is central to today's computer science. Boole manipulates statements which are given 'truth values', but Leibniz hoped to literally turn concepts into numbers, the better to manipulate them mechanically. Intriguingly, like later logicians, he considered that all concepts are made up of simpler ones which cannot be broken down further, similar to the way all numbers are made up of factors, except the prime numbers themselves.

His hope was to give all the simplest concepts a 'characteristic number' consisting of a pair of prime numbers, one positive and one negative. The characteristic number of a complex concept would be the product of the numbers of its components. To use his example: if 'animal' has the positive number 13 and the negative number −5, and 'rational' is made up of 8 and −7, then the characteristic number for 'man' will be (13 × 8) and (−5 × 7), or 104, −35. The great strength of this system was that it could be done on his machine (particularly as it did not involve tricky division or square roots). The great weakness, of course, is that it is nonsense.

Leibniz might have had more success if he had continued to study the binary system, and indeed he had been one of the first mathematicians to do so. He was fascinated by the way that the whole of arithmetic could be derived from 1 and 0, and considered that likewise the whole universe was generated out of pure being and nothingness. "God is pure being: matter is a compound of being and nothingness" (*Leibniz's German Writings (1838–40)*, ii, 411)

He continues:

> I shall not here go into the immense usefulness of this system; it would be enough to note how wonderfully all numbers are thus expressed by means of Unity and Nothing. But although there is no hope in this life of people being able to arrive at the secret ordering of things which would make it evident how everything arises from pure being and nothingness, yet it is enough for the analysis of ideas to be continued as far as is necessary for the demonstration of truths.

Leibniz was so proud of this idea that he planned to commemorate it with a medal bearing the legends: THE MODEL OF CREATION DISCOVERED BY G.W.L., and ONE IS ENOUGH FOR DERIVING EVERYTHING FROM NOTHING. His design emphasized his debt to Pythagoras and Plato in depicting the Sun, or 1, radiating its light on formless Earth, or 0.

The medal was never struck, and when he died neither the Hanoverian court, nor the Royal Society in London, nor even the Berlin Academy (which Leibniz had founded and been the first president of!) made any tributes to either him or his work.

But today, many ordinary houses contain a small tribute to him, whirring quietly in the electricity meter cupboard, under the stairs.

Pompous Footnotes

1 However the strategy he suggested was almost identical to the one actually carried out by Napoleon a century and a half later.

2 One of his models still survives and can be seen in the Hanover State Library.

3 More precisely, it has something to do with the rate or change of one quantity with respect to another quantity . . .

4 Leibniz's approach was algebraic; his language was original, offering such terms as differential, integral, coordinate, and function, while his notation, which is still used today, was simple and elegant. It was based on the letter 'd' for 'difference' (as in the symbol for a differential), and the contemporary long 'S' for 'sum', or integral.

5 Mysterious or not, the word itself comes from the rather dull Greek *monads* meaning 'units', and was used by Pythagoras. The long quote on monads is from *The Monadology*, #63 and 64.

CHAPTER 18
BISHOP BERKELEY'S
BERMUDA COLLEGE
(1685–1753)

"Berkeley is a most striking and even unique phenomenon in the history of philosophy," declares the Vice-Chancellor of Oxford University, Geoffrey Warnock, firmly from behind the reassuring solidity of his desk, in a book entitled *Great Philosophers*, without ever saying quite what was striking or "even unique" about him. Was it perhaps because Berkeley published a grand metaphysical theory at a precociously early age? Or was it because (when he wasn't composing poems) he wrote much of his philosophy pithily and wittily in the style of Plato's dialogues? Or was it because Bishop Berkeley had a social conscience and campaigned actively for the poor people of his native Ireland, suffering as ever at the hands of those two perennial companions, famine and English settlers? But most certainly, it was not because Berkeley was the first major European philosopher to visit America, where he tried and, in due course, failed to set up a college to convert slaves and Indians to Christianity, and in the process discovered a miracle cure made from the sap of pine trees. But here's that other and much more interesting story.

The Philosophical Tale

George Berkeley's strange theory that people, clothes, furniture, trees – everything – have no more existence than as ideas in people's minds came to him whilst he was still just in his early twenties, so leaving him plenty of time later on to travel the world, spread Christianity, and promote the benefits of 'tar water'.

His own idea was that what philosophers were beginning to call 'sense perceptions' were not created by some strange interaction with 'matter' as everyone around him, such as John Locke and Isaac Newton over in London, or Paul Gassendi and Pierre Boyle in France, assumed, but were placed directly in our minds by God, thus cutting out the 'middle man', so to speak.

It was at Trinity College, Dublin, where he had formed a student society to discuss the 'scientific philosophy' that he announced his 'new

155

principle' to overcome the threat of the 'materialism' which already seemed to be rapidly reducing the world to a kind of complicated machine. The new principle was applied two years later for the first time in *An Essay Towards a New Theory of Vision*, before being expanded in the *Treatise concerning the Principles of Human Knowledge*. In place of the mathematically tidy and predictable world of Newton and Locke, he offered up a kind of 'radical immaterialism', in which the world loses its objective reality and instead becomes intricately connected with whoever is looking at it. *Esse est percipi*, or 'to be is to be perceived'.

He had some very creditable observations of his own to back this up, especially about the way the mind constructs objects rather than simply 'perceives' them. If colors didn't really exist 'out there', but only in our minds (as even the most materialist of his fellow philosophers agreed), why not the sensations of touch too? All of this is of great philosophical interest.

But Berkeley's contemporaries were more excited about the new discoveries in nature by the 'scientists' and their extraordinary success in predicting and explaining phenomena. Berkeley's 'new principle' seemed like a throwback to a different age. Which it was, being essentially Plato's old line expressed a bit more forcefully. Dr. Johnson dismissed the theory by stamping his foot on the ground and saying "I refute it thus." Or was it by kicking a stone? Actually, the reality of the occasion does not matter. Clearly it is the idea that Dr. Johnson could have done this that is important.[1] So, although the theory caused some amusement, it was not taken terribly seriously at the time.

Fortunately, Berkeley was never one to be easily put off. In 1713 he obtained leave from his academic responsibilities and crossed the Irish Sea to England. Once in London he sought to "make acquaintance with men of merit" as well as arrange publication of a popularization of his theory in the form of *Three Dialogues Between Hylas and Philonous*. "Can anything be more Fantastical, more repugnant to Common Sense, or a more manifest piece of Scepticism than to believe that there is no such thing as matter?" begins Hylas in one, setting himself up to be comprehensively trounced by Philonous. The London intellectuals fell at once for this, praising the Irishman's charm and shrewd wit. The celebrated author Dean Swift recorded in his journal: "That Mr. Berkeley is a very ingenious man, and I have mentioned him to all the Ministers, and I will favour him as much as I can." Alexander Pope made him the gift of "a very ingenious new poem," and a new paper, the *Guardian*, asked him to be a regular correspondent.

All this fraternizing bore early fruit. Berkeley spent the next seven years, propelled by plum appointments (first as chaplain to Lord Peterborough, special ambassador for the coronation of the King of Sicily, and then as tutor to the son of the Bishop of Clogher), traveling around the continent. Berkeley was delighted by the rich store of antiquities and art treasures he found in Italy and was drawn there into the fashion for observation of natural phenomena. He even climbed Mount Vesuvius while it was erupting, and wrote up his discoveries for the *Transactions of the Philosophical Society*.

Alas, when Berkeley eventually returned to England it was to find the country in the midst of a crisis resulting from the bursting of the South Sea Bubble, as overpriced share options collapsed on the new Stock Exchange. In fact, the Bubble in a way reflected very well his theory that what is real is what is perceived – the shares were valuable as long as people thought they were valuable, but worthless once the perception had shifted. However, in an *Essay towards preventing the Ruin of Great Britain*, he modestly restricted himself to merely proposing some new laws, the encouragement of the arts, and a return to simpler styles of living. Nonetheless, it was the Bubble crisis that decided him on the need to lay the foundations for a new approach in the exotic climes of the Summer Islands.

His plan to create a 'University for Indians' in the New World created much more interest at the time than his other ideas. It was even discussed in the British Parliament and received royal approval. And, later on, it would be there, in the southern states of America, while working on the Bermuda College project, that he would make his discovery of the mysterious properties of tar water.

Yet why would a distinguished philosopher want to go to America anyway? It was a terrible place. Certainly, in the eighteenth century, the New World was considered to be an untamed and dangerous wilderness highly unsuitable for a European gentleman to even think of setting foot in, let alone found a college in. However, Bishop Berkeley thought it, or rather Bermuda, to have some very special qualities. "The climate is by far the healthiest and most serene, and consequently the most fit for study," he wrote to anyone who might listen, or more specifically, in this case, to his friend, Lord Percival, in a letter. "There is the greatest abundance of all the necessary provisions for life, which is much to be considered in a place for education. . . . It is the securest spot in the universe, being environed round with rocks all but one narrow entrance, guarded by seven forts, which render it inaccessible."

Today, the Summer Islands are better known and would be considered, at 600 kilometers distance from the mainland, to be too remote from America to be suitable as an educational annexe, but Bishop Berkeley, after all, considered distance, like existence, to be determined by perception, and not the other way around, and hence Bermuda was still, for him, the ideal spot for a college. Declaring himself ready, if necessary, to "spend the rest of my days in the island of Bermuda," he said it would be his task and duty henceforth to save the souls of both the newly imported African slaves and the indigenous savage peoples of America.

Waxing lyrical indeed in his enthusiasm for *Converting the Savage Americans to Christianity*, Berkeley wrote several new *Verses on the Prospect of Planting Arts and Sciences in America.*

> *The muse disgusted at an age and clime*
> *Barren of every glorious theme,*
> *In distant lands now waits a better time*
> *Producing subjects worthy fame.*
>
> *In happier climes where from the genial sun*
> *And virgin earth such scenes ensue*
> *The force of art by nature seems outdone,*
> *And fancied beauties by the true.*
>
> *In happy climes, the scene of innocence,*
> *Where nature guides and virtue rules,*
> *Where men shall not impose for truth and sense*
> *The pedantry of courts and schools;*
>
> *There shall be sang another golden age,*
> *The rise of Empire and the arts*
> *The good and great inspiring epic sage,*
> *The wisest heads and noblest hearts.*
>
> *Not such as Europe breeds in her decay;*
> *Such as she bred when fresh and young,*
> *When heavenly flame did animate her clay,*
> *By future poets shall be sung.*
>
> *Westward the course of empire takes its way . . .*

And, in 1723, the means to do so came into his hands, after Berkeley came into some serious money, partly from an inheritance, and partly as a result of being appointed to the rich deanery of Derry, which carried with it no other duties than finding ways of spending the income. Berkeley's method was pursuing his Bermuda project with greater vigor. He returned to London and obtained a royal charter for his new college, along with numerous private pledges of support including one of £20,000 from Parliament itself.

Then, pausing only to marry the daughter of the Chief Justice of Ireland, he set off directly, with three other evangelical companions, for America. Once there, they established a kind of 'base camp' at Newport, Rhode Island, and bought land and slaves to supply the planned college. Actually, methodologically, so to speak, Berkeley considered slavery to already be an excellent way to convert the Negro, so the new college was hardly necessary. But the native peoples of North America were another matter. These were best converted by missionaries of their own stock. Alas, as American Indians did not typically wish to become Christian missionaries, this required considerable extra effort, including the kidnapping of their children. This was because, as Berkeley explains, "only such savages as are under ten years of age, before evil habits have taken a deep root" can be made into missionaries, and even then their indoctrination has to be in a remote location, free from heathen influences. This is where the remoteness of Bermuda came in handy. "Young Americans, educated in an island at some distance from their own country, will more easily be kept under discipline till they have attained a complete education," he explains. Elsewhere, they "might find opportunities of running away to their countrymen" and "returning to their brutal customs, before they were thoroughly imbued with good principles and habits."

Doubtless, Berkeley himself was particularly aware of the need to prevent locals returning to their "brutal customs" as a result of being the son of an English settler born in Ireland. He considered Irish people to be greedy and naturally slothful, whereas the English were just greedy. Anyway, today, the bishop's missionary effort is immortalized in an engraving on the floor of one Yale University College, which notes appreciatively Berkeley's gift of a plantation to the university, but not, of course, that the value of the gift derived from the exploitation of slave labor.

Buy the bishop's tar water!?

While waiting for his funds to arrive, Berkeley spent his time usefully, studying and of course preaching. He completed a religious tract, *Alciph-*

FIGURE 18 He set to at once, preparing tar water for them. . . .

ron, or the Minute Philosopher, and preached to the natives. And at some point he discovered the miraculous tar water. This mattered because on his eventual return to Ireland he would find the land in the midst of two years of famine and plague.

And the return was not far off, for alas, while the bishop was away, Parliament had begun to perceive the project differently, and was now reluctant to send the money. By 1731 it had become all too obvious that they were never going to do so. The project collapsed.

On his arrival back in Derry, the good bishop found his lost flock to be suffering from a new and particularly terrible outbreak of plague. He set to at once, preparing tar water for them, carefully mixing pine tar, that is to say, sap, with water, allowing it to settle, and then draining off the fluid and bottling it.[2] He also wrote a philosophical guide, *Siris*, subtitled: *Philosophical Reflexions and inquiries concerning the virtues of tar-water, and divers other subjects connected together and arising from one another*, which detailed the virtues of tar water for curing most diseases. The theory of immaterialism reappeared here, now woven into an account of how tar water works, and so, at last, found a wider audience. In fact, *Siris* became a bestseller, both in Europe and back in America, rapidly going through several editions.

Berkeley was sufficiently encouraged by this to pen a new poem, entitled *On Tar*, containing in abbreviated form the essence of the longer work. It is a poem which on both medical and literary grounds demands extensive quotation here.

> *On tar*
> *Hail vulgar juice of never-fading pine!*
> *Cheap as thou art, thy virtues are divine.*
> *To shew them and explain (such is thy store)*
> *There needs much modern and much ancient lore.*

Well, maybe not too extensive. But we should let Berkeley finish by making the connection between his earthly cure and the heavenly truth:

> *Go learn'd mechanic, stare with stupid eyes,*
> *Attribute to all figure, weight and size;*
> *Nor look behind the moving scene to see*
> *What gives each wondrous form its energy.*
>
> *Vain images possess the sensual mind,*
> *To real agents and true causes blind.*
> *But soon as intellect's bright sun displays*
> *O'er the benighted orb his fulgent rays,*
> *Delusive phantoms fly before the light,*
> *Nature and truth lie open at the sight:*
>
> *Causes connect with effects supply*
> *A golden chain, whose radiant links on high*
> *Fix'd to the sovereign throne from thence depend*
> *And reach e'en down to tar the nether end.*

Alas, most of the purchasers of *Siris* read it for its medical advice and missed the significance of the philosophical and ecclesiastical reflections. Berkeley's account of tar water's universal curative powers by reference to Plato's theory of Forms, as well as 'the Trinity' and other ancient doctrines, was too heady a brew for the poor and sick. Nonetheless, tar water was the practical fruit of Bishop Berkeley's year spent in America discovering the hard way the difference between the idea of a college and one that is also there in reality.

Pompous Footnotes

1   Curiously enough, Samuel Johnson was actually one of the very few converts to immaterialism in Berkeley's lifetime. And when Johnson went on to write the first American philosophy textbook, *Elementa Philosophica*, published by Benjamin Franklin in 1752, he dedicated it to Berkeley.

2   More precisely, the yellow resin of *Pinus sylvestris*, also known as the Scotch Fir, mixed with turpentine and used (alarmingly) internally as well as externally for various disorders, including smallpox, scurvy, ulcers, fistulas, and even rheumatism. Like most medicines it does not work, but may help if you believe in it, or at least in the Bishop's theory.

CHAPTER 19
HEADMASTER HEGEL'S DANGEROUS HISTORY LESSON
(1770–1831)

One of the "curious things" about Hegel, writes the controversial, black-shirted[1] 'animal rights' philosopher Peter Singer, is that the aim of his masterpiece, the *Phenomenology*, is to understand and explain a process that is completed by the fact that it has been understood. "The goal of all history is that mind should come to understand itself as the only ultimate reality. When is that understanding first achieved? By Hegel himself in the *Phenomenology!*"

Experts like to say that Hegel's thought represents the 'summit' of Germany's nineteenth-century philosophical idealism. Afterwards came the descent. First into the 'historical materialism' of the 'Young Hegelian' Karl Marx, and then into the murky world of fascism in Italy. Giovanni Gentile, a 'neo-Hegelian' philosophy professor, created the fascist ideology here which then spread on to Spain, Austria, and Germany, but it is truly Hegel, not Gentile, who is the puppet master of modern history. Hegel it was who not only sent Marx padding off to the British Library every day, in search of the footprints of dialectical materialism, but who also inspired Nietzsche, Gentile, and many others with his talk of the new era to be ushered in through war and destruction. This is controversial stuff.

The Philosophical Tale

But then, like philosophy's other Prince of Darkness, Machiavelli, Hegel advises that "to be independent of public opinion is the first condition for achieving anything great."

Hegel speaks instead as a World Historical Personality who is able to interpret the spirit of the times and act accordingly. "In public opinion, all is false and true, but to discover the truth in it is the business of the Great Man. The Great Man of this time is he who expresses the will of his time; who tells his time what it wills; and who carries it out." To be a "Great Man" like this is the dream of Nietzsche and Heidegger, Hitler and Mussolini, and of course, Hegel himself.

But World Historical Personalities, however, have modest beginnings. Georg Hegel's is in Stuttgart, where he was born. His was a rather traditional, conservative family with Hegel Senior a minor civil servant. The family was Protestant and Georg was sent to Tübingen seminary, studying there alongside the future poet Friedrich Hölderlin and his slightly younger fellow philosopher, Friedrich Schelling. The three of them together witnessed the unfolding of the French Revolution and the rise of Napoleon afterwards.

Indeed, Hegel saw in Napoleon the incarnation of the World Spirit acting out history. The story goes that, with the completed manuscript of *Die Phänomenologie des Geistes* (*The Phenomenology of Spirit*) lying on his desk,

> on the night of October 13, 1806, I saw outside of my study the camp-fires of Napoleon's occupation forces. . . . Next day, I saw *die Weltseele* (The World Spirit) on horseback marching through the city of Jena.

Or so he wrote in a letter to one of his friends. The *Phenomenology of Spirit* is the book where Hegel offers his 'dialectical' account of the development of consciousness which starts, as the Marxists noted, with individual sensation, proceeds through social concerns expressed in ethics and politics, before culminating one day in pure consciousness of the 'World Spirit'. For Hegel, as later for both the Marxists and the fascists alike, individual 'freedom' is transcended by people recognizing that their essence lies in serving the State. This is the goal of history. In the *Philosophy of Right*, Hegel explains in an excellent headmasterly way that individuals must understand that the State doesn't exist for them, but rather that the individual exists for the State.

In a way, Hegel's new society aims to combine both individual desires – for wealth, for power, for justice – with the social values of the community: a kind of early 'third way' politics. But Hegel's solution also involves reclassifying all desires that are not compatible with the requirements of the social whole as 'irrational' and hence not what the individual really wants. Instead, the collective will, the *Geist*, is given complete power and authority. This is what makes Hegel the founding father of the two totalitarian doctrines: fascism and communism.

But before ushering in the new era, with the exception of a brief period as a newspaper editor, Hegel devoted his life wholly to teaching, first at Jena, then at Nuremberg, a spell at Heidelberg, and finally at Berlin.

FIGURE 19 Hegel explained, in an excellent headmasterly way, that individuals must understand that the State doesn't exist for them, but rather that the individual exists for the State.

Although Hegel has come to personify 'academic' philosophy – abstruse, complicated, and lofty – his first two posts were in schools; only after 1816 did he become a university philosopher. All his key works date from his time as a schoolmaster rather than from his university perch.

Actually, Hegel, rare amongst Western philosophers, is clear about the educational foundations of his system. But as most commentators are creatures of universities, they pass over this. Anyway, Hegel began by 'professing' to his pupils at Nuremberg grammar school. He also wrote voluminously on methods of teaching and learning (in the form of both manuscripts and letters) and reflected on numerous 'pedagogical matters'. These included the conflict between the need to achieve discipline and the advantages of 'student-centered' learning, the bad practice of 'spoon-feeding' on the one hand, and the desirability of obliging children to imbibe from the deep well of the classics.

Here in its earliest form is the Hegelian play of the dialectical reasoning. Everything has two sides, creating tension that must be resolved. In fact, Hegel was, in general, locked into a conflict between the two poles of traditional and progressive ideas of education. So it is that Headmaster Hegel bans dueling and fighting while introducing military drill into the school day. This he explained by saying that it would help students "to have the presence of mind to carry out a command on the spot without previous reflection."

As his school address of 1810 reveals, Hegel favored "quiet behavior, the habit of continuous attention, respect, and obedience to the teachers." This reflected his admiration for the discipline imposed in the classroom of Pythagoras who demanded that his pupils keep totally silent for the first four years of their studies.

Yet Hegel also writes that teachers should not "induce in children a feeling of subjection and bondage – to make them obey another's will even in unimportant matters – to demand absolute obedience for obedience's sake, and by severity to obtain what really belongs alone to the feeling of love and reverence." Students should not be regarded as "an assemblage of servants" nor should they have the appearance or behavior of such. "Education to independence demands that young people should be accustomed early to consult their own sense of propriety and their own reason."

Summing up this (suitably dialectical) ambivalence, he notes that "to regard study as mere receptivity and memory work is to have a most incomplete view of what instruction means. On the other hand, to concentrate attention on the pupils' own original reflections and reasoning is equally one-sided and should be still more carefully guarded against."

Some philosophers are more interesting when talking than they are when writing, and some are more interesting on paper than in real life. Hegel fits neither category. He is dull in both. One of his students recalls his lectures thus:

> There he sat, with relaxed, half-sullen air, and, as he spoke, kept turning backwards and forwards the leaves of his long folio manuscript; a constant hacking and coughing disturbed the even flow of speech; every proposition stood isolated by itself, and seemed to force its way out all broken and twisted; every word, every syllable was, as it were, reluctantly let go, receiving from the metallic ring of the broad Swabian dialect a strange emphasis, as if it were the most important thing to be said.

It would have been hard going listening to him. On the other hand, his writing is notorious too for being hard work,[2] and he is certainly ambitious in the range of the topics he attempts to cover. Schopenhauer accused him of exerting "not on philosophy alone, but on all forms of German literature, a devastating, or more strictly speaking, a stupefying, one could also say, a pestiferous, influence."

His first and most admired work is the *Phenomenology of Spirit* (sometimes translated as 'Mind'), mentioned already. Others during his life included the *Encyclopaedia of the Philosophical Sciences*, the *Science of Logic*, and the *Philosophy of Right*. Out of it all, the most notable feature is his use of the ancient technique called 'the dialectic'. Plato, for example, uses it in the form of arguments between two people with opposing positions, before suggesting a compromise position – which is then challenged too. Hegel brandishes the dialectic in response to a range of social issues including those concerning the family itself, where the contradiction between man and woman is overcome by the production of a child. However, Hegel's most famous use is as a system for understanding the history of philosophy and the world itself. His claim is that history is a series of moments evolving successively out of the conflicts inherent in the previous one.

For Hegel, the origin of society is in the first conflict between two humans, a "bloody battle" with each seeking to make the other recognize him as master and accept the role of slave. It is the fear of death that forces part of mankind to submit to the other, and society is thereafter perpetually divided into two classes: slaves and masters. Hegel does not consider the possible conflict between men and women in his theory. He thinks women are not part of the bloody conflict but "naturally" men's servants, with the contradiction resolved as described above. (Hegel himself had an illicit liaison with his landlady and had a child with her. He later "legitimized" the child as his own, although he would not marry the mother.)

For Hegel, and this is the point on which the Marxists would later disagree with him, it is not material need that propels one class to oppress the other – it is a conflict born solely out of the peculiarly human lust for power over one another. But Hegel, unlike Thomas Hobbes, approves of the motivation, and calls it the "desire for recognition." The struggle involves the risk of personal destruction, but this is the true path towards 'freedom'. So it was that the French Revolution is driven by the aspiration for 'liberty' and 'equality', but is accompanied (and then consumed) by brutal terror. Out of this contradiction, however, Hegel decided, emerges a new kind of State: for the first time, a State in which the power of rational government is combined with the ideals of freedom and equality.

In the aftermath of the destruction of World War II, as Stalin and Hitler, or communism and fascism, or indeed Young Hegelian and neo-Hegelian, collided, the philosopher of science Karl Popper wrote a fierce attack on all the individual "totalitarians" in his book *The Open Society and Its Enemies*. But of them all, it is the chapter on Hegel that is the most vituperative. Popper slams into Hegel as a fraud who hides his emptiness behind a pompous and obscure style. He says Hegel's philosophy is motivated by a desire to please his employer, the reactionary Prussian monarchy, in order to gain, in turn, his own position, prestige, and influence. Popper weaves extracts from Hegel together to paint a picture of an odious philosophy indeed.

Hegel, Popper says, represents the "missing link" between Plato and the modern forms of totalitarianism, with their worship of State, history, and the nation. The doctrine is that the State is everything and the individual is nothing. "The State is the Divine Idea as it exists on earth. . . . We must therefore worship the State as the manifestation of the Divine on earth, and consider that, if it is difficult to comprehend Nature, it is infinitely harder to grasp the Essence of the State. . . . The State is the march of God through the world."

Too many philosophers neglected Schopenhauer's incessantly repeated warnings, says Popper; "they neglected them not so much at their own peril (they did not fare badly) as at the peril of those whom they taught, and at the peril of mankind." But then Popper did not appreciate the role of a Headmaster. It *is* to stand up in assembly each morning, sing a few rousing songs, and inspire everyone. "Our School is everything! We should worship Our School as the manifestation of the Divine on earth, and understand that it is the March of God through the World!"

Instead, Popper wonders how such a worthless person as Hegel could have exerted such an influence. Popper thinks that it must have something to do with the desire of philosophers to retain around themselves something of an atmosphere not only of mystery but also of magic. He recalls that "philosophy is considered as a strange and abstruse kind of thing, dealing with mysteries with which religion deals," but not in a way which can be revealed to the uninitiated of the "common people"; it is considered to be "too profound for that," to be instead the property, the "religion and theology of the intellectuals, of the learned and wise."

And so the story of Hegel shows how easily a "clown may be a maker of history," as Popper puts it. The Marxists reinterpreted Hegel's glorious "war of nations" with a war of classes, the fascists sought a war of races. All Hegel required was the patronage of the powers that be to provide him with an official pulpit, a post in a university.

As an example of this kind of obedient, State-sponsored philosophizing, Popper offers Hegel's argument for "inequality before the law." Hegel says that yes, citizens are equal before the law, but that this equality applies only to matters in which "they are equal outside the law also." Adding: "Only that equality which they possess in property, age . . . *et cetera* can deserve equal treatment before the law." Indeed, the mature

State creates and enforces the inequality of the various classes. All this is very much the way to run a good school too – the prefects do not follow the same rules as the rest of the boys; the scholarship class eats dinner separately from the drongos . . .

Actually, Hegel explains that fundamentally all relations can be expressed in terms of master and slave. For nations, likewise, the choice is to assert themselves on the world stage – or to be enslaved.

Likewise, Hegel rejects the democratic notion that individual liberties should only be limited where their exercise would adversely affect others, and adds that true liberty is attained by allowing the "spirit of the State" free rein. And the spirit of the State is epitomized in the form of "an organic totality, the Sovereign power," its "all-sustaining, all-decreeing Unity" – that is, the monarch. The monarchical constitution is therefore "the constitution of developed reason; and all other constitutions belong to lower grades of the development and the self-realization of reason," he announces. Before giving an example.

"On the Stage of Universal History, on which we can observe and grasp it, Spirit displays itself in its most concrete reality." And indeed the concrete reality is the Prussian monarch. "The German Spirit is the Spirit of the new World. Its aim is the realization of absolute Truth as the unlimited self-determination of Freedom." Adding that this freedom, this German spirit, "has its own absolute form as its purpose."

Hegel opposes all restraints on this rising German Spirit, such as international organizations with the task of preventing conflict, explaining in the *Philosophy of Right* that war is crucial: "Just as the blowing of the winds preserves the sea from the foulness which would be the result of a prolonged calm, so also corruption in nations would be the product of prolonged, let alone 'perpetual' peace."

In 1831 cholera was epidemic in Berlin and Hegel's colleague and intellectual enemy, Schopenhauer, despite or perhaps because of being famously pessimistic, quickly left the city for the healthier climes of Italy. Schopenhauer thus survived the epidemic. Hegel stayed, perhaps out of his preference for his own nation, contracted the disease, and died.

Pompous Footnotes

1   On the cover of his *Introduction to Practical Ethics*, which was predictably controversial in Germany on account of its advocating euthanasia for handicapped babies, Dr. Singer wears a black shirt.

2   In her book *The Origins of Totalitarianism*, Hannah Arendt recalls (sympatheti-
    cally) an anecdote about Hegel's last moments. On his deathbed, his mysteri-
    ous last words were supposed to have been: "Nobody has understood me
    – except one, and he also misunderstood."

CHAPTER 20
ARTHUR SCHOPENHAUER
AND THE LITTLE OLD LADY
(1788–1860)

"Schopenhauer's gospel of resignation is not very consistent and not very sincere. . . . He agreed that what commonly passes for knowledge belongs to the realm of *Maya*, but when we pierce the veil, we behold not God, but Satan, the wicked omnipotent will, perpetually busied in weaving a web of suffering for the torture of its creatures. Terrified by the Diabolic vision the sage replies 'Avaunt!' and seeks refuge in non-existence. *It is an insult to the mystics to claim them as believers in this mythology. . . .*"

So says Bertrand Russell in *A History of Western Philosophy*. But that's not the only thing Professor Russell has against him:

> Nor is the doctrine sincere, if we may judge by Schopenhauer's life. He habitually dined well, at a good restaurant: he had many trivial love-affairs, which were sensual but not passionate: he was exceedingly quarrelsome and usually avaricious. On one occasion he was annoyed by an elderly seamstress who was talking to a friend outside the door of his apartment; he threw her downstairs causing her permanent injury. She obtained a Court Order compelling him to pay a certain sum every quarter as long as he lived. When at last she died, after twenty years, he noted in his account-book *Obit anus, abit onus* ['The old woman dies, the burden departs'].

The Philosophical Tale

Arthur Schopenhauer is not generally counted as one of the truly great philosophers – sometimes not even one of the great German philosophers. Despite his undoubted influence on Sigmund Freud, Friedrich Nietzsche, and even Ludwig Wittgenstein, there is more interest in asking why he pushed the old lady down the stairs than in all his theories. He lurks in the shadow not only of his celebrated contemporaries, Professors Hegel and Kant, but of Marx and Nietzsche too.[1] In fact, he is sometimes only remembered for his lengthy and vitriolic attacks on academic philosophy, epitomized by the detested Hegel. That man, "installed from above, by the powers that be, as the certified Great Philosopher," was in reality:

> a flat-headed, insipid, nauseating, illiterate charlatan, who reached the pinnacle of audacity in scribbling together and dishing up the craziest mystifying nonsense.

And, Schopenhauer adds, as "Governments make of philosophy a means of serving their state interests, and scholars make of it a trade," so Hegel was paid by the monarch of Prussia to play "jiggery-pokery" in front of an "audience of fools." In this way, Schopenhauer manages to combine his favorite target of other philosophers with criticism of the general public and the "powers that be" too, demonstrating that considerable talent for insult which helps explain why this most original of thinkers has been largely confined to a bit part in the theatrical performance that is Philosophy.

Arthur Schopenhauer was born in a port town in what is today called Poland, the son of a rich merchant, Heinrich Floris Schopenhauer. Heinrich was an anglophile who intended Arthur (so-called, it was hoped, to ease him into a career in business) to be born in London, but his wife, Johanna Troisner, became ill and they had to return home. Arthur was born in Gdansk instead. To make up, Heinrich sent Schopenhauer to boarding school in Wimbledon for a few months (which he hated), and took out a subscription to the London *Times*. When Arthur was 17, he was sent to business school in Hamburg.

Shortly after this, his father threw himself into the river, apparently because his business affairs went sour. Schopenhauer was devastated and seems to have blamed his mother, a glamorous socialite some twenty years younger than her husband. Yet, whatever Arthur's black thoughts, she continued to go from strength to strength, gaining a considerable reputation as a popular romantic novelist. It was through her that Schopenhauer was introduced to many of Germany's great writers of the time, including Goethe, Schlegel, and the brothers Grimm – as well as to the art of writing itself.

But Schopenhauer's chosen theme only occurred to him a few years later while at university in Berlin. It was here that he first came to the conclusion that most of what passed for philosophy then was all 'bunk'. After attending the celebrated Johann Fichte's (1762–1814) lectures for two years, he saw at once that the man was a charlatan. In his last book, *Parerga and Paralipomena* (1851), he explains his discovery: "Fichte,

Schelling and Hegel are in my opinion not philosophers, for they lack the first requirement of a philosopher, namely a seriousness and honesty of enquiry. They are merely sophists who wanted to appear to be, rather than to be, something. They sought not truth but their own interest and advancement."

By comparison, it seemed to him that he had a message far more important than that of any of his contemporaries. He began to see himself as a kind of metaphysical cryptographer who had stumbled on to the key to understanding the universe – and the key was this: each individual – not just some supposed philosophical elite – is already in touch with the ultimate underlying reality. Not just tentatively, contemplatively in touch, but directly, actively. We are all so many puppets twitching and dancing to its whim.

The World as Will and Representation was the end product of this realization, written in a non-academic style, with an ironic, aristocratic tone. Indeed, in later life, Schopenhauer tried to live as an aristocrat too, adopting a self-consciously leisurely existence as a 'great thinker'. Like Kant, whom he admired, he dressed in an old-fashioned way, ate at strictly regular times, and took a daily walk, in his case, in the company of his much-loved poodle, Atma. Apart from occasional visits to the theater and reading the newspapers at the public library, he was the model of a scholarly recluse. As he had put it when originally challenged as to why he was abandoning the business career his parents had planned for him: "Life is a difficult question; I have decided to spend my life in thinking about it."

And this is what he discovered. 'Will', instinct, 'desire', call it what you, er, will, is the basic force. Life is meaningless, since birth leads to death and the only purpose of activity between the two seems to be to produce offspring who can then repeat the cycle. There is nothing behind it – no strategy, no reason, no purpose. It is not only outside space and time, it creates these regularities, these 'appearances'. It is primary, it sweeps perception before it, it determines our concepts, it dictates all actions. It even drives evolution, not the other way around as Darwin would have it. Animals reflect their wills in their forms – the timid rabbit by its large ears, always ready to detect the faintest whiff of danger. The hawk's cruel beak and talons reflects its permanent desire to rip other creatures apart. We are like so many mayflies, created one day, dead the next, leaving only our eggs. Nature has more use for species than for individuals, but species too must come and go as part of the larger cycle.

Will is also irrational; it can create reasons but is by no means bound by them. The will to live and the will to procreate are irrational, they obey no rules and accept no logic. To demonstrate this, Schopenhauer describes the grisly tale of the Australian ant, nasty example of its kind, which, when decapitated, turns into two grotesque fighting machines – the head will try to bite the thorax, which will attempt to sting to death the other.

Schopenhauer does write, as Russell says, of the need to penetrate the "veil of Maya" in order to see the common reality of 'will', which is part of *Maharakya* or 'Great World', Hindu wisdom. He is one of very few European philosophers to relate his work equally to Eastern as well as Western works, which is why, as well as calling his poodle Atma after the Hindu life-force or soul, his study contained, alongside the usual bust of Kant, and less usual portraits of doggy friends, a golden Buddha on a marble stand. His library included more than 130 items of oriental philosophy including sacred Hindu texts that he called "the consolation of my life." Schopenhauer shared the Buddhists' view that pain is the norm and happiness the exception. And from Buddhism too comes his solution: nothingness. Nothingness is exactly the best you can obtain. It is the literal meaning of 'nirvana'.

In *On the Vanity of Existence* he explains:

> The vanity of existence is revealed in the whole form existence assumes: in the infiniteness of time and space contrasted with the finiteness of the individual in both; in the fleeting present as the sole form to which actuality exists; in the contingency and relativity of all things in continual becoming without being; in continual desire without satisfaction; in the continual frustration of striving in which life consists. Time and that probability of all things existing in time that time itself brings about is simply the form under which the will-to-live, which as thing-in-itself is imperishable, reveals to itself the vanity of its striving. *Time is that by virtue of which everything becomes nothingness in our hands and loses all real value.*

It was only the second edition of the *World as Will and Representation* (in 1844) that was received with any appreciation. Hitherto Schopenhauer had been known in Frankfurt mainly as the son of the celebrated Johanna; now he came to have a following which, if at first small in numbers, was sufficiently enthusiastic to make up for it. Artists painted his portrait; a bust of him was made by Elizabeth Ney. In the April 1853 number of the *Westminster Review* John Oxenford heralded, in an article entitled "Iconoclasm in German Philosophy," Schopenhauer's arrival as a writer and thinker. One of his most enthusiastic German admirers was Richard Wagner, who in 1854 sent him a copy of his *Der Ring der Nibelungen*, with the inscription: "In admiration and gratitude."

Years later, Friedrich Nietzsche would find a copy of *Die Welt als Wille und Vorstellung* in a second-hand bookstore and be unable to put the book down until he had finished it. In London, Sigmund Freud would study Schopenhauer's description of the primal "will to live" and "sexual impulse" avidly, before drawing up his own account of the "life-instinct" and the centrality of the "libido" in human life.

But initially, no one was interested in Schopenhauer, let alone in his philosophy of existence. Despite his mother's celebrity he had trouble even getting anyone to print a few hundred copies. After a series of delays in obtaining first publication, Schopenhauer wrote one of his characteristically abusive letters to the publisher, who replied cooly "that he must decline all further correspondence with one whose letters, in their divine coarseness and rusticity, savored more of the cabman than of the philosopher," and closed by committing himself to print only with the hope that "my fears that the work will be good for nothing but waste paper may not be realized . . ."

In fact, the book was widely ignored and despite so few copies being printed, sixteen years later most of them did end up as waste paper. Yet in the face of this general want of appreciation, Schopenhauer had some crumbs of comfort. His sister wrote to him to say that Goethe "had received it with great joy, immediately cut the thick book, and began instantly to read it. An hour later he sent me a note to say that he thanked you very much and thought that the whole book was good. He pointed out the most important passages, read them to us, and was greatly delighted. . . . You are the only author whom Goethe has ever read seriously, it seems to me, and I rejoice."

Even so, in a characteristically bitter yet pompous preface to the second edition, Schopenhauer would dedicate the book "Not to my contemporaries, not to my compatriots – to mankind I commit my now completed work, in the confidence that it will not be without value for them, even if this should be late recognized, as is commonly the lot of what is good."

Yes, yes, but did Schopenhauer really push the old lady down the stairs?

We refer to the what is known, in legal circles anyway, as the Marquet affair.

FIGURE 20 Grabbing the stick in one hand, and the seamstress around the waist, he tried to force her away from his rooms.

It appears that, returning home one day, Schopenhauer found three of (what he considered) that nasty sub-species, women, gossiping outside his door. One of these was a seamstress, Caroline Luise Marquet, who occupied another room in the house. Schopenhauer, having strong views on 'noise' (which he had set out in a not-very-creditable literary effort called "On Noise"), 'willed' them to go away, and indeed instructed them to do so – but they refused. Schopenhauer then went into his room and returned with a stick. Grabbing the seamstress around the waist, he tried to force her away from his rooms. She screamed, Schopenhauer pushed her – and the woman fell.

It sounds pretty bad for Schopenhauer. But curiously, when Mrs. Marquet brought an action against him for damages, alleging that he had kicked and beaten her, Schopenhauer managed to convince the court that whatever had happened (and he admitted using force), it was justified. The court dismissed the case. Only later, when she appealed against the judgment, and he declined to testify in his defense, was Schopenhauer fined. Years later, in May 1825, an elderly Mrs. Marquet returned to court a third time, now saying that the events had caused her to suffer fevers and that she had lost the power of one of her arms. She asked for, and was awarded, a monthly allowance as compensation.

So what sort of a human being was the great philosopher? Schopenhauer had several relationships, and an illegitimate son, whom he ignored and who died young from neglect. Whilst at university he fell in love with one Karoline Jagermann, the mistress of the Duke of Weimar, but she did not like him. The most serious affair he had was with a younger actress, Caroline Richter, who already had a son. But then Schopenhauer never intended to marry her anyway. In his writings, he sneers that marriage is a debt, contracted in youth and paid off in old age. Had not all the true philosophers been celibates – Descartes, Leibniz, Malebranche, Spinoza, and Kant – he opines.

He seems to have had a nasty temper, as Russell says, and spent much of his life in cold, uncommunicative silence with his mother and sister, particularly after they mismanaged (as he saw it) the family business. Yet the loss of self-control on the landing seems to reflect, in an unfortunate way, the central truth of his philosophy, the irrational 'will' that drives us.

It is in no small part due to him that today the 'selfish gene' is regularly trotted out by pundits and scientists such as Richard Dawkins, that the 'will to power' features prominently in the iconoclastic ravings of Nietzsche, and even the notion (encapsulated in the title of Schopenhauer's book) of a world created by 'will' has been repotted and transplanted in the ornamental gardens of existentialism.

But that is not to say that his contribution is appreciated. Far from it. Rather, his originality is lost and forgotten. Fittingly enough, in fact. For as he put it in the *World as Will and Representation*:

> The earth rolls on from day into night; the individual dies; but the sun itself burns without intermission, an eternal noon. Life is certain to the will-to-live; the form of life is endless present; it matters not how individuals, the phenomenal of the Idea, arise and pass away in time, like fleeting dreams.

Pompous Footnote

1 Being born in 1788 pitched Schopenhauer into the middle of a peculiarly fruitful era for German philosophy. Schopenhauer's enemies were his elders and betters: Immanuel Kant (1724–1804), Georg Hegel (1770–1831), and Johann Fichte (1762–1814). Søren Kierkegaard (1813–55) in Denmark, Friedrich Nietzsche (1844–1900), and Karl Marx (1818–83) were his junior inferiors.

VII
THE ROMANTICS

CHAPTER 21
THE SEDUCTION OF SØREN KIERKEGAARD
(1813–1855)

Søren Aabye Kierkegaard was born in Copenhagen, Denmark, on May 5, 1813. In the "letter from the young aesthete" which is part of *Fear and Trembling*, one of his strange, multilayered works, he recalls the occasion:

> I stick my finger into existence – it smells of nothing. Where am I? What is this thing called the world? Who is it that has lured me into the thing, and now leaves me here? Who am I? How did I come into the world? *Why was I not consulted?*

The Philosophical Tale

It is a good question, and one that has contributed to his reputation as the 'father of existentialism'. But consulted or not, Søren was born and brought up in a wealthy but dour Protestant household. His father, Michael Kierkegaard, liked to dwell morosely at the dinner table on the sufferings of Jesus and the martyrs, and family life was punctuated by lessons in 'obedience' from the Bible like that contained in the story of Abraham. Christians will know that Abraham was the devout father instructed by God to sacrifice not merely a few dumb animals, but his only son, and was just about to do so when, at the very last minute, he received divine dispensation not to. Quite how that fitted into the Kierkegaard household routine is not clear, but it sounds a bit ominous . . .

But then, the Kierkegaards were all members of the Moravian Church, a rather depressing affair based in Germany which believed, amongst other things, that the enjoyment of sex was sinful and that men should be allocated marriage partners by lottery.

Despite being so devout, Kierkegaard's father was said to be burdened with guilt after cursing God as a young shepherd one particularly wet day on the rain-swept hills of Jutland. His religious devotion increased each year, as he tried to combat what he perceived as "the curse" with faith. He believed that because of this lapse, God was punishing him. In particular, he thought all of his children would die before him, and certainly that none would reach 34 years of age, that being the age Jesus was supposed to have died at. Søren writes of both admiring and fearing his father with his grim preoccupation with death, but also of sometimes feeling that his "insanity" was infecting the family. As, according to Plato, it is only at age 35 that philosophers can start producing their best ideas, naturally this forecast of an early death cast a great shadow over the young Kierkegaards.

And for years, the dire prediction seemed to be becoming fulfilled. The first of what would be two Søren Kierkegaards died in a playground accident aged 12, and a sister, Maren, died at 25 of an unknown illness. She was soon followed by the other two daughters, Nicoline and Petrea, both at age 33 and both in childbirth. Another son, Niels, escaped to America but died there aged 24. His elder brother, Peter, although surviving himself, lost his wife, Elise. In fact, other than Peter, only the older Søren managed to defeat the prophecy by living to see his 35th birthday.

Some commentators have wondered why Michael Kierkegaard was so sure that cursing God would occasion such extreme punishment. Surely it would take a much worse sin than "youthful cussing" to require the price of so many young lives? Not cussing, but maybe marrying a woman for money rather than for anything else, hurrying her into her grave just two years later, and then having an illegitimate baby with the maid? Such speculations could not of course be more irrelevant to the case of Kierkegaard's father, who as a devout Lutheran valued order and self-discipline above all else. Or so these scholars tell us.

Nonetheless, Michael Kierkegaard's first wife, Kirstine, was both rich and already 36 when they married and evidently failed to produce any children. After only two years of marriage she died of pneumonia. Her gravestone notes only tersely that she is buried there "under this stone which her husband has dedicated to her memory." The dedication to Kierkegaard's second wife, Ane, who was indeed the family maid when she became pregnant, however, is more effusive. This declares that she has "Gone home to the Lord" but will be "loved and missed by her surviving children and friends, but especially her old husband." It seems either that Michael Kierkegaard preferred his second, younger, wife or that over the course of years he mellowed somewhat.

But Ane would have suited Michael better. Both Michael and his sons considered women to be essentially domestic servants, with special responsibility for producing babies, and indeed Søren's sisters' duties included waiting on their brothers. The girls' treatment was extreme even by the standards of the day and occasioned protest from one Councillor Boeson, a friend of the family.

But such humdrum domestic arrangements do not seem to have preoccupied Søren. In his books, Kierkegaard offers long discussions of his father, but makes no mention of his mother or sisters. Otherwise, like his father, he is instead preoccupied directly with God.

This was the period of what is nowadays fondly recalled as Denmark's "Golden Age." Copenhagen was devastated by fire twice in the 1790s, in 1801 the country lost its entire fleet, in 1807 it was bombarded from the sea by the English, and in 1813 the national mint went bankrupt.

But at least there was a great "flowering" of the arts, and it was indubitably for Denmark an era of scientific, artistic, and literary fertility. This was despite, or perhaps because, Denmark was also going through a period of social strife. The certainties of feudal society based on lords in their manors and peasants working the fields were giving way to more complex ones in which rich traders and skilled craftsmen challenged the social hierarchies. Michael Kierkegaard was just such a case. As the youngest of the family, with no prospects of inheritance, he had had to leave impoverished rural Jutland to become an apprentice for his uncle in Copenhagen. But once there, he rapidly succeeded in creating a small fortune, and with it a new social status.

Despite this, both Michael and his son Søren were highly critical of the changes in society, and considered that serious values, serious commitments, were being trivialized or lost. The superficiality of the 'new Denmark' was summed up for Søren by an amusement park established in Copenhagen. Here, peep shows, a wax museum, visual tricks such as dioramas, firework displays, and even pleasure gardens presented to him a frivolous, superficial, and irreligious way of living.

For even as a young boy, Søren Kierkegaard was very serious. At Copenhagen's elite grammar school, the School of Civic Virtue or *Borgerdydskolen*, he was nicknamed "the Fork," as he liked to pin down his classmates in debate and expose inconsistencies in their arguments.

Later, his interests went beyond merely winning arguments and on to playing a role in the literary world, and in particular joining the literary circle of one of the most celebrated figures of all Copenhagen, one J. L. Heiberg. Mr. Heiberg was a philosopher too, and had been responsible for introducing Hegel's philosophy to Denmark. As if this were not enough, Heiberg was the most famous Danish playwright of the day, held the post of director of the Royal Theatre, was married to a famous and beautiful actress, and hosted *the* most refined literary salon in Copenhagen. How Kierkegaard envied him! All his efforts were driven by the need to be invited into this charmed circle.

Or almost all. It was around this time that Kierkegaard become engaged to one Regine Olsen, whom he had first met when she was just 14. "Marriage is and remains the most important voyage of discovery a human being undertakes," he explains, in *Stages on Life's Way*. Regine became a key theme of much of his subsequent writing, but not in a very positive way. As Kierkegaard put it, in the words of Johannes the Seducer, one of his many pseudonyms, "to poeticize oneself into a young girl is an art; to poeticize oneself out of her is a masterpiece." Later, in the "Diary of the Seducer" in *Either/Or*, he wrote:

> The awakening of sexual desire in adolescence makes our happiness lie outside ourselves, and its gratification dependent on the exercise of freedom by another. Sexual attraction fills us with heady delight, but also the dread of responsibility. Anxiety is this ambivalent oscillation between fascination and fear.

So Regine had to go, but rather than declare an end to the engagement, Søren set about humiliating her in public in the hope that *she* would then break off the relationship. (Regine eventually married one of Søren's rivals, a school teacher who went on to a successful if rather dull career as a diplomat.) *Either/Or* became an instant success, mainly due to its racier aspects. The experience with Regine triggered a creative outpouring of twenty books over a period of eight years.

But Søren never made it to the literary set. Frustration at failing to gain full acceptance into J. L. Heiberg's coterie at times led him instead to less refined circles: visiting brothels and mixing with a group of heavy drinkers that included the otherwise very shy Hans Christian Andersen, already becoming a celebrated writer for his fairy tales. Søren used to enjoy ridiculing him at the meetings, but the two also conducted a strange sort of correspondence. He also began to run up debts and had to be bailed out repeatedly by his father.

His nadir came when he challenged a satirical periodical called *The Corsair* to parody him, which it did, very skillfully, portraying him as an eccentric figure who wandered aimlessly around Copenhagen talking to people – and what's worse, whose trousers were too short! Shocked and hurt by the mockery, Kierkegaard wrote in his journal: "Geniuses are like thunder – they go against the wind, frighten people and clear the air."

FIGURE 21 *"Geniuses are like thunder – they go against the wind, frighten people and clear the air."*

But when he was 25, he experienced what he describes as a sudden "indescribable joy" and decided to reform himself. He abandoned the heavy drinking, reconciled with his father, and published his first article, a critical examination of a Hans Christian Andersen novel, called "From the Papers of One Still Living."

But it is in *Either/Or* that Kierkegaard sets out his new insight, that the essential choice we take is between sensuous self-gratification or altruistic immersion in the demands of purity and virtue – the latter of which he sees as essentially the Christian commitment. And the choice cannot be made rationally; it is 'existential' in nature. What does that mean? Well, existentialists say that such decisions define and create individuals, the person who takes them does not exist until after he or she has chosen. Thus they are beyond the rational judgment of others. Søren applied this approach to Regine, creating what everyone else perceived as an elaborate series of public humiliations for the young woman, in order to 'provoke' her into ending their engagement. But, for Søren, he was creating the next Kierkegaard.

Whenever we decide to suspend the ethical, he writes egotistically, such acts will necessarily be beyond social justification and will be strictly "ineffable." They will be done in "fear and trembling" (the title of another of his books) since they defy civic virtue and hover on the edge of madness.

Indirect communication

One of the distinctive features of Kierkegaard's writing is his humor. *Concluding Unscientific Postscript to Philosophical Fragments* is an addendum of more than 600 pages to the little book *Philosophical Fragments*, which runs for less than fifty pages. Both are written under the pseudonym Johannes Climacus, this being characteristic of what Kierkegaard calls his method of "indirect communication."

According to Kierkegaard, direct communication is a "fraud" toward God, the author, and readers because it is related merely to objective thinking, which does not properly express the importance of subjectivity. Indirect communication enables readers to bring in their own thoughts and to form a personal relation with ideas. Conversely, being objective deprives people of the use of their passions in the area of interest. Christianity in particular can only be appreciated when approached with passion and inwardness, which is essentially subjectivity. Hegel's truth, by comparison, his "continuous world-historical process," is cold and remorseless.

So he breaks up his texts into prefaces, preludes, preliminary explorations, interludes, postscripts, letters to the reader, collations by pseudonymous editors of pseudonymous sections, divisions, and subdivisions in order to ensure that there is no obvious 'authoritative' point of view, but rather the reader is forced to make his or her own individual judgment about meaning. (The attentive reader will note that this chapter, in a nod to Søren, is also fragmentary and incomplete. It makes for lousy style, and tires the reader who has to unravel the connections – but it is a great shortcut for the writer.)

And since Søren's books were self-published using his inheritance, he was anyway able to write them any way he pleased – and still have enough money left over to live in a comfortable and commodious six-room city suite with his faithful servant Anders.

In the *Unscientific Postscript*, Kierkegaard describes real existence as being like "riding a wild stallion," whereas "so-called existence" is like falling asleep in a hay-wagon. Evidently inspired by this, a typical working day for Søren would consist of a period of 'meditation' in the morning followed by writing until midday. In the afternoon, he liked to take a long walk, stopping to chat to anyone he thought was interesting on the way, before returning home late in the evening. He then stayed up late to write for much of the night. (This, presumably, is the "stallion" bit . . .)

The walks through Copenhagen, together with his continuous stream of books, eventually made him quite a public figure, noted both as a critic of the then popular Hegelian philosophy and of the State Church.

But then these two enemies merged when Hans Martensen, an old rival from Kierkegaard's university days and a prominent proponent of Hegelian philosophy, assumed the leadership of the Danish Church. Kierkegaard was furious. He immediately launched a full-scale attack on the new bishop's brand of Christianity and offered instead his own vision, this time, despite his philosophical theories about the semantic benefits, without hiding behind pseudonyms. This and later works such as the series of satirical pamphlets called *The Instant* were popular and sold well – but this meant that they cost all the more money as the print bill expanded faster than any receipts. In fact, the day Kierkegaard collapsed in the street with what would be his final illness, he was on the way back home after visiting the bank to withdraw the last of his inheritance.

True to his anticlerical principles, he refused on his deathbed to receive the last rites, and what's more, his funeral was interrupted by a mob of protesters who objected to the presence of a priest – even though the priest was his brother. The city studiously ignored his passing, and for years after his death the children of Copenhagen were not allowed to be christened Søren because of the dreadful reputation attached to the name.

Kierkegaard's work was largely ignored or forgotten. That is until the twentieth century, when his ideas began to influence the French existentialists, who welcomed and admired his individualism and anti-rationalism – and completely ignored his religious priorities. Søren Kierkegaard would have appreciated the irony.

CHAPTER 22
MILL'S POETICAL TURN
(1806–1873)

J. S. Mill is generally considered "the most eminent" of the nineteenth-century British philosophers who propounded and developed the theory of *utilitarianism,* and his most important works are usually agreed to be the *System of Logic* (in two volumes, 1843), the *Principles of Political Economy* (1848), *On Liberty* (1859), and, of course, *Utilitarianism* (1861). But in the early years, something terrible nearly happened. Karl Britton, writing in the *Oxford Companion,* discreetly explains.

> [*Coughs politely*]: At the age of 20, Mill suffered a "mental crisis" followed by a long period of depression during which he found consolation in Wordsworth's poetry. On his recovery he reacted for a time against the intellectual and moral opinions of his father and his circle and came under the influence of Coleridge, Carlyle and John Sterling. In 1831 he met Harriet Taylor and the two formed a passionate attachment which gradually came to be tolerated by her husband but not by most of their friends. It seems that on the whole Mrs. Taylor's influence helped to free Mill from his Coleridgean inclinations.

That is good. But how did Mill come to be in such a pretty pickle in the first place? The path, it seems, was a short one.

The Philosophical Tale

John Stuart Mill was born in London and educated at home by his father, James, who was himself a philosopher active in promoting the utilitarian theory (one might say, a bit of a Utilitarian Preacher . . .). His childhood consisted of Greek at 3, Latin at 8, logic at 12 – impeccable philosophical training all the better to create out of the weak human mind a powerful "reasoning machine."

The plan had been hatched by both his father and his secular godfather, the great scientific rationalist and utilitarian Mr. Bentham, famous for designing a prison – the Panopticon – where everyone is watched all the time, and was designed to eliminate uncertainty, fuzziness, imprecision, and so on.

At 18, Mill was ready to start work in the East India Company, alongside Mill Senior, rising up through its ranks to eventually become its Examiner. The "mental crisis" occurred just four years later. Unfortunately, Mill, now aged 22, had come across a book of Wordsworth's poems, and decided to become a different kind of thinker altogether – a philosophical spirit more than a logical machine.[1]

> The object of poetry is confessedly to act upon the emotions, and therein is poetry sufficiently distinguished from what Wordsworth affirms to be its logical opposite, namely . . . matter of fact or science. The one addresses itself to the belief, the other to feelings. The one does its work by convincing or persuading, the other by moving. The one acts by presenting a proposition to the understanding, the other by offering interesting objects of contemplation to the sensibilities. ("What is Poetry?" in *Thoughts on Poetry and its Varieties* [1833])

Mill even met the poet in the Lake District at his sister's beautiful house, overlooked by England's finest mountains. Wordsworth would have been able to explain over tea in the peaceful garden there that:

> Poetry is the most philosophic of all writing . . . its object is truth, not individual and local, but general and operative; not standing upon external testimony, but carried alive into the heart by passion; truth which is its own testimony, which gives competence and confidence to the tribunal to which it appeals.

Or so Mill would write later. Wordsworth's humanism came, Mill said, like "medicine" to his soul, while the poetry of Coleridge led him from an atomistic philosophy towards a recognition of the organic nature of society.

As for his master, Bentham, the Great Utilitarian: "Words, he thought, were perverted from their proper office when they were employed in uttering anything but precise logical truth." Mill recalled with an especial shudder his saying that "quantity of pleasure being equal, push-pin is as good as poetry." And Mill notes another aphorism of Bentham's too, which he thinks is even more typical, that "All poetry is misrepresentation." To say this, Mill wrote in his often overlooked essay on poetry, seemed an example of "what Mr. Carlyle strikingly calls 'the completeness of limited men'."

FIGURE 22 Wordsworth's humanism came like medicine to his soul.

Here is a philosopher who is happy within his narrow boundary as no man of indefinite range ever was: who flatters himself that he is so completely emancipated from the essential law of poor human intellect, by which it can only see one thing at a time well, that he can even turn round upon the imperfection and lay a solemn interdict upon it. Did Bentham really suppose that it is in poetry only that propositions cannot be exactly true, cannot contain in themselves all the limitations and qualifications with which they require to be taken when applied to practice? We have seen how far his own prose propositions are from realising this Utopia: and even the attempt to approach it would be incompatible not with poetry merely, but with oratory, and popular writing of every kind.

Although, in fairness, Bentham's earlier writings were light and even occasionally playful (or at least so they seemed to Mill, used only to his diet of algebra and declining languages). Unfortunately, however:

in his later years and more advanced studies, he fell into a Latin or German structure of sentence, foreign to the genius of the English language. He could not bear, for the sake of clearness and the reader's ease, to say, as ordinary men are content to do, a little more than the truth in one sentence, and correct it in the next. The whole of the qualifying remarks which he intended to make, he insisted upon imbedding as parentheses in the very middle of the sentence itself.

Mill continues, using some of his hard-earned classical training, to accuse his tutor of a *reductio ad absurdum* in his objection to poetry:

> In trying to write in a manner against which the same objection should not lie, he could stop nowhere short of utter unreadableness, and after all attained no more accuracy than is compatible with opinions as imperfect and one-sided as those of any poet or sentimentalist breathing. Judge then in what state literature and philosophy would be, and what chance they would have of influencing the multitude, if his objection were allowed, and all styles of writing banished which would not stand his test.

Bentham's friends were naturally concerned. It seemed that young Mill had "read Wordsworth and that muddled him," wrote one, John Bowring, "and he has been in a strange sort of confusion ever since."

The cure

The debate over the poetry is not just an obscure side issue. It goes to the heart of Western Philosophy, with its 'linear, masculine' ways of thinking, its cold, dispassionate logic, its narrow, exclusive preoccupations . . . Mill abandoned the pretensions of philosophical deductions, with their spurious certainty *à la* Euclid, instead choosing the complexities of the real world, with its multiple factors and complex patterns of cause and effect – some of them indeed inherently unpredictable. Mill even declined to describe himself as a philosopher, preferring to be a "social scientist." The most important task, he decided, was to investigate the psychological character of the human mind, or as he put it in his *System of Logic* (Book VI, "On the Logic of the Moral Sciences"), "the theory of the causes which determine the type of character belonging to a people or to an age." The *System of Logic* takes up Kant's work on *a priori* and *a posteriori* knowledge, and analytical and synthetic propositions (Kant's favored terms) to draw a much more subtle (and useful) distinction between 'verbal' and 'real' propositions, and conclusions (inferences) that merely appear true, as opposed to those that really must be true. As he explains, if logic did not contain any 'real' inferences, then it would be saying nothing. But like mathematics, it does produce new knowledge (Mill argues), and this is for the same reason: it is based on grounds that could indeed be otherwise. It is just a psychological disposition within us that makes mathematical and logical truths seem so certain and unchallengeable.

But often Mill's and Bentham's approaches are telescoped together, with Mill anointed as Bentham's natural successor, even though Mill's brand of utilitarianism is fundamentally different. Far from being another preacher of the creed, like his father, he heretically denounced Bentham in a special essay in 1838, saying that his obsession with clarity had led him to erroneously conclude that what is not clear does not exist, and to dismiss as vague generalizations "the whole unanalysable experience of the human race." Nor were the Benthamites right to say that Mill had really fallen totally under the influence of the Coleridge School, a branch of the new movement of Romantic Poets, who after all were politically conservative and set against his radical socialism as much as the implied inhumanity of the new theories of economics.

For philosophically, Mill was also opposed to their preference for 'intuitions' over evidence as he was to spurious *a priori* reasoning. Not to be open to examining the evidence, he wrote, is to support the 'Establishment', and its "false doctrines and bad institutions." Here he accepted part of Bentham's approach; that of taking apart complexities and analyzing the parts. Thus society could indeed be understood by considering it as a set of individuals, but individuals also need to be understood – by treating each as consisting of a set of *feelings*.

As a result of his 'poetical turn' Mill changed his views on human nature and social science. It was not an anomalous period in his life, mercifully quickly got over. It was the formative one.

Pompous Footnote

1   Heidegger too turned to poetry, but thought there was no contradiction, writing in an essay on Hölderlin that this is "the establishment of Being by means of the world." The poet has the same role as the philosophers, and the same authority.

CHAPTER 23
HENRY THOREAU
AND LIFE IN THE SHED
(1817–1862)

Many of the philosophers whom we rely on to represent little oases of good sense and rationality in a disorganized world disappointingly turn out, on closer inspection, to be not only rather eccentric, but downright irrational. David Henry Thoreau, an anarchist who eked out a living by making pencils while living in a shed by a pond, on the other hand, appears even at first glance to be rather eccentric. The degree to which he turns out to be a philosopher is still a matter of debate.

In his *Journal* entry for January 7, 1857, Thoreau says of himself:

> In the streets and in society I am almost invariably cheap and dissipated, my life is unspeakably mean. No amount of gold or respectability would in the least redeem it – dining with the Governor or a member of Congress! But alone in the distant woods or fields, in unpretending sprout-lands or pastures tracked by rabbits, even in a bleak and, to most, cheerless day, like this, when a villager would be thinking of his inn, I come to myself, I once more feel myself grandly related, and that cold and solitude are friends of mine.
>
> I suppose that this value, in my case, is equivalent to what others get by churchgoing and prayer. I come home to my solitary woodland walk as the homesick go home. I thus dispose of the superfluous and see things as they are, grand and beautiful. . . . I wish to . . . be sane a part of every day.

The Philosophical Tale

This explanation did not impress Robert Louis Stevenson, the author of exciting yarns like *Treasure Island* and *Kidnapped*, who also abandoned more conventional professions to become a writer. Stevenson overcame ill health as a child to marry a beautiful native woman in a remote silver mine and live on a mountain in exotic Samoa. From there he wrote of Thoreau hiding in his cabin, full of "certain virtuous self-indulgences," adding:

there is apt to be something unmanly, something almost dastardly, in a life that does not move with dash and freedom, and that fears the bracing contact of the world. In one word, Thoreau was a skulker. He did not wish virtue to go out of him among his fellow-men, but slunk into a corner to hoard it for himself.

Nor, indeed, were many others impressed with Thoreau's alternative lifestyle. So it was that in his lifetime, and for years after, Thoreau was considered little more than a cranky backwoodsman, hostile to society and progress. His contributions to diverse campaigns – the abolition of slavery, the well-being of the Native Americans, and the preservation of America's wilderness – only made him still less accepted. But then, philosophers should not be measured by the views of their contemporaries. Time and history must be their judge instead. So here is what history records under the heading "Henry Thoreau."

He was born in Concord, Massachusetts, which for ecological purposes means in the temperate forest zone of the eastern coast of North America. In his time, Concord was considered quite a center for writers and literature. He was really called David Henry Thoreau, but was always known as Henry. These days, his house has been made into a museum of sorts, but, being removed several hundred meters from its original site, presents a small philosophical problem (like the Ship of Theseus) all of its own: is this really where Thoreau was born? If not, could there now be TWO such places?

Some people call him the "the poet laureate of nature writing," others hail him as the "prophet of our ecological conscience." One of his fellow writers, Nathaniel Hawthorne, called him "ugly as sin," continuing: "long-nosed, queer-mouthed, and with uncouth and rustic, though courteous manners, corresponding very well with such an exterior. But his ugliness is of an honest and agreeable fashion, and becomes him much better than beauty."

Hawthorne, who wrote a best-selling novel, *The House of Seven Gables* (not to be confused with *Anne of Green Gables*), adds that the "world owes all of its onward impulses to men ill at ease. The happy man inevitably confines himself within ancient limits." In fact, Hawthorne quite admired Thoreau, and even went so far as to claim inspiration from having lived as a hermit himself for several months in an attic room.

Being a political radical, Thoreau naturally studied at Harvard, and then, having acquired the foundations for a very conventional philosopher (rhetoric, classics, mathematics, and so on), returned to his native town where he became part of a group of writers that included Ralph Waldo Emerson, the leading light of a movement called New England Transcendentalism. This cult-like movement held that it is through nature that we come into touch with our essential soul. Thoreau also obtained a post teaching at Concord College but was dismissed for refusing to hit the children with a stick, or "administer corporal punishment" as it was euphemistically termed then. With his brother John, he briefly ran an alternative school instead, which offered things like 'nature walks', but it closed when John contracted and later died of tetanus. At this low point Thoreau accepted an offer to join Emerson as his editorial assistant, tutor to Emerson's children, and indeed general handyman. Not to mention gardener, of course. But his main job was at his parents' pencil factory, which combined usefully two of his interests: the native woods and the native (or at least New Hampshire) rock, graphite.

Then in 1845 he moved about half an hour's walk from his home to a small wooden shed, which he fondly but inaccurately called a "log-cabin," on the shores of Walden Pond, which is not a pond but a lake set in some forest. Ponds, after all, are defined by being small, and this one the locals said was bottomless. Thoreau can at least be allowed this small contribution to human knowledge – he found the lake at its deepest point was 100 feet. Anyway, more to the point, the land belonged to Emerson. Whatever his motives for moving there, it was not particularly secluded, being very close to the town, and indeed Thoreau praises not only wilderness in some supposed pure state, but also "partially cultivated countryside."

> Take the shortest way round and stay at home. A man dwells in his native valley like a corolla in its calyx, like an acorn in its cup. *Here*, of course, is all that you love, all that you expect, all that you are. Here is your bride elect, as close to you as she can be got. Here is all the best and all the worst you can imagine. What more do you want? Bear her away then! Foolish people imagine that what they imagine is somewhere else. (*Journal*, Nov. 1, 1858)

Because it was near the town, he had scarcely settled in when he bumped into the local tax collector who challenged him over his failure to pay his taxes. Thoreau said his conscience prevented him, as he could not fund either the Mexican–American War or slavery – an explanation which resulted in his being arrested and put in jail. This example is said to have inspired other tax evaders, notably Gandhi (against the British in India) and Martin Luther King (against segregation and racial discrimination in the US). Unfortunately, for the power of the protest, after only one night in jail he was released as an interfering aunt paid all his back taxes for him.[1] What would have happened to India if Gandhi had such an aunt! So Thoreau contented himself with writing an essay, *Resistance to Civil Government*, on the duty of civil disobedience instead.

This expands on the thought that struck him during his night in prison – of the absurdity of confining his body when his mind and spirit were free. He pitied the State for trying to punish his body because they could not get at *him*. They had superior physical strength to use against his body, but little to challenge his beliefs, for moral force comes from a higher law. When a government says, "Your money or your life," it is playing the highwayman, he says, adding:

> Cast your whole vote, not a strip of paper merely, but your whole influence. A minority is powerless while it conforms to the majority; it is not even a minority then; but it is irresistible when it clogs by its whole weight. If the alternative is to keep all just men in prison, or give up war and slavery, the State will not hesitate which to choose.

Returning to his little shed, he wrote his first book, *A Week on the Concord and Merrimack Rivers*, which was really a tribute to his brother, John. Not surprisingly, publishers were unenthusiastic, but at Emerson's prompting he self-published it. For years afterwards he was in debt, and blamed Emerson for encouraging him.

After two years watching the seasons change from the perspective of the shed, he left the pond to work off his debt in the pencil factory. But the experience inspired his next book, *Walden*, or *Life in the Woods*, which combines complimentary descriptions of the woods with disparaging observations on human nature and society such as that the "mass of men lead lives of quiet desperation." *Life in the Woods* starts by saying that most people waste their time by trying to acquire material goods instead of living simply (which is Plato's ancient lament too), and that even those who rise above that waste time reading modern fiction instead of Homer and Aeschylus. That is the Harvard influence. Fortunately, as the story unfolds, Thoreau begins to find nature in all her mystery and splendour even more interesting than the Greek classics. For this reason, more important than his books are his daily *Journal* entries. Over time, these recorded a wealth of detail on the forest and the lake, and how nature changes, adapts, and regenerates. Some credit him with laying the foundations of ecological studies by describing how species, places, and climate

FIGURE 23 Thoreau carefully recorded the weather for the day, which flowers were in blossom, and how deep was the water of Walden Pond.

all interact, and certainly Thoreau was a follower of Darwin, inspired by his accounts of the voyages on the *Beagle*, and became one of the first advocates of evolutionary theory in the predominantly 'Creationist' United States. However, the entries are more than that.

Each was a two-step process. First, Thoreau would carefully record his observations, such as the weather for the day, which flowers were in blossom, how deep was the water of Walden Pond, and the behavior of any animals he saw. But then, after this, he would attempt to identify and describe the spiritual and the aesthetic significance of what he had seen. Thoreau recalls approvingly the story about Wordsworth, that when a traveler arrived and asked Wordsworth's servant to show him her master's study, she showed him a room saying, "Here is his library, but his study is out of doors." So it was with Thoreau.

Someone later counted up all Thoreau's entries and said they amounted to two million words, which is a lot of observations. It is, alas, also a lot of paper, not to mention graphite, which an ecologist should really have hesitated to expend so freely, but in amongst it are glimmers of philosophical insight. His *Journal* is the foundation of his philosophy. As Thoreau puts it in the "Conclusion" to *Life on the Pond*:

If you have built castles in the air,
your work need not be lost; that is where they should be.
Now put the foundations under them.

197

So was Thoreau a self-indulgent skulker – or a philosophical pioneer? Stevenson himself spent much of his youth confined to bed with poor health, and had to struggle to gain his independence. His solution was to give up normal work and to travel to exotic lands and write extravagant novels. By contrast, Thoreau was sprightly although he had a wheezy chest and worked in a pencil factory. He traveled a little, but preferred, as he puts it, to see the world in his backyard.

Yet Stevenson and Thoreau also have a lot in common. Because Thoreau did leave his shed for his daily walk. Ironically, it was after one of these, a particularly late night expedition to count tree rings in the forest, which had to be abandoned due to heavy rain, that he caught the cold that led to his death – aged just 44. But then, for him, as he puts it, every walk is a sort of crusade. Even if "we are but faint-hearted crusaders."

> Our expeditions are but tours, and come round again at evening to the old hearth side from which we set out. Half the walk is but retracing our steps. We should go forth on the shortest walk, perchance, in the spirit of undying adventure, never to return – prepared to send back our embalmed hearts only as relics to our desolate kingdoms. If you are ready to leave father and mother, and brother and sister, and wife and child and friends, and never see them again – if you have paid your debts, and made your will, and settled all your affairs, and are a free man – then you are ready for a walk.

Pompous Footnote

1   Thoreau records in his *Journal*: "My Aunt Maria asked me to read the life of Dr. Chalmers, which, however, I did not promise to do. Yesterday, Sunday, she was heard through the partition shouting to my Aunt Jane, who is deaf, 'Think of it! He stood half an hour today to hear the frogs croak, and he wouldn't read the life of Chalmers'."

CHAPTER 24
MARX'S
REVOLUTIONARY MATERIALISM
(1818–1883)

People, wrote Marx in the *Poverty of Philosophy*, are both the authors and the actors of their own drama. Likewise philosophers "do not spring up like mushrooms out of the ground," he added, in an editorial for the *Kölnische Zeitung*, but are "products of their time, of their nation, whose most subtle, valuable and invisible juices flow into the ideas of philosophy."

So in order to understand Marx (and hence his theory of society), it is possible, rather than wading through the volumes of quasi-empirical historical research, to trot briskly through the rather smaller body of information on Marx's personal life and his social 'existence'. After all, as Marx and Engels also wrote, "the production of ideas, of conceptions, of consciousness is at first directly interwoven with the material activity and the material intercourse of men, the language of real life." 'Pure philosophy' is merely a kind of 'onanism' – intellectual masturbation – they said, even as, of course, they were committing the sin themselves . . . And then again, Marx describes himself as a 'world-historical' individual – a kind of crystallization of all the preexisting tendencies of history.

And this is a much more interesting, if sadly neglected, study.

The Philosophical Tale

Marx was born in Trier, which was, and for that matter still is, a very bourgeois market town in Germany. His parents were impeccably bourgeois. His father was a lawyer, and although he could have been a member of a persecuted minority, by virtue of being Jewish, had opted instead for improved social standing by converting. The house was bourgeois, full of all the most learned and cultured things, including books on the likes of Racine, Dante, Shakespeare, and philosophers like Rousseau and Voltaire. One of the Marxs' neighbors, the Baron of Westphalen, the celebrated socialist thinker, also lent Marx books, as well as, in due course, "the most beautiful girl in Trier." This being the baron's daughter, Jenny, who had fallen in love with the thickset, dark, handsome, ever-scowling Karl. Whether for his flamboyant style, his taste for excessive drinking, his dueling, or for his romantic love poetry, history does not say. For the next forty years she would be both Marx's faithful wife and secretary, writing up Marx's notes into legible, coherent form. This seems to have suited her as she records her view of the most important qualities for a woman as being "devotion." For a man, she says, it is "moral courage." Conversely, for Marx, the most important quality for a man is simply to be "strong," and for a woman to be "weak." And his idea of happiness, he says, is "to fight." Engels, incidentally, and irrelevantly, considered the ideal man to be one who "minded his own business," the perfect woman to be one able to "not mislay things," and happiness to be found somewhere in a bottle of revolutionary (1848) vintage wine.

But this talk of revolution is jumping ahead. First the Marxs had to quit their dull German town for glamorous Paris. Here they mixed with poets like Herweigh and Heine, and political philosophers like Bakunin. Engels, whom Marx had met already, was there too, and the two men established a firm bond. Engels, unlike Marx, was thin and pale, blue-eyed and short-sighted, and he wrote well. Their relationship was to be enduring. However, Marx fell out with the Russian anarchist over the question of whether the communist vanguard would usher in the classless society or simply degenerate into a corrupt, cruel, and incompetent bureaucracy.

But falling out with Bakunin had to wait its turn. First Marx fell out with the French authorities, and on being expelled from Paris instead declared himself "a citizen the world." He then fell out with the Belgians, after settling briefly in Brussels, and having inherited a small fortune (the first of several such happy financial events). The Belgian authorities complained that he tried to use some of the money to buy guns for the workers of Brussels.

Returning to his native Germany, he and Engels rushed out the *Communist Manifesto* to try to catch the wave of revolutions that swept Europe in 1848. The *Manifesto*, written (despite his public protestations) primarily by Engels, opens with the famous claim, "The history of all hitherto existing society is the history of class struggles." If the *Manifesto* did not seem to help with the revolutions, it helped make Marx unwelcome in Germany, so much so that in 1849, Marx and Jenny (and their children and their "loyal housekeeper") set up home in London instead. This was the London of Charles Dickens's novels, a world of dark Satanic mills in which little match girls toiled, and grim workhouses in which Oliver Twists were refused seconds of porridge. Marx was to stay more or less permanently there for the rest of his life. The Marxs' circumstances at this time were 'straitened', to use the euphemism for 'debt-ridden', but their lifestyle

200

remained undeniably still bourgeois. On their arrival they even had the crests of the Duke of Argyll emblazoned on their silverware in order to ease them into their new surroundings.

At this time, Marx supplemented a modest income from articles in the *New York Daily Tribune* (although actually most of the columns were ghost-written by Engels) with money sent to them, in used £1 notes, by Engels. This arrived half a note at a time, not so much because Engels was being mean, but because the two men believed, probably correctly, that their letters were being intercepted.

Although this was money resulting from the exploitation of workers in Engels's factory in Manchester, – or as Marx later put it, although:

> Capital . . . pumps out a certain quantum of surplus labour from the direct producers or workers, surplus labour that it receives without an equivalent and which by its very nature always remains forced labour, however much it might appear as the result of free contractual agreement . . . (*Capital*, Vol. III)

– at least it allowed Marx to continue his 'research' in the Reading Room of the British Library, as well as in various taverns around London, and (it would turn out) in the bedroom of one Hélène Demuth, by whom he would have a lovechild. The child, Freddy, was eventually fostered out, and features not at all in history. But the fate of Karl and Jenny's seven children was not to be envied either – malnutrition took the lives of four of them in infancy.

In 1856, the Marxs received more money from another inheritance, which they spent partly on a comfortable house near Hampstead Heath and on sending the three remaining children to the South Hampstead College for Ladies. Alas, the inheritance soon ran out, and even though Marx wrote furiously, "I will not allow bourgeois society to turn me into a money-making machine," he had to redouble his money-making efforts, which consisted of writing letters to Engels.

One such ran:

> Dear Engels,
>
> Your letter today found us in a state of great agitation. My wife is ill. Little Jenny is ill. Lenchen [the housemaid] has some sort of nervous fever. I could not and cannot call the doctor because I have no money to buy medicine. For the last 8–10 days I have been feeding the family solely on bread and potatoes, but whether I shall be able to get hold of any today is doubtful . . .

FIGURE 24 Marx snorted angrily, *"Capital* will not even pay for the cigars I smoked writing it!"

The best and most desirable thing that could happen is for the landlady to throw me out. Then I would at least be quit of the sum of £22. But such complaisance is hardly to be expected of her. [One of the evil landlord class . . .] On top of that, debts are still outstanding to the baker, the milkman, the tea chap [*sic*], the Greengrocer, the butcher. How am I to get out of this infernal mess . . .?

The next day Marx received £4 from Engels. Four measly quid! Times were evidently hard in the textile factory business. Being a writer, even a revolutionary one, was no bed of roses. As Marx snorted angrily, *"Capital* will not even pay for the cigars I smoked writing it"!

Actually, the tobacco took a toll on his health, and the once dashing Marx became something of a social outcast, covered in boils and furuncles. The once beautiful Jenny succumbed to smallpox in 1860, and although she recovered, she was left, in Marx's words, looking like "a rhinoceros, a hippopotamus."

The 1860s saw Marx lose his income as 'Europe correspondent' for the *New York Daily Tribune*, but two more legacies provided the family with financial lifeline, which they used . . . to move to a bigger house and hold grand parties.

In 1870, Engels retired as factory master, taking down the hammock he used (slightly bizarrely) to sleep in one last time from his factory office, and moved to London. So that his friend could 'retire' too, he provided Marx with a kind of pension – the not inconsiderable sum of £350 per annum. And it is around now that Marx's long career of political agitation begins to earn him public recognition. A surprisingly reasonable piece written in praise of the egalitarianism, democracy, and simplicity of the Paris Commune gained him the excellent sobriquet of "the red terror Doctor," in place of his other nickname, "Doctor Cranky." Of the Commune he had written:

> Its true secret was this. It was essentially a working-class government, the product of the struggle of the producing against the appropriating class, the political form at last discovered under which to work out the economic emancipation of labour. . . . Yes, Gentleman, the Commune intended to abandon that class property which makes the labour of the many the wealth of the few.

Later, however, Marx corrected the impression that he favored the Commune, saying that it was "in no wise socialist."

The entry in the ledger of history

If Marx's personal life seems to have been one of self-indulgence and more than a little hypocrisy, that does not mean Marxism is irredeemably flawed: it as, after all, most of it, really 'Engelism'. It was Engels, nick-named "the General" in the Marx household, who wrote the first draft of the *Communist Manifesto*, and most of the *German Ideology*, as well as many of the articles in the newspapers. It was Engels who praised and planted reviews of 'Marx's' ideas, and who many consider created the concept of 'Marxism' in his book *Socialism: Utopian and Scientific*. And lastly, it was Engels who 'assembled' the various volumes of *Capital* out of Marx's notes.

But what then remains of Marx's own achievements? In a letter to Weydemeyer, Marx wrote of them:

> Now for myself I do not claim to have discovered either the existence of classes in modern society or the struggle between them. Long before me, bourgeois historians had described the historical development of this struggle between the classes, as had bourgeois economists their economic anatomy. My own contribution was:
>
> 1. to show that the existence of classes is merely bound up with certain historical phases in the development of production;
> 2. that the class struggle necessarily leads to the dictatorship of the proletariat;
> 3. that this dictatorship itself constitutes no more than a transition to the abolition of all classes and to a classless society.

However, of these elements of the legacy, it can be said that the first is a truism, and the second and third are 'demonstrated' only in mere rhetoric.

In 1863, when Engels's 'common law wife', Mary Burns, died unexpectedly and suddenly, Marx and Engels had their one falling out when Marx, in a letter to him written straight after, quipped: "instead of Mary, ought it not to have been my mother?" The rest of the letter is concerned with Marx's latest financial requirements.

VIII
RECENT PHILOSOPHY

CHAPTER 25
RUSSELL DENOTES SOMETHING
(1872–1970)

Bertrand Arthur William Russell, Third Earl of somewhere or other, son of a Victorian prime minister, and Professor of Philosophy at Trinity College, Cambridge, is still considered there, if not much anywhere else,[1] as "profoundly influential in the development of philosophy in the twentieth century." His special expertise is said to have been in the area of philosophical logic; indeed, he is credited with having coined the term, although as the words have long currency individually, and the activity preceded him by 2,000 years, it is hard to see how his arrangement can count as a novelty. Nevertheless, says Nicholas Griffin, writing in the *Routledge Encyclopedia of Philosophy*, he was indisputably responsible for a number of "important logical innovations," prime amongst which was a way to "reparse sentences continuing the phrase 'so-and-so' into a form in which the phrase did not appear." Such achievements deserve further examination.

The Philosophical Tale

It had all started in 1890 when he met the famous logician Peano at a philosophy conference in Paris. Giuseppe Peano inspired the young Russell to undertake the task of putting mathematics on a logical foundation. At first things went very well. From 1907 to 1910, Russell worked in his study at Cambridge from ten to twelve hours a day, writing out logical theorems, under the benevolent supervision of Alfred North Whitehead, of whom history has recorded that he hosted "legendary afternoon teas." These theorems would eventually become the magisterial *Principia Mathematica*.

But when the great work was completed, as that other 'Great British Twentieth-Century Philosopher' A. J. Ayer relates, the directors of Cambridge University Press failed to appreciate the importance of the proofs, and saw only how long it was and how few people would want to read it. Instead of seeing the benefits of putting mathematics on a logical foundation *et cetera, et cetera*, they saw only that it would cost them £600 to print, which was twice as much as they were prepared to pay. Happily, the Royal Society, of which both Russell and Whitehead were fellows, could be persuaded to contribute another two hundred quid, but the authors still had to find the remaining £100. Thus, concludes Sir Freddy, woefully, "their financial reward for this masterpiece, which had cost them ten years' work, was minus £50 apiece."

The *Principia* is very long and not much read nowadays. But its point can be summed up in just one sentence: logic is more important than mathematics, which in fact can be reduced to just a few logical principles.

Numbers, for instance, so dear to mathematicians, are revealed by Russell to be merely adjectives. Two dogs, for example, is just another way of saying of some dogs that they have the quality of 'twoness'. See that group of dogs over there? It belongs in the class of 'twoness', along with my ears, your hands, Russell's first two wives, in fact, every other group of things that has this ephemeral quality. But what about that group of four dogs? Does it too belong in the group of two things? For it contains two collections of two dogs.

But this is already getting complicated. We need an expert like the contemporary Professor Mark Sainsbury of London University to ease us gently in. Take 1 + 2, for example. (Leave 2 + 2 for the advanced students.) This, he explains, can be better expressed as: "the class of classes each of which is the union of a member of one with a member of two (cases in which the member of one has a member in common with the member of two to be ignored)." In other words, Professor Sainsbury finishes with a flourish, "the class of three-membered classes"!

How is that an improvement? Yet for many modern philosophers, it is. They think that ordinary language is much better expressed 'formally' using logic. Sentences about the world should be stripped of their 'cannibal superstitions' to reveal their logical essence, as Russell rather ethnocentrically put it in *Mind and Matter*. Even simple sentences like 'snow is frozen water' need clarification, for what kind of verb is 'is'? (That's two uses of the little word in a row.) Is this 'is' an 'is' as in something exists? or is 'is' *is* (that's three) as in 'equals'? Or is it 'is' as in describing a property of snow? Which is is it?

Anyway, these are the sorts of questions Russell raises. But if Russell's reputation as a great logician is dubious, his contribution to the popularization and, more, clarification of philosophy, through works like *The*

Problems of Philosophy (1911) and *History of Western Philosophy* (1946), has stood the test of time.

But back to 1905, and Russell's first important publication, "On Denoting." It is here that Russell outlines his theory that words that precede nouns such as 'some', 'no', 'a', and 'every' – or 'quantifiers' as he calls them – need to be done away with. This is because, like unicorns and the King of France, they do not really stand for anything. Socrates stands for Socrates, and the word 'philosopher' stands for certain scholarly attributes in a person, but in the phrase 'Socrates is a philosopher', what does the 'a' stand for? A quantity, yes, but that complicates things. Because to say a unicorn has one horn does not really mean that there really is a unicorn, which has one and only one horn.

Russell decided that everything we say must consist only of statements (perhaps combined) about things we have immediate direct knowledge of – knowledge, quintessentially, by sense perception.

So we could say, 'The other day, I met a man in Paris who told me he was the French king, and I could see that he had gone bald' – but not, of course, 'the present King of France is bald'. This fitted with his idea, proposed in 1914, that the old philosophical problem of how we really know anything about the 'external' world could be solved by always referring to 'sensibilia'. In effect, by only referring to ideas in our heads. Later on, he refined his approach by saying that all 'sensibilia' had to be understood as bundles of simple sense perceptions.

Russell narrowed these down as well, to things such as colors, smells, hardness, roughness, and so on, although this tactic had occurred to others before him to no great effect. He says that 'sense-data' provide us with 'knowledge by acquaintance', otherwise we have to settle for 'knowledge by description'. Very little is given to us to know directly, even the existence of ourselves is limited to awareness of 'willing', 'believing', 'wishing', and so on. Curious example to offer, Russell insists mountains cannot be known directly, so we have to confine ourselves to talking about the sense perceptions we may have had which led us to create the 'hypothesis' of a mountain (Russell's house is surrounded by tall, hard objects which have snow on the top of them). (The only concession Russell allows, in line with best scientific practice, is that we may continue to make certain assumptions, such as that things continue to exist when not being looked at, and that what was true today continues to be true tomorrow, at least, 'in general'.)

Science is, however, rather an imprecise and 'happy-go-lucky' area. Not so mathematics. And it was here that Russell found himself

FIGURE 25 But what about his own hair? If he did not normally cut it, he could certainly cut his hair this time . . .

confronted with a problem, and a bitter problem it turned out to be too. In fact, in due course it would became his philosophical monument – known for ever after in philosophy as 'Russell's paradox'. It is expressed in mathematical parlance as 'the problem of the set of all sets that are not members of themselves', and the problem is simply whether it is a member of itself or not. But we can do better than that if we remember the case of the hairdresser of the Hindu Kush, who was supposed to cut the hair of everyone in the town who did not normally cut their own hair. For the hairdresser, the range of possible clients for haircuts is simple enough: either people normally cut their own hair or they don't. But what about his (let us assume it is a male hairdresser) own hair? If he does not normally cut it, he can certainly cut his hair this time. But if that is so, he would appear to be cutting the hair of someone who normally cuts his own hair – which he is not supposed to do. So the hairdresser should not cut his own hair. But if he does not cut his hair, then clearly he fits the category of people whose hair he can cut.

It all goes round and round, in an ultimately rather futile self-referential fizzle. So Russell decided to save his excellent theory by outlawing all statements that are 'self-referential' (not just ones about hairdressers, or indeed sets of sets that are not members of themselves). This is his 'theory of types'.

The next problem was that of negatives. To say that 'Socrates is a man' is complicated, but to say that 'Socrates is not a woman' is much, *much* worse. Russell wanted to 'outlaw' such negative assertions too. Because he wished to make all our statements simple ones directly relating to either logical or empirical truths. And how can we be directly referring to something that does not exist? Clearly negatives will not do. Or perhaps I should say, clearly only positives will do.

From now on, instead of being negative and vague, we should be positive and precise. Instead of saying 'a dog may have run into my study and now I can't find my manuscript notes', we should say 'there is some x such that x is canine and there is a y such that y is a room for writing in and there is a z such that it is a collection of my papers and x went into y and ate z'!

The advantages of this are not immediately clear to non-philosophers. But what this did was it enabled logical philosophers to avoid making unintended and unnecessary existential commitments in their observations, like:

The King of France is bald
Socrates is human
Snow is white
Unicorns have only one horn
Hesperus is Phosphorus,
et cetera, et cetera

Take that first sentence, 'the King of France is bald'.[2] Is it true or false? The joke, rather a weak one, but enough for Russell and later philosophers, being that there is no King of France. He had his head cut off centuries ago. That being so, it is not clear whether the claim is true or false or neither. But now a solution is at hand. The sentence can be broken down into its three constituent parts, says Russell. These are that there IS at present a King of France, that there is only one such thing, and that this unique, existing thing is, in fact, bald. Now we can see that the first part is simply not the case. Therefore, the sentence 'the King of France is bald' is false. So is the statement 'unicorns have one horn'. But not 'snow is white'.

For this great work Russell naturally expected a Nobel Prize. But he was to be disappointed. However, at least he was not put into prison. As happened twice later in his life. But then, 'Earl Russell' was also something of a social misfit and political radical. Perhaps this was the inevitable consequence of applying logic to everyday life.

The decay started during World War I, a decline we can date from 1916 when he was expelled from Trinity for opposing conscription (signing a statement of protest against "this evil and unjust war" with the poet Siegfried Sassoon, who would die in it two years later). Soon afterwards, he was sent to Brixton prison for six months for libeling the American army, or making statements "likely to prejudice His Majesty's relations with the United States of America" as the indictment put it.

While in prison Russell wrote *Political Ideals: Roads to Freedom*. In the book he attempted to explain why he was willing to suffer for his political beliefs: "The pioneers of Socialism, Anarchism, and Syndicalism, have, for the most part, experienced prison, exile, and poverty, deliberately incurred because they would not abandon their propaganda; and by this conduct they have shown that the hope which inspired them was not for themselves, but for mankind."

After the war, he traveled to Russia to see 'the revolution', with Dora Black (who later became his first wife), and met Lenin and Trotsky, but didn't like them much, nor their system. Instead, for the next fifty years, Earl Russell became something of a ragamuffin, alternating between radical alternative communes and schools, demos, and international meetings, marrying four times, and producing a flood of philosophical writings carelessly spanning the whole spectrum of human life the like of which had not (mercifully) been seen since Aristotle. Power, Pornography, Sex – all came under his beady eye. In sum, he abandoned logic to write on public morality. Later, he told colleagues, he did this, solely "for money."

In 1940, protesters objecting to his views on God (not existing[3]) prevented him from taking up a philosophy post in New York. So he went back to Britain, and campaigned against nuclear weapons, organizing a series of conferences for eminent academics, especially scientists, that he invited from all over the world to come and unite against war. For this, he obtained in due course another spell in prison. Naturally, he used the time to write another book.

As a philosopher, Russell sometimes speaks absolute nonsense. Russell seems to have been aware of this, hence his "impish grin" whilst offering increasingly ludicrous examples. Not so his heirs. They issue their dull arrangements with a seriousness born of a serene lack of self-knowledge. Fortunately aside from his logic, Russell did other things. The same is not true of his followers.

Pompous Footnotes

1   Possibly also in Wales. As well as being born in Gwent in the south of the 'land of white gloves', Bertrand Russell lived in North Wales from 1955, making him arguably Wales' greatest philosopher.

it might seem that neither (a) 'the King of France is bald' nor (b) 'the King of France is not bald' is true. Russell argued[1] that (b) is ambiguous between being the negation of (a), and thus entailing truly that there is not exactly one present King of France, and being not the negation of (a), but rather equivalent to 'There is exactly one present King of France and whoever is the King of France is not bald', which like (a) is false.

Indeed, Russell even invented a special mathematico-philosophical jargon (with lots of squiggles not even available on most people's computers) to express such truths, which no one but professional philosophers could understand. This – at last – gave professional philosophers a reason for their existence, albeit not a 'necessary' one.

2   Professor Sainsbury discusses the much worse implications of the King of France NOT being bald as follows:
3   When he was asked in a radio debate how, if God did not exist, he could explain the existence of the universe, his reply was: "I should say the universe is just there, and that's all." (Exists (universe) necessarily . . .)

CHAPTER 26
THE RIPPING YARN OF LUDWIG WITTGENSTEIN
(1889–1951)

Just who was Wittgenstein? For most of the philosophical authorities, Ludwig Josef Johann Wittgenstein, born 1889, died 1951, was simply "the leading analytical philosopher of the twentieth century." Dr. Peter Hacker, of St. Johns College, Oxford, says that his "two major works" altered the course of the subject. His "revolutionary conception of philosophy" meant afterwards that there were no longer any specifically philosophical propositions or specifically philosophical knowledge. The task of philosophy became merely "conceptual clarification and the dissolution of philosophical problems." The goal of philosophy was no longer knowledge, but merely understanding. But first of all, philosophers need to understand Wittgenstein.

The Philosophical Tale

Wittgenstein 'the life' is not so much a philosophical tale as a full-blown ripping yarn. Amongst the drab, dreary ranks of philosophers, he stands out gleaming – a rough diamond thrown amongst so many dull, gray pebbles. His CV* alone seems to set him apart: an Austrian multimillionaire who gave away all his wealth, a schoolmate of Hitler's, a war hero, a modernist architect, a village schoolteacher, the designer of the world's first jet engine,[1] and (last but not least) the brilliant pupil of Bertrand Russell who, after just two years of study, solved (as he modestly writes later) the major problems of philosophy.

> The truth of the thoughts that are here set forth seems to me unassailable and definitive. I therefore believe myself to have found, on all essential points, the final solution of the problems. (*Tractatus*, Introduction)

Typical of being a philosophical hero is that while the *Tractatus*, the first and indeed the only book he published in his lifetime, was being printed,[2] the author was to be found not lounging aimlessly in the tweedy

*Or 'Résumé' or 'Work History'.

214

armchairs of a dusty European University but amongst the chickens and villagers of the Austrian countryside. Fortunately for philosophy (this tale continues), he did return to Cambridge, pausing only in Vienna to design a stunning home for his sister, including an interesting new design for the central heating and radiators.

Whilst there at Cambridge, Wittgenstein became an institution within an institution, celebrated both for his unorthodox personal style and for his revolutionary approach to teaching. Refusing to lecture but offering only to hold seminars, his ascetic office had few books, equipped instead with the famous deckchair. Those who attended his seminars became his 'disciples', and showed their commitment by dressing the same way – tweed jackets, flannel trousers, no ties. (The clothes, like the philosophy, were not for girls . . .) After each session, he would invite selected confidants to join him at 'the flicks', where he would sit in the middle of the front row (nearest the screen) munching on a pork pie. As for Cambridge's official social gatherings, Wittgenstein declined to attend the 'dinners' of the university, although he did agree to participate in the 'Moral Science Club' from time to time, including one infamous evening when, to murmurs of approval from his disciples, he demanded of Karl Popper that he provide an example of a 'moral rule', gesticulating with a poker for emphasis. Popper supposedly said, "Not threatening visiting speakers with pokers," and Wittgenstein threw the poker down and stormed out (followed by disciples).

Another time, pressed to lecture to the famous Vienna Circle on the merits of the scientific approach to knowledge, he agreed to do so but only read out an epic oriental poem to them with his back to the group the whole time. Only at the very end did he turn to announce (perhaps like Mill) that philosophy is best approached through poetry.

That's not all, but it's certainly enough. After all, this account, although based on real enough elements, is misleading. It's not a myth, but it's certainly a legend.

Towering genius – or just overweening conceit?

In life, the intense, even slightly mad Wittgenstein intimidated those around him into silence. Not for Wittgenstein the Socratic dialogue. He would pronounce and others would make notes. And likewise, today the official hagiography neglects some facts. Wittgenstein did give away 'control' of his inherited millions, but only to his sisters, and so it was that during World War II, even as the Nazi project was at its most clear and most appalling, he was still able to arrange that a large chunk of the Witt-genstein family fortune – not, say, three ingots of gold (as we all might send) but three tons of the stuff – was made available to the Nazi war effort. In return, the family received official 'non-Jewish' status. Charitable types will say that Wittgenstein did this to "save his sisters," but the truth is that the Wittgensteins had the whole world to live in, and chose instead to align themselves with the persecutors of their neighbors.

But why would Wittgenstein do this? As is also not often officially dis-cussed, Wittgenstein – the innovator who would generally acknowledge no philosophical sources or inspirations – did freely disclose one philo-sophical mentor: his fellow Austrian, Otto Weininger. Weininger's phi-losophy, popular at the turn of the century, was that the highest form of human was a cooly logical male superhero, and that being homosexual, emotional, or Jewish (such traits being 'feminine' in some sense) were all defects. Each human has two parts, male and female, Weininger acknowl-edged, but it is best to be as male as possible. To be all female would reduce someone to the level of an animal. "Man is first entirely himself when he is entirely logical. Indeed, he is not until he is thoroughly and everywhere only logic," Weininger explains tersely. The book was actu-ally so popular that in just a few years it went through some twenty-nine printings and multiple translations, including an English-language version. It was also aided by celebrity endorsements including the comment of one Adolf Hitler that Weininger was the "only good Jew" he had ever heard of. Wittgenstein bemused his colleagues at Cambridge by distribut-ing copies of the book amongst them.

Then again, another element suppressed in the usual story is that although, technically, Wittgenstein "resigned" from teaching in the village school, in reality he left in disgrace. An investigation into incidents of violence towards his charges found in one case he had hit a child so hard that the child lost consciousness. The family might well have felt short-changed in the following inquiry, but the local officials would have been aware of the danger of offending one of the most powerful families in the land.

Wittgenstein *did* have a meteoric career at Cambridge, but it seems to have been less on merit than on influence. His doctorate was awarded after Russell and Russell's friend and colleague, G. E. Moore, accepted the *Tractatus* 'in lieu' of a conventional thesis.

But despite this scholarly link, in fact, Russell and Wittgenstein did not get on well. On a personal as well as an intellectual level they were opposed. Wittgenstein, for reasons we have just seen, rejected votes for women, and this at a time the suffragettes were fighting and dying for the right. Russell, on the contrary, was an activist for women's suffrage. Secondly, Wittgenstein believed in strict corporal punishment (which is why he beat the Austrian village children), while Russell founded a radical school run on alternative principles. Wittgenstein volunteered to fight for the Axis Powers in World War I and was awarded medals for his zeal, while Russell was a conscientious objector or "conchie" and was jailed for it. Later, Russell would campaign for CND, which Wittgenstein called the "scum of the intellectuals." And finally, Russell was a heterosexual who campaigned for homosexuals, while Wittgenstein was an active but guilt-ridden homosexual who considered his behavior a kind of "weakness" and spent much of his life attempting to suppress or escape his sexual nature. His biographers labored mightily, but ultimately in vain, to conceal this fact on his behalf.

But we should return to the central philosophical tale, and the status of the Wittgenstein legend. Did he really 'invent' analytical philosophy and inspire the Vienna Circle to campaign for the complete reevaluation of the subject's approach?

The answer to that is not in the scraps and letters hoarded for so many years and so jealously by his literary executors (such as G. E. M. Anscombe, one of his 'pupils') but in the only book that he ever published – the *Tractatus*. And this, furthermore, is very short. So it should be possible to pin some answers down just by looking through it.

Wittgenstein starts with the startling claim that the world is a collection of "facts." That is, a chain of "simples" or "objects," *Gegenstände*, the ultimate building blocks of reality.

> *Objects* make up the substance of the world. That is why they cannot be composite. The substance of the world can only determine a form, and not any material properties . . . in a manner of speaking, objects are colourless . . . objects are what is unalterable and subsistent; their configuration is what is changing and unstable.

The *Tractatus*, even in its later role as a doctoral thesis, does not offer any references or sources. Yet we do not need to look very far to see a view not so very different, if not as strikingly posed as the numbered assertions of the *Tractatus*. The writing of his dissertation adviser in 1911, Bertrand Russell, for example. And Russell himself follows on a long tradition of which Leibniz is only one prominent figure. For both, the world consists only of logical atoms (in Russell's terms) or "simple facts" (as

Leibniz describes it), and both assumed that when logic goes as far as it can, it will find the ultimate building blocks of reality (Leibniz's monads). Russell and Leibniz both argue that knowledge is essentially a matter of analyzing the "building blocks" of reality and thereby guaranteeing the "determinateness of sense" in language. This is the project of the *Tractatus* too.

Now Russell and Leibniz also thought that it was possible and desirable to construct an artificial language to better exhibit the logical form of arguments. In describing his famous monads, Leibniz explained they do not appear, but we must postulate them in logic in order to explain reality and understand the meaningfulness of language.

Russell used metaphors from chemistry, talking of the task of creating "molecular propositions" out of "logical atoms," while Leibniz elegantly described possible complex arrangements of his logical monads. Wittgenstein's *Tractatus* explains that language paints pictures of facts, and that "the propositions show the *logical form* of reality." Russell himself, warning against grand "system building" of the Leibnizian style, emphasized instead the need to identify the "logical structure" of language, and the confusing ways in which it could differ from the "grammatical" one. This is essentially the project of the 'later Wittgenstein'. But the 'Young Impetuous Wittgenstein' declares in the *Tractatus* that it should,in principle at least, be possible to construct a new, logically rigorous language. Of course, this new language will not deal with a lot of topics for (in the *Tractatus*' most quotable line) "wherefore one cannot speak, thereof one must be silent." Or as Weininger more poetically puts it: "Kant's solitary man laughs not, nor dances, shouts not, nor rejoices. For him, no need to make a noise, so deeply does the world expanse its silence keep."

Yet although Wittgenstein praised and used to pass round copies of Weininger's little tract at Cambridge, it was not taken very seriously, possibly because of its advocacy of extreme misogyny with racist undercurrents. Possibly . . . Instead, it was his own version that achieved wider currency:

> Most propositions and questions that have been written about philosophical matters, are not false, but senseless. We cannot, therefore, answer questions of this kind at all, but only state their senselessness. Most questions and propositions of the philosophers result from the fact that we don't understand the logic of our language. (*Tractatus*)

If this was essentially Russell's project, it is still this sort of language that has left scholars to interpret Wittgenstein as the "inspiration" and "one

FIGURE 26 *"... solitary man, laughs not, nor dances ... nor rejoices."*

of the leading lights" of the Vienna Circle, that informal group of interwar philosophers devoted to making philosophical reasoning as logical and scientific as they could.

However, Wittgenstein (like Weininger, and unlike Russell) was also arguing that important truths were unapproachable through logic. Hence he was profoundly opposed to the logical positivists and hence his reading out to them of a mystical text – with his back turned to them. The Circle, far from being inspired by this, as the dictionaries assure us, were unimpressed. Afterwards, one member, the logician Rudolf Carnap, wrote:

> The impression he made on us was as if insight came to him as through a divine inspiration, so that we could not help feeling that any sober rational comment or analysis of it would be a profanation. . . . [He] tolerated no critical examination by others, once the insight had been gained by an act of inspiration.

And of course, most of the *Tractatus*, in logical positivist eyes, is metaphysical nonsense. Take the sentence "language pictures facts," for example. But then, Wittgenstein explains his words are there as a ladder to be climbed up and then jettisoned. And not just his words either. The whole study of philosophy, he suggests, has only the limited purpose of allowing us to see things with a new clarity, before it itself must be jettisoned.

Wittgenstein himself did at least put his money where his mouth was, and attempted, after publishing his theory, to exit philosophy. But after some years he was back, taking up a research fellowship and later a chair at Cambridge. Although he never committed himself again to print, many of his notes, comments, and lectures were later collected up and published as the *Philosophical Investigations*. The Wittgenstein here describes language as a series of interlinked "language-games," in which words and sentences function in so many different and subtle ways: as "deeds," as "symbols," as "commands." Words, he says (borrowing as ever, in this case from the Swiss linguist Ferdinand de Saussure [1857–1913]), are like pieces in a game of chess, taking on their meaning only in the context of the game. In one aside, he even ruefully acknowledges:

> It is interesting to compare the multiplicity of tools in language and of the ways they are used, the multiplicity of kinds of word and sentence with what logicians have said about the structure of language. (Including the author of the *Tractatus Logico-Philosophicus*).

Pompous Footnotes

1   Alas, the 'design' remained just that as Wittgenstein abandoned his engineering studies to pursue his metaphysics. It was left to Frank Whittle to actually make such a thing.

2   The English translation came out in 1922 but it was also published a year earlier in an obscure German journal. The literary world had been unenthusiastic about the *Tractatus*, much to Wittgenstein's indignation, until Russell, trading on his own reputation, persuaded a publisher by offering to write an introduction to it. But Wittgenstein himself was far from grateful, accusing Russell of completely misunderstanding his book and of misrepresenting it there.

CHAPTER 27
HEIDEGGER'S TALE
(AND THE NAZIS)
(1889–1976)

Martin Heidegger has both his critics and his admirers. Of the published variety, he has about three critics and over a thousand admirers. One of the latter, David Krell, proclaims him as "without doubt the most powerfully original and influential philosopher of the century," at least in the "continental tradition," whatever that may be (long lunches, flowery prose). Certainly, to date, there have been perhaps a thousand volumes of commentary on Heidegger published in the English language alone. This is far more attention than anyone else in the last few centuries has received.

Hush then while M. J. Inwood, of Trinity College, Oxford, introduces the work of "probably" the greatest philosopher of the twentieth century.

> From 1916 to 1927 he published nothing but studied widely and intensively, especially the phenomenology of Husserl, Scheler's philosophical anthropology, the hermeneutics of Dilthey, and the texts of St. Paul, Augustine and Luther. Christian texts supplied him not only with examples of momentous, historic decisions . . . but also with an ontology distinct from our own Greek-derived ontology. At the same time he lectured, with enthralling brilliance, on these and many other themes.

In which case, there is a bit of a mystery as to why his writings, which are all based on the lectures, are so dreary and dull. But that mystery is as nothing to the other one about Heidegger, a mystery which is easily summed up: why, for twelve years, and throughout the whole of World War II, was he a member of the Nazi Party?

But this is jumping ahead a bit. The tale of Martin Heidegger begins in Baden, Germany, in 1889.

The Philosophical Tale

Heidegger was brought up in a rural area, with a proud tradition of ultra-nationalism. His family was devoutly Catholic and Heidegger himself originally intended to become a priest. He both studied and taught theology at the archbishopric at Freiburg. Traces of this can be discerned in his writings where a 'deep fall' (as in the story of the Garden of Eden) is followed by a life of inauthenticity (sin), creating angst (guilt). This angst prompts a quest for salvation, which Heidegger says comes through asking the question 'What is Being?'

Since this was his solution, his interests shifted from religion to philosophy, and he himself moved with them to Marburg where in 1923 he studied under Edmund Husserl, the creator of phenomenology, whom be had met earlier. *Being and Time* (*Sein und Zeit*) was the result, emerging five years later and dedicated to his supervisor. Husserl, it should be noted, was Jewish by ethnicity, albeit Christian by both baptism and practice, otherwise he would not at this time have been allowed to hold a chair in Germany. Even so, pressure mounted on 'Jewish' academics in the 1920s and 1930s to leave German public life. When Husserl eventually resigned as professor at Freiburg, Heidegger was ready to step into his shoes.

Particularly in later years, Heidegger liked to say his theory was built out of the ruins left by the "destruction" of Husserl's "neo-Kantian" writings, with their characteristic elevation of the abstract entities so beloved of the ancients over the mundane imprecision of the everyday. Instead, Heidegger focuses on human consciousness, and its awareness of its existence, its transience, and its impotence. Heidegger says cryptically that the problem for humanity (or *Dasein* as he puts it) "lies in its always having its being to be."

Heidegger continued to lecture contentedly on the various problems of being at Freiburg until early 1933, when in the wake of Hitler's triumphant arrival as elected chancellor of all Germany, the rector of the university (an outspoken critic of the Nazis) resigned. And now the plot thickens. Heidegger is appointed in his stead, and on May 1, 1933 joins the National Socialists. He even has *Being and Time* reprinted, this time minus its dedication to Husserl. Only a footnote remained mentioning the personal link, which his supporters later offered as evidence of a "compromise of the kind that happened a great deal in Germany."

But Heidegger did not seem to be looking for a compromise. On becoming rector of the university, he presented an enthusiastic National Socialist vision of its future, inspired by his own philosophy. While Heidegger was rector, the Nazi salute was required at the beginning and end of all classes, the Jewish student association building was occupied by an angry mob, and some – but not all – Jewish professors and students were expelled. In June 1933, at Heidelberg, Heidegger declared that the course for German universities to follow would be "a tough struggle to the end in the spirit of National Socialism, which will not be drowned by Christian and humanist notions." Heidegger wrote secret letters to Nazi officials denouncing a colleague, Hermann Staudinger (who later went on to win a Nobel Prize in chemistry). He declined to supervise any further Jewish students, and took to wearing a swastika lapel pin.

But let us step back a bit to comprehend this complicated thinker, the greatest of the last century.

Becoming rector at Freiburg was the first step in Heidegger's effort to bring a National Socialist vision to the universities. His rector's address proclaims the "historical spiritual mission of the German people," stresses the Nazi ideals of work service and military duty, and announces that the "spiritual world of a people is the force of the deepest preservation of its powers of earth and blood." Students and staff are instructed firmly that: "The Führer himself, and he alone, is the German reality, present and future, and its law." He finishes with words from Plato's *Republic*: "All that is great stands in the storm."

Heidegger believed Germany was the heir to the Greek tradition of language and thought. The Greek and German languages were original and intelligent languages. All other languages in Europe had been Latinized, which to Heidegger meant corrupted. The Greeks had attempted to get to the meaning of 'Being', and now the Germans were the only ones capable of rising from the rubble of Western Civilization to resurrect the tradition. Hitler was said to share a similar view.

Heidegger warned that Germany was at the center of the struggle for Being, caught between the nihilism of Bolshevism and the materialism of capitalism. "We are caught in a pincers. Situated in the middle, our *Volk* experiences the severest pressure. It is the *Volk* with the most neighbors and hence the most – endangered – and with all this, the metaphysical *Volk*. We are certain of this mission. But the *Volk* will only be able to realize that destiny if within itself it creates a resonance . . . and takes a creative view of its heritage. All this implies that this *Volk*, as a historical *Volk*, must move itself and thereby the history of the West beyond the center of their future 'happening' and into the primordial realm of the powers of Being," he wrote earnestly.

Heidegger now evidently saw himself as rescuing civilization from where she had fallen, seduced by the technical rationality of logic and science, debased by technology. Nazism shared this aim – of getting back to a wholesome "golden age" to find again the true German consciousness. Nor was the compromise evident in his November 1933 speech,

FIGURE 27 Only the Germans were capable of rising from the rubble of Western Civilization . . .

"Bekenntnis zu Adolf Hitler und dem national-sozialistischen Staat," which translates as "Declaration of Allegiance to Adolf Hitler and the National Socialist State." (That is, unless you are François Fedier, writing at the time of the 1988 'Heidegger affair' in France, in which case it translates as "Appel pour un plébiscite," or "Call for a Plebiscite," which is a public vote to decide a matter of State.)

One of the favorite themes of the far right in Germany, and particularly the Nazis, is the firm belief in a national destiny and of a community of the people: *Volksgemeinschaft*. This requires the throwing off of the shackles of parliamentarianism and modernism that other countries had imposed on the German people. Only then could the ideal community be created bound by race and blood. The task of doing this called for authentic heroes, such as Albert Leo Schlageter, a German soldier who carried out acts of random violence after World War I ended for everyone else. He was executed, despite Berlin's protests, by the French authorities in 1923, for conducting acts of sabotage in the Rhineland. He is praised on page 1 of *Mein Kampf*, and after they came to power the Nazis established a national holiday in his honor. For Heidegger, Schlageter was the model of the authentic *Dasein*. In another speech soon after becoming rector, Heidegger honors Schlageter, affirming that he had died at a time of "darkness, humiliation, and treason," but promising that his sacrifice would lead inevitably to a "future awakening to honor and greatness."

224

Schlageter, he told the approving university audience, "walked these grounds as a student. But Freiburg could not hold him for long. He was compelled to go to the Baltic; he was compelled to go to Upper Silesia; he was compelled to go to the Ruhr. . . . He was not permitted to escape his destiny so that he could die the most difficult and greatest of all deaths with a hard will and a clear heart."

This is also the language of *Being and Time*, where Heidegger elaborates on the "authentic" life.

> Once one has grasped the finitude of one's existence, it snatches one back from the endless multiplicity of possibilities which offer themselves as closest to one – those of comfortableness, shirking, and taking things lightly – and brings *Dasein* [that is here, roughly, "humanity"] into the simplicity of its fate. This is how we designate *Dasein*'s primordial historicizing, which lies in authentic resoluteness and in which *Dasein* hands itself down to itself, free for death, in a possibility which it has inherited and yet chosen.

As for nothingness, the element latched upon by the existentialists after the war, in *What is Metaphysics?* Heidegger says "we know Nothingness," we know it through fear: "Fear reveals Nothingness."

That sounds a bit ominous . . .

But Heidegger's period as rector of Freiburg was to be short-lived. He would resign in the summer of 1934, amidst a purge of the SA and Nazi apparatus generally against those contaminated by Jewish or capitalist ideas. Even so, Heidegger remained a dues-paying member of the National Socialist Party until 1945.

In an interview (with *Der Spiegel*) in 1966 reflecting on his speeches (and embargoed at his instruction until after his death), he explained that he saw in Nazism the possibility that "here is something new, here is a new dawn." He said he regretted, though, exhorting the students in 1933 to let the Führer "himself and he alone" be the "rules of your Being."

The generally accepted version of the Heidegger story is that his 1930s dalliance with Nazism was a youthful mistake, a brief flirtation by a scholar naïve about politics and the ways of the world. When he realized his mistake, he resigned his position as rector and refused henceforth to take part in Nazi activities. Furthermore, even during this period, he tried to protect the integrity of the university from the worst excesses of Nazism and personally intervened with the Nazi authorities on behalf of

Jewish students and colleagues. And this story of Heidegger's youthful indiscretion is supported by an impressive array of intellectuals, including Hannah Arendt (who has added value being Jewish herself) and Richard Rorty.

For their judgment they draw on an excellent source: the essay Heidegger submitted to the de-Nazification committee in 1945. Here, the scholar who normally could not string two sentences together without introducing at least twelve obscurities, is for once admirably brief and succinct. He writes: "In April 1933, I was unanimously elected rector (with two abstentions) in a plenary session of the university and not, as rumor has it, appointed by the National Socialist minister." So succinct, in fact, that he however neglects to mention his additional title of "Führer" of the university, which was indeed an honorific bestowed by the minister . . . And he continues: "Previously I neither desired nor occupied an academic office. I never belonged to a political party," without mentioning his activities in the youth group 'Gralbund', founded by Richard von Kralik, a conservative nationalist who called the English and Americans "German rejects."

Anyway, he explains, he only joined the Nazi Party in order to facilitate administrative relations for the university.

> A short while after I took control of the Rectorship the district head presented himself, accompanied by two functionaries in charge of university matters, to urge me, in accordance with the wishes of the minister, to join the Party. The minister insisted that in this way my official relations with the Party and the governing organs would be simplified, especially since up until then I had no contact with these organs. After lengthy considerations, I declared myself ready to enter the Party in the interests of the university, but under the express condition of refusing to accept a position within the Party or working on behalf of the Party either during the Rectorship or afterward.

And again Heidegger fails to take the opportunity to explain here why, if his party membership was motivated by his desire to facilitate his work as rector, he renewed it every year until 1945, long after his duties as rector had finished.

Instead he offers evidence of his discreet resistance after 1934. "After my resignation from the Rectorship it became clear that by continuing to teach, my opposition to the principles of the National Socialist worldview would only grow. . . . Since National Socialist ideology became increasingly inflexible and increasingly less disposed to a purely [*coughs*] philosophical interpretation, the fact that I was active as a philosopher was itself a sufficient expression of opposition."

Years later, one of his students, Hannah Arendt, remembered for her description of Auschwitz as showing the "banality of evil," was solicited to write an essay for an anthology honoring Heidegger on the occasion of his eightieth birthday. She started by recalling how she herself first heard of Heidegger, back in the Germany of the 1920s.

> There was hardly more than a name, but the name travelled all over Germany like the rumour of the hidden king. The rumour about Heidegger put it quite simply: Thinking has come to life again. . . . There exists a teacher; one can perhaps learn to think.

Quite what he thought, then, evidently was less of an issue. But she offers the following explanation of Heidegger's political activities, recalling learnedly how Plato had traveled to Syracuse to advise its tyrannical ruler, too. "Now we all know that Heidegger, too, once succumbed to the temptation to change his 'residence' and to get involved in the world of human affairs," she starts indulgently. After his relatively brief foray into politics, Plato had had to return to Athens, concluding that further attempts to put his theories into practice were futile. Heidegger, though, "was served somewhat worse than Plato because the tyrant and his victims were not located beyond the sea, but in his own country." And she continues:

> We who wish to honour the thinkers, even if our own residence lies in the midst of the world, can hardly help finding it striking and perhaps exasperating that Plato and Heidegger, when they entered into human affairs, turned to tyrants and Führers. This should be imputed not just to the circumstances of the times and even less to performed character, but rather to what the French call a *déformation professionelle*. For the attraction to the tyrannical can be demonstrated theoretically in many of the great thinkers (Kant is the great exception). And if this tendency is not demonstrable in what they did, that is only because very few of them were prepared to go beyond "the faculty of wondering at the simple" and to "accept this wondering as their abode."

In this way, Arendt even manages to make Heidegger into the victim who fell prey to the greatness of his thought. Indeed, he emerges from the affair with some credit:

> Heidegger himself corrected his own "error" more quickly and more radically than many of those who later sat in judgement over him.

The plot thickens

Heidegger's followers make quite a lot of all this. After all, they point out, Arendt was herself Jewish, and was even briefly incarcerated in a camp in Vichy France. Surely her assessment must be considered dispassionate. What's more, Arendt is a respected philosopher too. However, "dispassionate" is not quite right. The Heidegger affair has another dimension. Curiously, when Arendt was but a young student of 18, studying under Professor Heidegger at Marburg, she fell hopelessly in love with the 35-year-old married man and conducted a secret romance. Heidegger wanted it kept secret too, telling his "saucy wood nymph" firmly that she must destroy all his letters. Of course she didn't (unprincipled woman!), so years later the other Heidegger affair came to light. So the world can read in letters like this one from Heidegger to Hannah, dated June 22, 1925, that:

> What no one ever appreciates is how experimenting with oneself and, for that matter, all compromises, techniques, moralising, escapism, and closing off one's growth can only inhibit and distort the providence of Being.

Surely no one should lightly intrude on such personal feelings. But we must! Truth demands it. So here, too, is a fragment from one of Hannah's letters, four years later, after their ways had necessarily separated:

> I often hear things about you, but always with the peculiar reserve and indirectness that is simply part of speaking the famous name – that is, something I can hardly recognise. And I would indeed so like to know – almost tormentingly so, how you are doing, what you are working on, and how Freiburg is treating you.

With significance, she signs off, "I kiss your brow and eyes," whereas Heidegger signs himself tersely "your."

But even if one begins to suspect Hannah Arendt's portrait of Heidegger, his defenders maintain that any character flaw in the man is an entirely separate matter from his philosophy, which must be judged "on its own merits." Any attempts to relate his philosophy of *Dasein* to Nazism is, they insist, illegitimate. There is nothing in it, particularly not in *Being and Time*, that bears any affinity to Nazism.

This isn't how Heidegger saw it, however. For example, his speech on November 11, 1933, says that "the National Socialist revolution is not simply the takeover of the existing power of the State by another party which has emerged for that purpose; rather, this revolution brings about the complete overturning of our German *Dasein*." Heidegger expected the Nazis' political revolution to continue on into a second more profound one involving a "transformation of man himself." His philosophical studies, involving retrieval of Greek ideas, were designed to help further this political process.

Right up to the end of the war, Heidegger saw the evidence of a metaphysical sickness in the collapse of the decadent Western democracies facing the "internal greatness" of the National Socialist Movement (a point made not only in his 1935 essay "Introduction to Metaphysics" but also in 1952, on the occasion of its reprinting – despite other amendments). After 1945, Heidegger simply swapped sides around to show the sickness contaminating not democracy but Nazism. In the 1945 "Letter on Humanism," his new project, on the ruins of the Third Reich, becomes to overthrow the "Western humanism" that was responsible for Nazism!

And since the end of World War II, many philosophers since have recorded their admiration for Heidegger's important political work. Derrida, employing his characteristic 'deconstruction' technique, even says that once Heidegger succeeded in liberating himself from 'metaphysics' following his *Kehre*, or 'turn', his philosophy became the best form of *anti-Nazism*.

Despite this, many of Heidegger's most convinced supporters found it puzzling that he had not (at least) spoken out after the war to condemn Nazism, speculating, for example, that it might have been a disdain for media coverage, or for apologies in general, rather than for the more simple reason that he was a Nazi. They choose not to recall that, when challenged after his infamous rector's address by his friend Karl Jaspers (who had a Jewish wife) whether he really supported the Nazi program, he said that there *was* an international Jewish conspiracy and anyway, that Hitler had "marvelous hands." These philosophers prefer to imagine the roots of Nazism are to be found in the houses of the concentration camp guards rather than in the abstractions of their icons. Yet fascism drew on a long German philosophical tradition stretching at the least from Hegel and Nietzsche, with the additional imput of the Italian philosopher Giovanni Gentile.

Gentile, a respected 'neo-Hegelian', was (as Heidegger seems to have dreamed of becoming for Hitler) Mussolini's 'ideas' man, adopted as the official thinker of the Italian fascists – and was executed for his trouble after the war by the communists. The Nuremburg tribunal, noting that

Heidegger shared something of Hitler's messianic style of delivery, merely banned him from lecturing for five years.

After the war, Heidegger made only one statement referring to the Holocaust. He equated it with the mechanization of the food industry, saying that "in essence" that was "no different than the production of corpses in the gas chambers and death camps." Both, he suggests, are examples of "nihilism."

Hitler's political influence has faded somewhat; philosophy, however, remains deeply in Heidegger's thrall.

CHAPTER 28
BENJAMIN LEE WHORF AND THE COLOR PINKER
(ca. 1900–1950)

The Sapir–Whorf hypothesis is so called after its author, Benjamin Lee Whorf, and his intellectual confidant, Edward Sapir, which sounds democratic but actually is a bit odd in itself. After all, Whorf wrote it and he named it the 'principle of linguistic relativity'. Anyway, since academics prefer their name for it, it is possible for Robert Kirk of Nottingham University to call it a "relativistic doctrine" (which would otherwise look a bit silly), before continuing:

> According to Sapir [sic], we see and hear . . . very largely as we do because the language habits of our community predispose certain choices of interpretation. Whorf develops the idea, attempting to illustrate it from American Indian languages. The doctrine risks collapse into the truism that some things can be said more easily in some languages than in others.

The Philosophical Tale

Benjamin Lee Whorf is not taken very seriously these days. Not as an anthropologist, not as a linguist, not *even* as a philosopher. In fact, he is not taken very much at all. His groundbreaking work on the language patterns of the Hopi Indians of North America is now dismissed by populists like Stephen Pinker as "unintentionally comic."

Stephen Pinker, a contemporary philosopher who normally describes himself more imposingly as a "cognitive scientist" (well aware of the power of language!), explains in *The Language Instinct* that "The idea that thought is the same thing as language [not, of course, that this is what Whorf does say] is an example of what can be called a conventional absurdity." Pinker helpfully sketches out instead the answer provided by today's science (neglecting the role of consciousness, which Cognitive Scientists do not believe in):

> the cells of the eye are wired to neurones in a way that makes neurones respond [to certain colors]. No matter how influential language might be,

231

it would seem preposterous to a physiologist that it could reach down into the retina and rewire the ganglion cells.

Even within Whorf's own discipline of linguistics, Noam Chomsky describes his work as "entirely premature" and "lacking in precision." As one would-be follower of Whorf (Dan Moonhawk Allford) put it, if you want to find out more about his work, you need to be able to put up with the fact that not a single sociolinguist seems "to be able to say Whorf's name without an accompanying sneer on their lips."

Why should this be so? What causes this reaction? Is his work, as Robert Kirk says, little more than truisms? Or is it perhaps not based on enough evidence, as Chomsky (completely differently) alleges? Even were Whorf to be shown to be absolutely right about the nature of language, "his correct guess would have been based on no evidence of substance and no defensible formal analysis of English structure," Chomsky complains. Or is it perhaps because Whorf preferred to work outside academia for the whole of his short life as (coughs politely) an insurance investigator?

Then again, perhaps the explanation has something to do with the fact that his arguments are unwelcome to many. For one, they appear to elevate the thinking of the American Indian over the thinking of the American academic, a scandalous supposition made much worse by being couched in scientific language. As John Lucy puts it: "For some [linguistic relativity] represents a threat to the very possibility of reasoned inquiry." Whorf, he explains, threatens the legitimacy of the activities of conventional researchers looking for 'objective facts' and 'reality'.

But what is this dangerous, poorly founded theory? In essence, it is that:

> We dissect nature along lines laid down by our native languages. The categories and types that we isolate from the world of phenomena we do not find there because they stare every observer in the face; on the contrary, the world is presented in a kaleidoscopic flux of impressions which has to be organized by our minds – and this means largely by the linguistic systems in our minds. We cut nature up, organize it into concepts, and ascribe significances as we do, largely because we are parties to an agreement that holds throughout our speech community and is codified in the patterns of our language.

The agreement is, of course, "an implicit and unstated one," Whorf continues, but "its terms are absolutely obligatory; we cannot talk at all

FIGURE 28 *"We dissect nature along lines laid down by our native languages . . ."*

except by subscribing to the organization and classification of data which the agreement decrees."

So let's sort through and organize some of the data and isolate some categories now.

Benjamin Lee Whorf was born in Winthrop, Massachusetts, on April 24, 1897, the eldest of three boys. His father, Harry, was evidently something of a cultural polymath, earning his living as a commercial artist, author, photographer, stage designer, and playwright. Encouraged by his mother Sarah, young Benjamin explored the mysteries of ciphers and puzzles, and read widely on botany, astrology, Mexican history, Mayan archaeology, and photography. He came in due course to anthropology via an unusual route of physics, Jungian synchronicity, systems theory, and Gestalt psychology (with its concepts of 'foregrounding' and 'backgrounding') – but, above all, through linguistics. All of which interests he had been only able to pursue in his spare time.

For his day job was rather mundane – investigator and engineer for the Hartford Fire Insurance Company. Yet these years were by no means wasted. Within his work he came across many examples of what he would later see as language influencing thought patterns, and when his linguistic theory appeared in several influential articles it was set around the topic of fire prevention. People, he observed in the first of these articles, tended to be careless around 'empty drums' of gasoline, drums, that is, 'empty' of petrol but equally 'full' – of vapors more explosive than the liquid. He noticed how people were complacent towards industrial 'waste

233

water' and 'spun limestone', both, again, flammable and dangerous despite the impressions of reassuring stability that the words 'water' and 'stone' convey.

In the 1920s, while still working full time, he entered into correspondence with the leading US scholars of the day. From 1931 onwards he studied linguistics (part-time) under Edward Sapir, one of the key figures in the new discipline of sociolinguistics. It was at this time that he made his in-depth and highly original study of the language structures of the Hopi Indians. A stream of detailed yet almost poetic papers established his name and he became a research fellow at Yale.

Linguistic relativity is in itself not a new idea. Indeed it is rather an old one, older than the physics variety, going back at least to the nineteenth century and the founder of linguistics, Baron Wilhelm von Humboldt. The baron himself viewed thought as being entirely impossible without language, and that language completely determined thought, something which is not Whorf's position at all. After Einstein's demonstration of the 'relativity' of space and time, Von Humboldt's theory took on new life and Einstein himself cited it in a radio program. Whorf, with a background in chemistry, was not claiming to have invented anything; rather, he wanted to unite the new thinking in 'hard science' with the older philosophical theory.

In one of his essays, later collected together into the book *Language, Thought, and Reality* (1956), he says:

> Just as it is possible to have any number of geometries other than the Euclidean which give an equally perfect account of space configurations, so it is possible to have descriptions of the universe, all equally valid, that do not contain our familiar contrasts of time and space. The relativity viewpoint of modern physics is one such view, conceived in mathematical terms, and the Hopi *Weltanschauung* is another and quite different one, non-mathematical and linguistic.

He goes on to challenge the Newtonian worldview, permanent and unchanging like Plato's Forms. It is this that so alarmed the philosophers, rather than anything merely linguistic.

> In [the] Hopi view, time disappears and space is altered, so that it is no longer the homogeneous and instantaneous timeless space of our supposed intuition or of classical Newtonian mechanics. At the same time, new concepts and abstractions flow into the picture, taking up the task of describing the universe without reference to such time or space – abstrac-

tions for which our language lacks adequate terms. These abstractions . . . will undoubtedly appear to us as psychological or even mystical in character.

For 2,000 years European thinkers had assumed that language merely followed thinking. And thought was supposed to depend on laws of logic or reason that were supposed to be the same for everyone, no matter what language was used. (Not for nothing had Bertrand Russell [on the other side of 'the pond'] spent most of Whorf's youth wrestling with the task of producing just such a 'logical foundation'.) But now, Whorf said, neither language nor yet concepts were universal at all!

Of course, trapped within our 'house of language' this seems very strange. But Western languages can be thought of as being static, orientated towards patterns, whereas languages like Hopi are active, concerned with processes. The most significant difference between these two orientations is over the issue of identity. Nouns (and hence names) give an identity. This notion is central to Western philosophy. Aristotle's 'laws of thought', which seemed to him then and still seem to many now absolutely certain, consist of:

The law of identity: $A = A$;
The law of non-contradiction: A does not equal 'not A'; and
The law of the excluded middle: either A or 'not A' but not both A and 'not A'.

Actually, the laws go back well before Aristotle, certainly to the pre-Socratic philosophers, most notably Parmenides. It was he, in the fifth century BCE, who formulated the second of the laws as: "Never will this prevail, that what is not is." It may seem uncontroversial, but it appears that, at the time, Parmenides' law actually represented a radical break with convention. Up to then, philosophers like Heraclitus had argued that since things changed, they had to contain what they were not. Only such contradictions could account for change. Heraclitus' words have echoes of the language of the Hopi Indians: "Cold things grow warm; warm grows cold; wet grows dry; parched grows moist."

But for 2,000 years, Western philosophy accepted Aristotle's lead instead. And then Whorf came along and upset the conventions. Instead of language following their rules, he suggested that logic only seeks to institutionalize the accidents of Western grammar, and in so doing creates a misleading view of the world.

Take the gasoline container example, for instance. Whorf says the use of the word 'empty' on a sign by the metal gasoline drums led workers to think of the drums as 'empty', void, 'full of nothing', when in reality the drums were full – of inflammable residues. In order to reassert order in the linguistic world, Pinker instead insists the workers' error is because the gas drums look empty – so the confusion is empirical, not linguistic, after all. Since steel gasoline drums tend not to be see-through, this argument weakens somewhat, but Whorf's point is rather different anyway: he is pointing out that when the workers mentally categorized the drums as 'empty', they adopted a linguistic model of 'empty' containers that led them to perceive no hazard.

Let Pinker have his turn again: "No one is really sure how Whorf came up with his outlandish claims, but his limited, badly analysed sample of Hopi speech and his long-time leanings toward mysticism must have contributed." Professor Pinker himself has no such biases: "The idea that language shapes thinking was plausible when scientists were in the dark about how thinking works or even how to study it. Now that cognitive scientists know how to think about thinking . . ."

Well, yes, now that the scientists have solved the mysteries of the mind, Whorf's theory looks very flimsy. Comical even. Pinker's terribly modern (don't mention Hobbes, for example) hypothesis, by comparison, is that the human brain is a kind of computer, a "symbol-processing machine" which converts data in, be they linguistic or sensory, according to predetermined, biologically hardwired 'rules'.

> In the brain, there might be three groups of neurones, one used to represent the individual that the proposition is about (Socrates, Rod Stewart, and so on [*Pinker's witticism*]), one to represent the logical relationship in the proposition (is a, is not, is like, and so on), and one to represent the class or type that the individual is being characterized as (men, dogs, chickens, and so on).
>
> Each concept would correspond to the firing of a particular neurone; for example, in the first group of neurones, the fifth neurone might fire to represent Socrates and the seventeenth might fire to represent Aristotle; in the third group the eighth neurone might fire to represent men, the twelfth neurone might fire to represent dogs. The processor might be a network of other neurones feeding into these groups, connected together in such a way that it reproduces the firing pattern in one group of neurones in some other group. . . . With many thousands of representations and a set of somewhat more sophisticated processors . . . you might have a genuinely intelligent brain or computer.

This, says Pinker, is the 'computational' theory of mind. There really is a color red coded into the brain (in 'mentalese'), even if the language people use does not have it. And now Pinker plays his trump card against the increasingly pathetic straw man of Benjamin Whorf: "The clinching experiment carried out in the New Guinea Highlands by Eleanor Rosch" in 1972.

The Dani people, Eleanor Rosch discovered, have only two 'color terms', *mola* for bright warm ones and *mili* for dark cold ones. These can be taken crudely as 'black and white', as Pinker indeed terms them. Just two color terms, yet Professor Rosch found that the Dani were *just as good* at discriminating colors in tests as anyone else! Evidently, their lack of words for colors was not affecting their perceptions. End of story, and end of poor Mr. Whorf's insurance investigator theories, as far as Pinker was concerned.

However, Eleanor Rosch's research was not quite the end of the story. Methodologically, her tests, involving pairing colors on charts, seem to have been inadvertently biased towards precisely the colors typical of an English speaker's language categories – blue, red, green, and so on – over the 'shades' distributed around them. And then there was the problem that the tests were so complicated that a mere 20 percent of the Dani were able to complete them. Just perhaps lacking color terms made the test harder to complete . . .

All subsequent attempts since to replicate the research have failed, and worse still, a study[1] with twenty-two Berinmo speakers (who have slightly more color categories than the Dani, but nowhere near as many as an English speaker) came to a very different conclusion:

> Recognition of desaturated colours did appear to reflect colour vocabulary.
> . . . Whilst Berinmo speakers, like those of all other languages hitherto investigated, appear to group contiguous areas of the colour space together, no evidence was found for these sections to correspond to a limited set of universal basic colour categories.

All this debate took place long after Whorf had departed the scene, of course. But maybe he would not have been too bothered anyway. For in another passage Whorf reflects a difference of perspective:

> A fair realisation of the incredible degree of diversity of linguistic systems that ranges over the globe leaves one with the inescapable feeling that the human spirit is inconceivably old; that the few thousand years of history covered by our written records are no more than the thickness of a pencil

mark on the scale that measures our past experience on this planet; that the vents of these recent millenniums spell nothing in any evolutionary wise, that the race has taken no sudden spurt, achieved no commanding synthesis during recent millenniums, but has only played with a few of the linguistic formulations and views of nature bequeathed from an inexpressibly long past.

Pompous Footnote

1 See "Color Categories Are Not Universal: Replications and New Evidence from a Stone-Age Culture," by Debi Roberson, Ian Davies, and Jules Davidoff, where it is all clearly set out – in black and white . . .

CHAPTER 29
BEING SARTRE AND NOT DEFINITELY NOT BEING BEAUVOIR
(1905–1980 AND NOT 1908–1986)

Sartre's oeuvre is a unique phenomenon. No other major philosopher has also been a major playright [*sic*], novelist, political theorist, and literary critic. It is still too early to judge which facet of Sartre's extraordinary genius posterity will regard as the most important, but since his philosophy permeates his other works, its enduring interest is assured.

Anyway, that's the conclusion reached by Dr. Thomas Baldwin of Clare College, Cambridge, in *The Oxford Companion to Philosophy*. But where in this assessment is 'Mrs. Sartre' – Simone de Beauvoir? Vanished. Not a whiff of her feminine perfume, although elsewhere in the encyclopaedia Professor Grunebaum of Buffalo State College deals with Sartre's little shadow thus:

de Beauvoir . . . in her essays *Pyrrhus et Cinéas* (1944) and *The Ethics of Ambiguity* (1947) . . . attempted to reconcile her less extreme view with Sartre's by distinguishing two kinds of freedom [and recognizing] that personal freedom is ineluctably bound up with that of others. However, like him, she was unable ever to convincingly give content to the idea of freedom as a moral idea, or, logically, to escape the admission that the Sartrean existentialism has no grounds for preferring one project to another.

The Philosophical Tale

Sartre derides those who act out roles: the bourgeoisie with their comfortable sense of 'duty', homosexuals who pretend to be heterosexuals, peeping Toms who get caught in the act of spying, and, most famously of all, waiters who rush about. All of these, he says, are slaves to other people's perceptions – 'the Other'. They are exhibiting *mauvaise foi* – 'bad

239

faith'. This is a common flaw and, as the psychologists say, in choosing this fault to condemn in others Sartre tells us a little about himself too.

Not that Sartre would like to, for Sartre considered himself a man of principle and a political radical. In the early 1950s, when others muttered weakly about gulags, Sartre celebrated the new Russia under its heroic leader, Joseph Stalin, and even went on a fact-finding tour. After this, he returned to Paris to denounce rumors that Russians were not truly free. Indeed, he told an interviewer pressing him on the subject, "the freedom to criticize is total in the USSR."

This was existentialism in practice. For existentialism is a philosophy of action, an "ethic of action and self-commitment." Sartre said that in 1946, just after spending World War II writing philosophy. "I have said," he declares in *Critique of Dialectical Reason* (1960), "and I repeat – that the only valid interpretation of human history is historical materialism." But here is an attempt at making some sense of Sartre as a solitary individual.

Jean-Paul Sartre, like Marx himself, was always more a man of letters than a man of action. Brought up in tranquil, rural France, he describes spending most of his childhood in his grandfather's library. His adolescence was equally book-centered, spent being groomed for a place amongst France's elite in one of its best colleges, eventually emerging from his studies only to return to school as a teacher. At least, this being France, he was able to be a teacher of philosophy, but he still disliked the experience and in particular his surroundings, the port of Le Havre, which he would later deride, in his first novel, *Nausea*, as Bouville.

When World War II arrived and interrupted his intellectualizing, he became a meteorologist in the army, and when the French surrendered to the victorious Nazis, he found himself a prisoner of war, albeit on a long leash which allowed him parole to return to philosophy teaching (this time in sophisticated Paris), and indeed to organize his first play, mid-war. He explained later that he considered becoming active in the resistance, but this would have involved subordinating himself to either the communists or the Gaullists. The solution he arrived at instead was to concentrate on his writing and finishing what would be his *magnum opus*, *L'Être et le Néant*, or 'Being and Nothingness'. "I am condemned to be free," he famously observed there.

When the war ended, he decided against life as a professor, instead choosing that of a writer and intellectual, campaigning for liberation movements such as the cause of the Vietnamese against the Americans, or of the Algerians against La France herself. Meanwhile, his fiction writing was triumphantly received everywhere, and in that auspicious year, 1964, he was offered the Nobel Prize for Literature, but – wait for it! – he chose not to accept it.

Sartre's philosophy emphasizes the use of imagination, which is the purest form of freedom available to us. The 'anguish' of existence is that the rest of the world is that "these things are not otherwise but thus," as Heidegger put it (whom the French existentialists hailed as their philosophical leader, despite this being just after World War II and despite Heidegger's being, as we have seen, a Nazi). In his *Critique of Dialectical Reason* Sartre offers by way of an example workers engaged in monotonous tasks yet having sexual fantasies, thus demonstrating the power and counterfactual freedom of the imagination.

He emphasizes what is not over what is, the latter being a rather humdrum sort of affair consisting of the kind of things that scientists examine, while the 'what is not' is really much more interesting. He sums up his view (if "sums up" is ever an appropriate term in existentialist writing) thus: "The Nature of consciousness simultaneously is to be what is not and not to be what it is." And hence we come back to our own natures, our own 'essences'. We exist, yes, but how do we 'define ourselves'? (In one of the movement's empty catchphrases, "existence precedes essence.") It is here that the waiter comes in:

> His movement is quick and forward, a little too precise, a little too rapid. He comes toward the patrons with a step a little too quick. He bends forward a little too eagerly; his voice, his eyes express an interest a little too solicitous for the order of the customer. Finally there he returns, trying to imitate in his walk the inflexible stiffness of some kind of automaton while carrying his tray with the recklessness of a tight-rope walker by putting it in a perpetually unstable, perpetually broken equilibrium which he perpetually re-establishes by a light movement of the hand and arm. (*Being and Nothingness* [1943])

This spotlight on 'consciousness' is what made Sartre's name. But, curiously enough, another book that came out in 1943, *She Came to Stay*, by his lifelong intellectual confidante and companion Simone de Beauvoir, also describes various kinds of consciousness, in passages ranging from wandering through an empty theater (the stage, the walls, the chairs, unable to come alive until there is an audience) to watching a woman in a restaurant ignore the fact that her male companion has begun stroking her arm: "it lay there, forgotten, ignored, the man's hand was stroking a piece of flesh that no longer belonged to anyone." As well as this one:

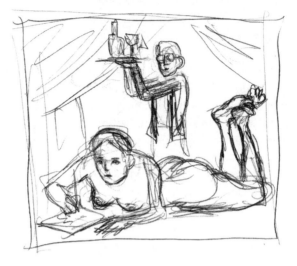

FIGURE 29 We exist, yes, but how do we 'define ourselves'?

> "It's almost impossible to believe that other people are conscious beings, aware of their own inward feelings, as we ourselves are aware of our own," said Françoise. "To me, it's terrifying when we grasp that. We get the impression of no longer being anything but a figment of someone else's mind." (*She Came to Stay* [1943])

Curiouser and curiouser, although the two books came out in the same year, Simone de Beauvoir's was written some time earlier, and Sartre read the drafts avidly on his brief army leaves before commencing *Being and Nothingness*.

Now who's showing bad faith? Sartre or the waiter?

Sartre even records in his diary how Beauvoir had to correct him several times for his clumsy misunderstanding of existentialist philosophy. It turns out that Sartre simply borrowed all Beauvoir's ideas and used them (unacknowledged) in his own work. The only unknown is why Beauvoir was content to allow this, indeed, repeatedly denied any credit for Sartre's work. But then the Sartre–Beauvoir relationship, although much celebrated and something of a philosophical icon, is also completely misunderstood. Truly it is itself a philosophical tale. On the one hand there is the well-known plot of Sartre the womanizer who denies the dutiful

Beauvoir marriage in order to preserve his 'existential freedom'. On the other, and much less well known, is the factual history recorded in their letters to one another. This records that, in 1930, Sartre proposed marriage to Beauvoir. She was aghast at this, both for the conventionality of the proposal and for the conventionality of Sartre's assumptions, and it was she who insisted instead that if they were to spend their years together she wanted to be able to continue to have other relationships (with both male and female lovers). And the true sexual tale belies the professional one, oft-related, of Sartre the genius aided by Beauvoir the frustrated would-be wife turned into dutiful secretary. On the contrary, in truth, Beauvoir had both the intellectual and the literary edge on her younger partner. Beauvoir, from a convent school that no one was supposed to progress beyond, managed to pass France's highest philosophy exam a year early, while Sartre, with all the resources of privilege, struggled to pass on his second attempt.

Sartre later claimed this was due to an excess of originality in his answers, but in truth this must have been a new departure if so. Up to then the greatest display of creativity he had shown had been when as a child he had carefully copied out stories from comics, adding in extra details from his grandfather's encyclopaedias. He had then passed the whole lot off as his 'novel' to admiring parents.

In *The Words*, Sartre acknowledges, with refreshing frankness, these early examples of 'bad faith', noting how his mother would:

> bring visitors into the dining-room so that they could surprise the young creator at his school-desk. I pretended to be too absorbed to be aware of my admirers' presence. They would withdraw on tiptoe, whispering that I was too cute for words, that it was too-too charming . . .

Which play-acting brings us back to the waiter. Now I've observed waiters too. They often need to perform tasks quickly, for a practical reason, not an optional one related to their 'false consciousness'. The job is skilled – demanding more than demeaning. They are indeed actors, as they have a role to carry out, and, of course, like actors, they have an audience watching them. (Even people like Sartre and Beauvoir, sometimes.) So let's use a different analogy instead. That of the philosophy intellectual.

> Their speech is a little too sonorous, the emphasis on words a little too firm. Their gesticulations seem ungainly in their self-consciousness, their eyes gaze a little too eagerly, their voice occasionally dropping in a pretend confidence as they struggle to communicate the essence of their latest

theory, or rising, a note of disappointed incredulity coming in, if there is any dissent, as if sensing a lost equilibrium which can only be re-established by a flurry of paper . . .

For what seems also to be going on in Sartre's philosophy – in his attack on 'bad faith' – is a none-too-subtle series of value-judgments, in which the philosopher-author is desperate to emerge ahead and above the rest of humanity. Perhaps it has something to do with justifying his ambivalent role in the war, vacillating between Gaullism and communism before deciding to write a new book instead. (The one featuring the waiter . . .) Perhaps it was to do with borrowing his partner's ideas. Perhaps he wasn't quite sure that it *was* better being Sartre rather than not being, or even than being the Nothingness of the Waiter.

So who really was the great existentialist? Beauvoir, unlike Sartre, would have been aware that many of existentialism's elements, for example the notion of 'the Other', can be found in Hegel where they can in turn be traced back to the Eastern philosophical tradition, with its 'deemphasis' of individualism as a delusion born of ignorance – and perhaps conceit. That said, Beauvoir's later development of the notion to class all women as 'the Other' in male-dominated society *was* her own. Yet her early attempts to get her philosophical ideas published were firmly rebuffed by French publishers with the advice to leave philosophy to men!

In one of Beauvoir's fictional tales, *She Came to Stay*, is a clue to the famous relationship. In the book, her first, there are three main characters, of whom Françoise stands in for Beauvoir herself, Pierre represents Sartre, and the third, Xavière, is Beauvoir's then live-in lover, Olga. In Chapter 1, Françoise creates a new version of a classic play, in which the Sartre figure will not only be the lead character but will also be credited with responsibility for the production. In *She Came to Stay*, the motivation of Françoise in hiding her originality is simply love. However, some see in the real-life story another explanation. They see Beauvoir calculatedly feeding Sartre the plagiarist, watching his meteoric rise with pride – and at the same time cocking a snook at the crusty, male-dominated French philosophical establishment. And so a tale lies within a tale, within a tale.

CHAPTER 30
DECONSTRUCTING DERRIDA
(1930–2004)

Jacques Derrida coined the term 'deconstruction' in the 1960s (although its 'traces' can be found everywhere), at a time when the upturning of conventional structures was the position to be adopted by academics by default, if not already (to borrow a French word) a bit *passé*. Deconstructionists were to be intellectual radicals. They were to throw away all the fruits of philosophy: epistemology, metaphysics, ethics – the whole apple cart. After all, those were the products of a worldview rooted in false oppositions.

False oppositions, that is, like the 'is/is not' scientific one, the 'past/future' chronological time one, the 'good/bad' ethics one. Derrida explains that all the other thinkers' and philosophers' claims and counterclaims, their theories and findings were no more than elaborate word games – that they have been 'playing jiggery-pokery' with us.

Andrew Cutrofello, writing in *The Concise Routledge Encyclopaedia of Philosophy*, explains more, in the lucid prose of the genre.

> His work can be understood in terms of his argument that it is necessary to interrogate the Western philosophical tradition from the standpoint of 'deconstruction'. As an attempt to approach that which remains unthought in this tradition, deconstruction is concerned with the category the 'wholly other'. Derrida has called into question the 'metaphysics of presence', a valuing of truth as self-identical immediacy which has been sustained by traditional attempts to demonstrate the ontological priority and superiority of speech over writing. Arguing that the distinction . . . can be sustained only by way of violent exclusion of otherness, Derrida has attempted to develop a radically different conception of language, one that would begin from the irreducibility of difference to identity, and that would issue in a correspondingly different conception of ethical and political responsibility.

The Philosophical Tale

French political philosophy prides itself on having given to the world the original Declaration of the Rights of Man in 1789, not to mention inspiring

Marx and Engels in Paris, and creating the impressive edifice of 'Structuralism' itself in the nineteenth century. Not surprisingly, then, ever since Sartre *all* philosophers in France have been expected to take a political position. Ironically, this made political philosophy a bit *passé*, as its exponents now seemed to be people not able to realize that everything was political. However, unlike many of his contemporaries at the École Nationale Supérieure during the 1950s, Derrida did not join the Party, the French Communist Party that is, but rather kept aloof, declaring himself merely to be "of the left," as he put in a book called *Deconstruction and Pragmatism* (1996). In an interview for the magazine *Moscou aller-retour*, Derrida promised the Russians that "If I had the time, I could show that Stalin was 'logocentrist', though it would demand a long development."

> My hope as a man of the left is that certain elements of deconstruction will have served, or because the struggle continues, particularly in the United States – will serve to politicise or repoliticise the left with regard to positions which are not simply academic.

This stance irritated his French colleagues but went down very well in the English-speaking world, particularly America, where it was not pragmatic for career-minded academics to join radical parties but still desirable to seem progressive. Along with a mish-mash of similar intellectuals in Germany known as the 'Frankfurt School', Derrida became a 'major figure' for new disciplines calling themselves things like 'Critical Theory', 'Cultural Studies', and 'Contemporary European Thought'.

In place of politics, Derrida eagerly adopts the Structuralist project which claimed that all theories claiming universal application, like Marxism and Nazism but also liberalism and indeed utilitarianism, were 'imperialist' and suppressed alternative perspectives and cultures. Structuralists instead sought to show that the world was too subtle and too complicated to be captured in simple theories.

Derrida even takes this one step further, adding in the element of *Destruktion* that Heidegger had proposed to anyone who would listen to him. 'Deconstruction' too would destroy the implicit hierarchies of other theories through playful highlighting of their contradictions and shaking up their dogmas.

The first thing to deconstruct is that which is not there – the ideas that have been hidden and suppressed. And the first thing that Derrida finds 'excluded' is writing itself, which he says is always being treated by philosophers as a shadow form of speech.

So Derrida deconstructs Ferdinand de Saussure's description of the workings of language, and finds that in seeking to provide a list of distinctions between writing and speech, the Father of Structuralism has inadvertently produced a list of characteristics of thinking – it is arbitrary in form, material, and relative – that apply as much to speech as to writing! The difference between speech and writing is thus revealed as nothing more than a philosophical illusion. (You see how deconstruction cunningly takes the hidden assumptions buried in a text – and turns them upon themselves.)

Following this successful deconstruction of the speech/writing distinction came the end of the soul–body one (*vide* Descartes); the collapsing of the difference between things knowable by the mind and things knowable by sense perception; the rejection of distinctions between literal and metaphorical, between natural and cultural creations, between masculine and feminine . . . and yet more:

> All *dualisms*, all theories of the immortality of the soul or of the spirit, as well as all *monisms*, spiritualist or materialist, *dialectical* or *vulgar*, are the unique theme of metaphysics whose entire history was compelled to strive towards the reduction of the *trace*. The subordination of the *trace* to the full *presence* summed up in the *logos*, the humbling of writing beneath a speech dreaming as *plenitude*, such are the gestures required by an *onto-theology* determining the *archaeological* and *eschatological* meaning of *being* as *presence*, as *parousia*, as life without *différance*: another name for death, *historical metonymy* where God's name holds death in check. (*Of Grammatology*)

However, in the late 1980s, Derrida seemed to lose his radicalism in one respect at least. In a special lecture on justice for an audience in New York, he announced that uniquely amongst all the concepts, justice, the search for which Western philosophy (and this book) starts with, is (like Socrates) indeconstructible. Or as he puts it in studiously unintelligible style:

> if there is a deconstruction of all determining presumption of a present justice, it operates from an infinite 'idea of justice', infinitely irreducible. It is irreducible because due to the Other – due to the Other before any contract, because this idea as arrived, the arrival of the Other as a singularity always Other. Invincible to all skepticism . . . this 'idea of justice' appears indestructible . . .

If there is no justice in the world at present, all is still not lost. The idea remains. After all, it is inde(con)structible.

Now who's playing jiggery-pokery?

It seems that Derrida is playing jiggery-pokery with us. It is all a great game, of 'signification', 'ideality', and transcendental–empirical parallelism in general.

> The play of *differences* supposes in effect *syntheses* and *referrals* which forbid, at any moment, or in any sense, that a simple element be *present* in and of itself, *referring* only to itself. Whether in the order of spoken or written discourse, no element can function as a *sign* without referring to another element which itself is not simply *present*. . . . This interweaving, this *textile*, is the text produced only in the transformation of another *text*. Nothing neither among the elements nor within the system is anywhere ever *simply present* or *absent*. There are everywhere, *differences* and *traces* of traces. (*Semiology and Grammatology*)

Perhaps Derrida is saying that there can be no 'meaning' as there is nothing fixed within the great web of language, or indeed life and perception. Everything is a mirage, or what's worse, a kind of 'fine powder' residue left behind by boiling off our politico-sexual assumptions. Loaded terms like 'is' which discriminates against 'is not', or 'me' which is set against 'you'. We must destroy the web of words!

But it seems hard to follow what Derrida is saying. What was that transcendental–thingummy again? After all, Derrida himself liked, *koan* like, to offer contradictions and to refuse definitions when asked to explain things. At various times, he has insisted that deconstruction itself is not a method, nor an act performed, as it were, on a text by a subject. Indeed, he once declared in his "Letter to a Japanese Friend" that it is never possible to say either that 'deconstruction is such and such' or 'deconstruction is not such and such', for the construction (yes) of the sentence would be such that is false already.

It is a grand position to be sure, to coin a phrase and then to deny others the ability to make any pronouncements whatsoever on the new term. Yet we can try to approach the issue in a little more roundabout way. Derrida acknowledges a certain influence from the German philosopher Heidegger, using his tool of *destruktion* to expose the bankruptcy of Western civilization and 'humanism' in general with his own philosophical project, which he had called *Dekonstruktion*, which means what it sounds like.

FIGURE 30 This textile is the text.

(Actually, before that the term seems to have come from a Nazi psychiatry journal edited by a cousin of Hermann Göring. Small world!) Anyway, what is said to be noteworthy about Heidegger's project is that it both highlights and challenges the role of time in our structuring of the world, in our minds and in our writing of texts.

Which is just as well, as when, in fact, you look at Derrida's writings, very little of it is original. Indeed, his main claim to originality may be in coining the term 'deconstruction'. Although, in fact, it is not hard to coin new words, only hard to make them useful. (Funnily enough, in his native France, there's still no such word.)

From Heidegger, Derrida also takes the notion of 'presence', the *destruktion* of which he says is the central task for philosophy. Heidegger's footprints are there too in the concept of 'Being', and the difference between *beings* and *Being*, which Heidegger calls the 'ontico-ontological difference', and describes movingly at length in a book called *Identity and*

Difference. Derrida refers obliquely back to this at one point in *his* book called (not entirely coincidentally) *Writing and Difference* when he defines *différance* as the pre-opening of the ontico-ontological difference.

His 'transcendental phenomenology' came out of Husserl, who had also noted that "Reason is the *logos* which is produced in history. It traverses *Being* with itself in sight, in order to appear to itself, that is, to state itself and hear itself as *logos*.. . . In emerging from itself, hearing oneself speak *constitutes itself* as the *history of reason* through the detour of writing. Thus it *differs* from itself in order to *reappropriate* itself."

And here we find the origins of '*différance*', one of Derrida's favorite punning terms, playing on the two senses of 'to differ' in position (in space) and 'to defer', delay, in time – that is, defer-ence.

One translator, Alan Bass, who may be taken as something of an enthusiast, says that Derrida is "difficult to read." It is not only by virtue of his style but also because "he seriously wishes to challenge the ideas that govern the way we read.. . . Some of the difficulties can be resolved by warning the reader that Derrida often refers back to his own works, and anticipates others, without explicitly saying so . . . compounded by frequent use of the terminology of classical philosophy, again without explicit explanation or reference." (We saw one dropped in earlier, *parousia*, a Greek word which has some sort of religious connotation to do with being governed by the presence.)

A cinematic biography of the great *philosophe, Derrida the Movie*, was released in 2002. It depicted Derrida as a joker, as 'one of us'. His Jewish origins are shown by his having bagels for breakfast; his self-doubt by his worrying about the color coordination of his clothes. At one point, as the camera follows him into his library, packed with thousands of books, the philosopher is asked: "Have you read all the books in here?" "Why no," Derrida replies, "only four of them. But I read these very, very carefully."

We might say the same thing. Have I read all of Derrida? Why no, only a few paragraphs. But I read those very, very carefully.

SCHOLARLY APPENDIX:
WOMEN IN PHILOSOPHY,
AND WHY THERE AREN'T MANY

There are only a few women in many reference works to philosophy, scattered around, like so many afterthoughts. In philosophy, it seems as if women must be as Aristotle said, lacking a certain virtue, the vital philosophical faculty of rationality.

And just in case they didn't realize it, over the ages would-be women philosophers have been comprehensively suppressed. Hypatia, hailed as the most brilliant thinker of her time, was dragged from her chariot and killed with sharpened shells. Aspasia, another skilled mathematician and logician, was sent to a nunnery and forbidden to leave. Teano, on becoming head of the Pythagoreans, was taken prisoner and tortured.

The physical oppression has been only part of it, though. Plato's mentor, Diotima, was demoted to the status of a fictional creation. In more recent times, Jenny Marx and Harriet Mill have been ahistorically discounted as influences in the development of Marxism and liberalism. Even in the twentieth century, Simone de Beauvoir had her first book, the foundation account of existentialism, sent back by the publisher with a note advising her to stick to 'women's topics'.

So many of the women-who-might-have-been-philosophers wrote poems and letters rather than books. For any and all of these reasons, few of their writings in philosophy have had any direct influence on the subject, and their contribution can only be gauged second-hand by noting the occasional male acknowledgment. One of the most famous of these comes in Plato's dialogue the *Symposium*, or "Drinking Party," where the wise woman, Diotima, is credited by Socrates as having opened his eyes to the values of poetry, love, and, most importantly of all, the nature of knowledge and the 'Forms' themselves. Diotima indeed is perhaps the 'Mother' of Western philosophy. Given this, it was necessary to relegate her to the status of 'imaginary person', a task undertaken by male scholars in the fifteenth century, and comprehensively ignore her ever since.

So let us start by correcting that imbalance slightly by recalling that celebrated example of 'women's philosophy', perhaps indeed the ONLY example to have survived the millennia (disguised in Plato's clothing).

It is 360 BCE, and the scene is a drinking party at the home of Agathon, in Athens. Socrates is speaking.

> You made a very good speech, Agathon, but there is yet one small question which I would fain ask: Is not the good also the beautiful?
> AGATHON: Why, yes.
> SOCRATES: Then in seeking the beautiful, love wants also seeks the good?
> AGATHON: I cannot refute you, Socrates. Let us assume that what you say is true.
> SOCRATES: Say rather, my dear Agathon, that you cannot refute the truth; for Socrates is easily refuted. But now, before taking my leave of you, I want to tell a tale of love which I heard told originally by Diotima of Mantineia, a woman wise both in this matter and in many other kinds of knowledge. In the old times, it is said, she told the Athenians to offer sacrifice before the coming of the plague, and thus delayed the arrival of the disease by ten years. But for me, she was my instructress in the art of love, and I shall now repeat to you what she said to me, beginning with the points made to me by Agathon, which are almost the same as those I made to the wise woman when she questioned me.
> First I said to her, in nearly the same words which he used to me, that Love was a mighty god, and likewise beautiful and she proved to me that, by my own account, Love was neither beautiful nor good. "What do you mean, Diotima," I said, "is love then evil and foul?"
> "Hush," she said; "must that be foul which is not fair?"
> "Certainly," I said.
> "And is that which is not wise, ignorant? do you not see that there is a mean between wisdom and ignorance?"
> "And what may that be?" I said.
> "Right opinion," she replied; "which, as you know, being incapable of giving a reason, is not knowledge (for how can knowledge be devoid of reason?), nor again, ignorance, for equally, how can ignorance attain the truth?, but is clearly something in-between ignorance and wisdom."
> To which I replied, "Quite true."
> "Do not then insist," she said, "that what is not fair is of necessity foul, nor that what is not good must be evil. Because love is not beautiful and good does not mean that love is therefore foul and evil; for there is a mean between them."

Ancient Women

But this is jumping ahead a bit. The Philosophical Tale of the missing women philosophers should include many other ancients, such as Aspasia (to 401 BCE), whose elegant hairdo is memorialized in a fresco over the portal of the University of Athens. Aspasia was active in Athenian intellectual and political life at the time of Plato. She became the mistress, and then later wife, of Pericles, and thus one of the key figures in the Sophist movement. Aspasia was considered an authority on rhetoric, politics, and the State. Philosophers of her time called her the "mistress of eloquence." Socrates was said to have visited her often to discuss the arts of rhetoric and philosophy.

Like Socrates, Aspasia was tried for impiety but in her case she was acquitted after Pericles came to her defense. She is in Greece.

Another 'lady friend' of Socrates was Arete of Cyrene. According to the epitaph inscribed on her tomb she possessed the beauty of Helen, the virtue of Thirma, the pen of Aristippus, the soul of Socrates, and the tongue of Homer. She was the daughter of Aristippus, himself a student and friend of Socrates, and one of the few who were present on the fateful occasion that Socrates drank the hemlock. Aristippus founded the Cyrenaic school in what is nowadays northeast Libya. The school was an advocate for hedonism, or the pursuit of pleasure, and in due course Arete succeeded her father as director, teaching both natural and moral philosophy for the next thirty years. She is said to have written some forty books, and taught some hundred or so other philosophers.

Then there is Cleobuline (or, more precisely, Eumetide of the Cleobuline sect). She was one of the seven sages of ancient Greece and wrote enigmatic texts in hexameters (little poems of six lines), as well as something about the medical properties of a 'sucking glass' which is commented on favorably by Aristotle in Book II of the *Rhetoric*. Some texts recall that she was given the job of washing the feet of visitors at her father's house, a role which must be considered as a relatively good outcome for a women philosopher.

Hipparchia (ca. 300 BCE) defied her wealthy parents to mary Crates, a celebrated Cynic philosopher who had also given up a considerable inheritance, to become a couple of itinerant philosophers spreading the teachings of their sect. In keeping with their philosophical beliefs, the couple lived simply, with Hipparchia making her name as a philosopher by writing a treatise called "Philosophical Hypotheses," as well as in the rather second-hand way of explaining the principles of the movement. The most interesting thing about her was that she apparently took the obligation to live 'according to nature' very seriously, for example talking with her husband in public as an equal, and in Book III of the *Anthology of Palatine*, it is said that she declined to ornament her clothes or her feet, or wear make-up. We are told she walked with a stout stick, in bare feet, dressed in a simple habit like a monk, and slept on the earth. Her philosophy has been summed up as "nothing natural is shameful." We should have obtained our word 'Hippy' from her. But, alas, it seems not.

Then there are several 'Pythagorean women', such as Themistocle, who was the sister of Pythagoras, and is said to have been the true source of the Pythagorean moral code, which, as we have seen, is not necessarily entirely an unblemished achievement. Where some say Pythagoras consulted the priestess at the oracle in Delphi, others say he consulted his sister, and the likelihood is indeed that Pythagoras obtained his ideas from her, but preferred to report them as coming from the Oracle, in order to make the views appear more authoritative.

Another Pythagorean women philosopher was Theano, alternatively either his daughter or wife according to different accounts (or two different people!), and who became the director of the Pythagorean school after Pythagoras departed Earth to undergo another cycle of reincarnation. Whilst he was alive, however, she helped the master identify the density of the 'ether' that the Pythagoreans supposed to surround the Earth and fill space, as well as several other complicated bits of geometry. There is a document attributed to Theano in which metaphysics is discussed, and there are reports of many other of her writings in which she expresses her views on the usual women's philosophy areas of marriage, sex, ethics, and, of course, women. Some accounts say that after Theano became director of the Pythagorean school she was captured and tortured in a bid to extract their secrets, but even after the most unspeakable tortures, resolutely refused to speak.

According to Montaigne, Theano (like Hipparchia) encouraged all women who married to strip off without any shame in front of their men, a policy condemned by Plutarch with the weighty advice that a true women retains her modesty even without her clothes on. Indeed, Theano herself is supposed to have told a young man who stared at her beautiful elbows "they are beautiful, but they are not for everyone." Plutarch would have approved, but not been content with that. He thought that women should not speak in front of men in public. And so, despite the fact that she evidently wrote much, and converted Pythagoras to the view that it was not numbers but the order of numbers that governs the universe, such tittle-tattle is all history has been able to pass on of her philosophy. Perhaps it would have been better if she had divulged a few more of the secrets.

Another notable Pythagorean, probably a bit later (no one seems sure of the dates exactly), was Aesara of Lucania, who wrote a book, "On Human Nature," which presented a theory of natural law based on a new principle of 'harmonia'. Harmonia, as we might guess, is the principle that everything is in harmony: geometry, arithmetic, music, the cosmos – everything. Like Plato (in the *Republic*) she links the 'harmony of the soul' with the well-being of the State. However, where Plato looks at the 'larger model' of society to investigate justice, she puts it the other way round, saying we should look at the individual soul in order to find the nature of justice. In this way, she produced a theory of natural law, justice, and human psychology.

Hypatia we have noted more properly already amongst our ancient men. A younger contemporary of Hypatia was Asclepigenia. She also taught in a Neo-Platonic school, but one in Athens, headed by her father. Like Hypatia, she was an atheist or 'pagan' philosopher, and she applied mystical, magical, and theurgic principles to the workings of the universe. She compared the teachings of Plato and Aristotle to the metaphysical claims of Christianity. Upon the death of her father, she took charge of the Academy together with her brother and another philosopher. Her most famous student was the philosopher Proclus, who is held in conventional male philosophy as a key link in the chain of Western philosophy.

But that chain, whether male or female, takes a bit of a jump now, and so the next famous women philosopher we can find is probably Hildegaard of Bingen (1098–1179). Hildegaard was prone to having visions, and thought she had been sent by God to warn the people against the folly of forgetting the Scriptures. Her tactic was first to write letters to various religious and secular authorities, coupled with preaching tours throughout her native Germany. Her writings are basically descriptions and interpretations of her 'visions', introducing in the process what scholars say is 'vivid' new imagery. She barely counts as a philosopher, more a mystic, but given the paucity of women philosophers she is often included in lists of such.

Then there's the rather tame Christine de Pizan (1365–ca. 1430), nowadays honored as France's 'First Woman of Letters', a poet and exponent of women's rights, especially the right to a full education. She followed the interests of Aquinas and many others, holding wisdom to be the highest virtue, as well as sharing Aquinas's desire to identify suitable causes for 'holy war'.

Christine de Pizan was one of France's first professional writers and is sometimes said to be the first person ever to be self-supporting through writing alone, although this seems a rather meaningless claim. Her writings were rich in philosophical argument and thought, reflecting upon the social and political debates of the time, the end of the feudal period. The French remember her as having written a poem, "Song in Honor of Joan of Arc," which was indeed the first tribute paid to the French icon. Christine composed the poem as she saw Joan's victory as epitomizing the honor of France and the worth of women.

Renaissance Women

Another French woman of letters and another mystic was Jeanne Marie Bouvier de la Motte, also known as Madame Guyon. After being left a wealthy widow at the age of 28, she began spreading her mystical philosophy in southeastern France. She introduced the French to the doctrine of Quietism, a form of mysticism that stresses withdrawal from worldly concerns, suppression of will, and passive meditation on the divine. In so doing, she incurred the wrath of the Archbishop of Paris and was imprisoned in 1688, although she was released the next year thanks to the intervention of the king's wife. Alack, she was put back behind bars for her writings again in 1695 and remained there until 1703, when she was released under the condition that she leave Paris.

One of the most romantic tales of the women philosophers is the tragic twelfth-century love story of 'Peter the Venerable' and Heloise. Even by the age of 16, Heloise had become renowned throughout France for her learning and was considered France's greatest living philosopher. She knew Latin, Hebrew, and Greek, and she was well educated in ancient philosophy and rhetoric. It was at this point that the venerable Peter Abelard asked to become her private tutor. When Peter met her, he "forced himself upon her," and soon she was pregnant by him.

Even so, Heloise did not want to marry Peter because (it is said) she feared the marriage would ruin his clerical career. So, bizarrely, despite marrying Peter, both of them publicly denied the marriage. Heloise's uncle accused Peter of being something of a cad, and as if to disapprove this, Peter sent Heloise to a monastery and forced her to take the vows and enter religious life. Stranger and stranger, Heloise's uncle hired thugs to "pull Peter from his bed and castrate him." Whether this actually happened I do not know, but it seems that, either way, Peter went on to a successful philosophical and religious career, while Heloise remained for the rest of her life a sad and solitary figure in the abbey. The only trace that is left of her philosophical wisdom is in a series of letters over the long years, between Heloise and Peter.

With the Renaissance women came back into playing a role in public discourse, or at least the rich ones did. Elisabeth of Bohemia (1618–80), the Princess of Palatine, corresponded with Descartes, who as we have seen had something of a taste for ladies, especially royal ones. Her questioning of his description of the interaction of mind and body and of the operations of 'free will', in the face, as she puts it, of the brute physical reality of being human, is counted as of sufficient merit to give her at least the reflected glory of the great male philosopher.

For some reason England has spawned a lot of women philosophers, such as Catherine Cockburn (1679–1749), or Catherine Trotter as she was rather unpromisingly originally called. Trotter was really a successful playwright. However, she became involved, albeit anonymously, in a debate about 'ethical rationalism' that Samuel Clarke had launched in the 1704–5 Boyle Lectures, a debate that had brought in the likes of Francis Hutcheson and Lord Shaftesbury. Her contribution to philosophy is said to have been her defense of John Locke's *Essay Concerning Human Understanding*, which is rather a meagre claim, as of course the *Essay* was widely admired and Locke himself needed little defense.

Another Englishwoman, Mary Wollstonecraft (1759–97), is one of the best-known names in 'women's philosophy', although that does not, as we have seen, mean very well known. Certainly she will not feature on many courses. She lived in England and worked as a journalist and translator, as well as writing books such as *Thoughts on the Education of Daughters* (1787), in which she identified inadequate education as one of the ways in which men kept women in their power. She traveled to France, where she wrote *A Vindication of the Rights of Men* in 1790, a reply to the male philosopher Burke's condemnation of the values of the Revolution.

Her most influential book, *A Vindication of the Rights of Women with Strictures on Moral and Political Subjects*, although claimed as an early feminist philosophy, is in a sense merely a 'reaction' to Thomas Paine, John Locke, and Jean Jacques Rousseau's publishing efforts on behalf of 'men's rights', the title coming from Paine's *Vindication of the Rights of Man*. Her contribution to philosophy was to say that women have the same rights as men, which may not seem very radical, but still as a political doctrine has a long way to go before finding universal acceptance. Her reasoning, then, is more important: she argued that virtue is a mix of reason and feeling, and not merely reason alone. "Mind has no sex," she said, a view that could also be attributed to Plato. She adds, however, that relations between men and women are corrupted by artificial distinctions based on gender, comparing them to unnecessary political distinctions, based on class, or wealth, or power, and that true virtue requires political justice. For this her contemporaries condemned her as a "philosophizing serpent," a "hyena in petticoats," and even as an "impious amazon." Like many of our women philosophers, she died young – in her case at age 38, in childbirth.

Another England-resident radical, Mrs. Marx, who, it might be noted in passing, is supposed to have contributed at all stages of the writing process (based in London) to Marx and Engel's philosophy, has been comprehensively discounted by subsequent historians, and also died young.

Anne-Louise Germaine Necker, Baronne de Staël-Holstein (1766–1817), to leave England briefly, is probably the woman philosopher with the best claim to a long name, even if she is normally referred to merely as Madame de Staël. She was not herself German but wrote a book about the country and the 'German character', in which she introduced the works of Kant, Fichter, Schelling, Schlegel, and others to the French intellectuals, who were otherwise only interested in 'romantic' thinkers. Another book, *Literature Considered in its Connexions to Social Institutions*, in its way predated Marxist Critical Thinking by linking religion, law, morality, and literature. Madame de Staël was actively involved in the French Revolution and continued to defend its values in her writing long after it had gone sour.

Harriet Taylor (1807–58) qualifies as a philosopher by being the lover of one, in this case of the English liberal John Stuart Mill. Mill is noted for his views on 'political economy' but also on equality, liberty, and individualism. Although she already had married poor John Taylor in 1826, Harriet Taylor fell in love with Mill in 1830 and the two conducted a really rather scandalous liaison ever after. Mill himself acknowledges that the ethical elements of his philosophy were the result of their discussion on the nature of equality, liberty, and individualism. But Harriet is remembered more for 'the scandal' than for that.

KEY SOURCES AND FURTHER READING

Ancients and More Ancients

On Socrates

The introductory quote is from Hugh Tredennick in *The Last Days of Socrates* (Penguin Classics, 1954), p. 8; the quote from Plato is the *Apology*, especially 29a, and the following quote is in the *Symposium*, especially 220 C–D. Sarah Kofman's book, *Socrates: Fictions of a Philosopher* (1998), referred to in the text, is a fine, scholarly account which summarizes several different approaches to Socrates. If browsing on the Internet, try Frostburg State University (www.frostburg.edu): there is an essay by Jorn Bramann, "Socrates: An Insider on the Outside," which details, amongst other titbits, why Socrates married his notoriously bad-tempered wife, Xanthippe.

On Plato

There are many summaries of Plato's thought, but unusually amongst philosophers, it is always better to read the works themselves. The introductory quote is from *The Concise Encyclopaedia of Western Philosophy and Philosophers* (Routledge, second edition, 1991). The quotes from Plato himself are from *Republic* 592 a–b, *Republic* 372–375, and the statement advancing Eros as a god is in the *Symposium* at 242e. Epistle II is reproduced in *Plato*, Vol. 7, translated by R. E. Bury (Heinemann, 1961). The *Stanford Encyclopaedia of Philosophy*, at plato.stanford.edu, has some detailed discussion of various aspects of Plato, including his poetical interests.

On Aristotle

The view of women as tame animals is given in Aristotle's *Politics*, especially around 1254 b 10–14. Slaves and barbarians are discussed in *Physics*, especially around 1252 b 8. Special acknowledgments to, and a recommendation to look at, www.womenpriests.org for material on Aristotle and the role of women are due.

On Lao Tzu

There is no reading. He has 'disappeared'. However, there is still the *Tao Te Ching* itself, in various forms of which only the Chinese is an accurate portrayal – but quite impenetrable both by reason of being in Chinese and by reason of being very ancient and obscure. I have used various English translations to arrive at the hybrid quotations given here. There are several good versions on the Internet.

On Heraclitus and Pythagoras

There are only a few fragments . . . However, on the so-called pre-Socratics generally, a good source is *The Pre-Socratic Philosophers: A Critical History* by G. S. Kirk and J. E. Raven (Cambridge University Press, 1957).

Specifically as for Newton on Pythagoras, the notes to propositions 4 to 9 of *Principia Mathematica* say that the mathematics of the laws of gravity must have been known to Pythagoras as he had applied harmonics to the heavens: "by means of experiments he ascertained weights by which all tones on equal strings were reciprocal as the squares of the lengths of the string."

On Hypatia

Sarah Greenwald and Edith Prentice Mendez have their very scholarly essay, "Women and Minorities in Mathematics: Incorporating Their Mathematical Achievements into School Classrooms: Hypatia, the First Known Women Mathematician," at Appalachian State University – albeit they think Hypatia is a mathematician, not a philosopher, which is a bit of a demotion. Michael Deakin, in the math department at Monash University in Australia, has a convincing looking account too at www.polyamory.org/~howard/Hypatia/primary-sources.html.

Medieval Philosophy

On Augustine

The *Confessions* is the original autobiography, full of misinformation as all of its kind, but there are many good essays on him too, for example those by Gerald W. Schlabach and Lewis Loflin, both now on the Internet.

On Aquinas

G. K. Chesterton's mini-book simply entitled *Saint Thomas Aquinas: The Dumb Ox* (various editions) is still being published, and indeed, even more remarkably, still being sold. Especially as it is now on the web in all its effusive entirety, for example at gutenberg.net.au. Colin Kirk's short summary of Aquinas's life is in *The Essentials of Philosophy and Ethics* (Hodder, 2005, edited by myself).

Modern Philosophy

On Descartes

The introductory quote on Descartes is from Professor F. E. Sutcliffe, who was writing in *Descartes: Discourse on Method and the Meditations* (Penguin Classics, 1968), p. 19. The letter is the one of April 15, 1630, and is quoted in Jonathan Ree's modest edition of *Philosophical Tales* on p. 7. For those who insist on reconnecting with the conventional view of Descartes ("there must be some reason why he is so famous"), a good place to start is with the two volumes of *The Philosophical Writings of Descartes*, edited by Cottingham, Stoothoff, and Murdoch (Cambridge University Press, 1984).

On Hobbes

To understand Hobbes, assuming one is feeling depressed and should want to do so, see *Leviathan* (published in 1651), and if you really want to read the circle theorem, *De Corpore*, published in 1655. The series of mathematical papers is not described here in strict chronological order. Instead, for a full blow-by-blow account of the narrow issue, there is (perhaps unwisely) a whole book, *Squaring the Circle: The War between Hobbes and Wallis* (1999), by Douglas Jesseph.

On Spinoza

Spinoza continues to have an enthusiastic following, indeed, some are too enthusiastic, such as the Catholic scholars who claim that Pope John Paul II was the reincarnated Spinoza (see www.johnadams.net for an amusing picture of this). *Spinoza's Heresy: Immortality and the Jewish Mind*, by Steven Nadler (Clarendon, 2004), offers a detailed if more conventional account of that earlier controversy.

Enlightened Philosophy

An Approach to Political Philosophy: Locke in Context (Cambridge University Press, 1993), by James Tully and others, contains a number of different perspectives on Locke's politics. There are several good sites on the Internet, such as those at www.classical-foundations.com, and the *Internet Encyclopaedia of Philosophy* (at www.iep.utm.edu) has a comprehensive selection of articles on Locke going into far more detail than one might reasonably want. I have benefited from the interesting article "John Locke and Afro-American Slavery" on the website of Oregon State University.

On Hume

There are several accounts of Hume's life and indeed works too, but of these, his own effort, *My Life*, is very short and really a little pathetic. Better to consider wading through the 700-odd pages of *The Life of David Hume* by Ernest Mossner (first published in 1954, but republished more recently by Oxford University Press).

On Rousseau

As well as the ripping yarn of Rousseau's dog, mentioned in the text, there is the full e-text of the French rogue's *Confessions* at Adelaide University's website: adelaide.edu.au.

On Kant

Kant can be really a rather dull read. I picked up these 'titbits' here and there, but the only further reading I would recommend (someone has to) is my own entry, "K is for Kant," in *Wittgenstein's Beetle* (Blackwell, 2005). Admittedly, however, this is only about one tiny bit of his philosophy, and not at all about his life and 'context'. The six hundred pages of *Kant: A Biography* by Manfred-Kuehn (Cambridge University Press, 2002) should provide this, even if it starts unpromisingly: "The year 1724 was not one of the most significant years in the history of the human race, but it was not wholly insignificant either . . ."

The Idealists

On Leibniz

George MacDonald Ross's slim volume on Leibniz for the 'Past Masters' series (1984, but also available online at leeds.ac.uk as an e-text) offers some background on the eccentric philosopher as well as a good insight into his thinking. On the Internet, www.mathspages.com has a full account of his work with 'computers'.

On Berkeley

The best book of the bishop is his *Three Dialogues between Hylas and Philonous*. An interesting essay on Berkeley is the old one: George Herbert Mead, "Bishop Berkeley and his Message," in the *Journal of Philosophy* 26 (1929), pp. 421–30. The University of Illinois (Chicago) website (tigger.uic.edu) has a good selection of Berkeley memorabilia including some poems and some pictures.

On Hegel

If Kant is hard going, it might seem that Hegel would be even worse. But thank goodness for Karl Popper. *The Open Society and Its Enemies*, Volume 2, *Hegel and Marx* (Routledge, 1945) is quite a ripping yarn. And www.hegel.net has a very accessible biography, expanding on a 1911 *Britannica* article of the (as it thinks) great man. (The quote on Hegel's lecturing style is from here.)

On Schopenhauer

Christopher Janaway's *Very Short Introduction* to Schopenhauer (Oxford University Press, new edition, 2002) is an accessible if rather unimaginative entrée, and there are some good websites for desserts, such as www.friesian.com/arthur.htm, which has some strange lurid diagrams representing Schopenhauer's thought and philosophical roots, or the e-text of Schopenhauer's book, *The Wisdom of Life*, at www.turksheadreview.com.

In my chapter, the introductory quote is from Bertrand Russell, *A History of Western Philosophy* (first published 1946), pp. 726–7, in the Counterpoint edition of 1979. The first quote of Schopenhauer's is from *On the Vanity of Existence*, translated by R. J. Hollingdale (Penguin, 1976), p. 51, and the concluding quote is from the *World as Will and Representation*, 1.54, translated by E. F. J. Payne (Dover, 1969), vol. 1, p. 281.

The Romantics

On Kiekegaard

The keen reader could certainly try the original text, strange as it is. Cambridge University Press have a new (2006) edition of *Fear and Trembling*, edited by C. Stephen Evans and Sylvia Walsh. But Kiekegaard, like all the existentialists, with his philosophical hat on, is extremely dull too. However, there is a rather different side of him explored in *The Humor of Kierkegaard: An Anthology*, edited by Thomas Oden (Princeton University Press, 2002).

On Mill

The introductory quote is from *The Oxford Companion to Philosophy*, edited by Ted Honderich (Oxford University Press, 1995) where in Karl Britton glosses the story. *What is Poetry?* is quoted in *Philosophical Tales* by Jonathan Ree (Methuen, 1987), p. 107. Wordsworth's view is taken from *Preface to Lyrical Ballads* in *Wordsworth's Poetical Works* (Oxford University Press, 1908). Mill's criticism of Bentham is from "On Bentham and Coleridge" in his 1832 essay, *What is Poetry?*, while the final quote is from Caroline Fox, *Memories of Old Friends*, edited by Horace Pym (London, 1882), entry for August 7, 1840.

McMaster University in Canada (socserv.mcmaster.ca) has several e-texts of Mill, including some rarities such as his essay "On Bentham."

On Thoreau

The text of *Walden* is available online at www.turksheadreview.com, again as an e-text, and the text of "Walking" is offered by a church in Ottowa (uuottawa.com) as part of its 'sermon archive'. *Walden* is also available in a "too cheap to be a proper book" edition by Dover as a 'Thrift' paperback. But then Thoreau himself was fairly poor . . .

On Marx

The "production of ideas" quotation is from *The German Ideology*. Superscholarly readers might like to track down the leading article of *Kölnische*

Zeitung, no. 179; general readers might prefer *Marx: A Clear Guide*, by Edward Reiss (Pluto Press, 1997). Francis Wheen did a popular biography of Marx, but then Francis Wheen is one of the pompous windbag school of journalist-philosophers so one hesitates to offer him further publicity . . .

Recent Philosophy

On Russell

Russell has had plenty of mentions already for his history, but on the man himself, a good, nay terrifyingly huge, source on the web is the official 'Russell archives', which are kept by McMaster University, Canada, at www.mcmaster.ca/russdocs/russell.htm.

Russell's oeuvre, as it were, is wide, and works like *In Praise of Idleness* are refreshingly different from the usual philosophical discussions, even including his own *Problems of Philosophy*. This book, despite being for years considered the perfect introduction to the subject, is really rather limited, or "strained," as one anonymous reviewer remarked of my own fascinating *101 Philosophy Problems*, a book I mention here solely for advertising purposes.

On Wittgenstein

The quotes are taken from *Critique of Patriarchal Reason*, by Arthur Evans with Frank Pietronigro (White Crane Press, San Francisco, 1997); from *Tractatus* 2.021; from Otto Weininger, *Sex and Character* (1903), quoted in *Critique of Patriarchal Reason*, p. 187; and from *Philosophical Investigations* itself, paragraph 23.

Wittgenstein's Poker by John Eidinow and David Edmonds is a popular, because well-researched and well-written, introduction to the sinister Austrian philosopher.

On Heidegger

See, for example, Alex Steiner, source for many of these interesting historical comparisons, "The Case of Martin Heidegger, Philosopher and Nazi," published April 4, 2000, on the 'World Socialist Web Site'. Alas, Heidegger's philosophy is all quite unreadable. Others, however, think differently, as a visit to a bookshop will certainly show.

On Benjamin Lee Whorf

Robert Kirk writes in *The Oxford Companion to Philosophy* (entry quoted in full). For Whorf himself, there is only *Language, Thought and Reality: Selected Writings*, edited by John Carroll (MIT Press, 1956). And there is Dan Moonhawk Alford on "The Great Whorf Hypothesis Hoax: Sin, Suffering and Redemption in Academe," at www.enformy.com.

On Sartre and not Beauvoir

The introductory quote is from *The Oxford Companion to Philosophy*, edited by Ted Honderich (Oxford University Press, 1995). The Beauvoir–Sartre relationship and the similarities between their works are explained in detail in *Simone de Beauvoir and Jean-Paul Sartre*, by Kate and Howard Fullbrook (Basic Books/HarperCollins, 1994), and the 'alternative explanation' offered is theirs. Sartre's autobiography, *The Words*, was published in 1963; *She Came to Stay*, Beauvoir's first published work, came out in 1943.

A curious website called "Dad's Classmates: Sartre and de Beauvoir" is at www.wisdomportal.com/Dad/Sartre-Beauvoir.html. It also offers a few links.

On Derrida

The introductory quote is from *The Concise Routledge Encyclopaedia of Philosophy* (Routledge, 2000). Other quotes are from *Semiology and Grammatology*, translated by Alan Bass, in *Positions* (University of Chicago Press, 1981), p. 26, and *Of Grammatology*, translated by Gayatri Chakravorty Spivak (Johns Hopkins University Press, 1976), p. 71.

When Derrida died in 2004, his fame at least merited him a piece in India's national newspaper, *The Hindu*, which is online at www.hindu.com. Although the paper makes some errors in its account, it does note that many thought his writing was "negative, abstruse, incoherent, nihilistic, and destructive," which is as good a summary as any.

On Women Philosophers

There is, as I say, almost nothing published on this. A little mini-book in French offers a survey of the ancients, from which I have taken some of the material: *Histoire des Femmes Philosophes*, by Gilles Ménace (published by Arléa in 2003). The topic would make a very good research project, but beware the 'siren sources'!

ACKNOWLEDGMENTS

There is an interesting, if rather unkind, new habit in book publishing of adding a sort of "anti-acknowledgments" in which the author assails all those who have hindered, run down or otherwise obstructed him during the writing of the work in question – or indeed over his entire lifetime.

Alas, I shall have to forgo that pleasure here, partly, as far as the second concern goes, on account of space, but also because, in all honesty, with regard to writing this book, I can't think of any. Instead, I should like to offer a more conventional kind of acknowledgment, one in which I record publicly my thanks and appreciation for help received. For a history of philosophy, by its nature, is a huge undertaking, and even an alternative history, like this one, is still quite demanding.

Fortunately, these days, there is the Internet, which makes immediately available (to those with the luxury of access to it) almost all the great texts in philosophy, plus a vast range of secondary materials, opinions, and analyses. So my first acknowledgment is to those essentially unknown or anonymous philosophical enthusiasts who have provided, free of commercial intent, philosophical research and materials on the web.

But this book is equally a reflection of the very specific interest of its editors, in particular the excellent Jeff Dean, who guide such projects from mere ideas to either fruition – or oblivion. And I should like to thank here all those other specialists at Blackwell for their support and help during the production process too.

I did think of *not* thanking Raul for his pictures because it seemed to me that his role is so central, it would be like marginalizing him to do so. But then obviously the pictures are great and I've really appreciated and enjoyed working with him. So maybe it would be all right to mention that here as well.

Finally, I should like to especially acknowledge the careful, insightful, and entirely appropriate comments and suggestions of the professional "readers," including, of course, that great philosophical muse (and not-too-distant relative) Brenda Almond, one of the great, if otherwise under-acknowledged, women philosophers, and my unprofessional but very special reader, Judit'.

INDEX

Items in **bold** indicate a major entry